Related Books of

WebSphere Engineering
A Practical Guide for WebSphere Support Managers and Senior Consultants

by Ying Ding

ISBN-13: 978-0-13-714225-5

The Practical, End-to-End Guide to WebSphere® Infrastructure Engineering and Technical Management. Drawing on his tremendous real-world expertise, Ying Ding shows how to maximize the WebSphere platform's reliability, stability, scalability, and performance for large enterprise systems. You'll find insightful discussions of each option and strategy for managing WebSphere, including practical guidance on making the right tradeoffs for your environment.

Whether you're a WebSphere administrator, developer, consultant, support manager, engineer, or architect, this book brings together the information you need to run your WebSphere infrastructure with maximum effectiveness and efficiency.

WebSphere Business Integration Primer
Process Server, BPEL, SCA, and SOA

by Ashok Iyengar, Vinod Jessani, and Michele Chilanti

ISBN-13: 978-0-13-224831-0

Using WebSphere® Business Integration (WBI) technology, you can build an enterprise-wide Business Integration (BI) infrastructure that makes it easier to connect any business resources and functions, so you can adapt more quickly to the demands of customers and partners. Now there's an introductory guide to creating standards-based process and data integration solutions with WBI.

WebSphere Business Integration Primer thoroughly explains Service Component Architecture (SCA), basic business processes, and complex long-running business flows, and guides you to choose the right process integration architecture for your requirements. Next, it introduces the key components of a WBI solution and shows how to make them work together rapidly and efficiently. This book will help developers, technical professionals, or managers understand today's key BI issues and technologies, and streamline business processes by combining BI with Service Oriented Architecture (SOA).

Related Books of Interest

The New Language of Business
SOA & Web 2.0

By Sandy Carter
ISBN-13: 978-0-13-195654-4

In *The New Language of Business*, senior IBM executive Sandy Carter demonstrates how to leverage SOA, Web 2.0, and related technologies to drive new levels of operational excellence and business innovation.

Writing for executives and business leaders inside and outside IT, Carter explains why flexibility and responsiveness are now even more crucial to success — and why services-based strategies offer the greatest promise for achieving them.

You'll learn how to organize your business into reusable process components — and support them with cost-effective IT services that adapt quickly and easily to change. Then, using extensive examples — including a detailed case study describing IBM's own experience — Carter identifies best practices, pitfalls, and practical starting points for success.

 Listen to the author's podcast at:
ibmpressbooks.com/podcasts

Executing SOA
A Practical Guide for the Service-Oriented Architect

by Norbert Bieberstein, Robert G. Laird, Dr. Keith Jones, and Tilak Mitra
ISBN-13: 978-0-13-235374-8

In Executing SOA, four experienced SOA implementers share realistic, proven, "from-the-trenches" guidance for successfully delivering the largest and most complex SOA initiative. This book follows up where the authors' best-selling *Service-Oriented Architecture Compass* left off, showing how to overcome key obstacles to successful SOA implementation and identifying best practices for all facets of execution—technical, organizational, and human. Among the issues it addresses include introducing a services discipline that supports collaboration and information process sharing; integrating services with preexisting technology assets and strategies; choosing the right roles for new tools; shifting culture, governance, and architecture; and bringing greater agility to the entire organizational lifecycle, not just isolated projects.

 Listen to the author's podcast at:
ibmpressbooks.com/podcasts

IBM Press™

Visit ibmpressbooks.com
for all product information

Related Books of Interest

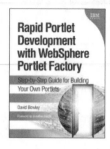

Rapid Portlet Development with WebSphere Portlet Factory
Step-by-Step Guide for Building Your Own Portlets

by David Bowley

ISBN-13: 978-0-13-713446-5

Portlet development traditionally has been difficult and time-consuming, requiring costly resources and specialized expertise in multiple technologies. IBM® WebSphere® Portlet Factory simplifies and accelerates portlet development, enabling developers to build world-class portlet solutions without in-depth knowledge of portal technology.

Expert developer David Bowley walks you through several of today's most common portlet development scenarios, demonstrating how to create powerful, robust portlets quickly and cost-effectively. Each walkthrough contains all the step-by-step instructions, detailed guidance, fast answers, and working sample code you need to get tangible results immediately.

Enterprise Messaging Using JMS and IBM WebSphere

Yusuf

ISBN-13: 978-0-13-146863-4

IBM WebSphere System Administration

Williamson, Chan, Cundiff, Lauzon, Mitchell

ISBN-13: 978-0-13-144604-5

Outside-in Software Development

Kessler, Sweitzer

ISBN-13: 978-0-13-157551-6

Enterprise Master Data Management

Dreibelbis, Hechler, Milman, Oberhofer, van Run, Wolfson

ISBN-13: 978-0-13-236625-0

Enterprise Java Programming with IBM WebSphere, Second Edition

Brown, Craig, Hester, Pitt, Stinehour, Weitzel, Amsden, Jakab, Berg

ISBN-13: 978-0-321-18579-2

Service-Oriented Architecture (SOA) Compass

Bieberstein, Bose, Fiammante, Jones, Shah

ISBN-13: 978-0-13-187002-4

IBM WebSphere

Barcia, Hines, Alcott, Botzum

ISBN-13: 978-0-13-146862-7

SOA Governance:
Achieving and Sustaining
Business and IT Agility

SOA Governance: Achieving and Sustaining Business and IT Agility

William A. Brown
Robert G. Laird
Clive Gee
Tilak Mitra

IBM Press
Pearson plc

Upper Saddle River, NJ • New York • San Francisco
Toronto • London • Munich • Paris • Madrid
Cape Town • Sydney • Tokyo • Singapore • Mexico City

www.ibmpressbooks.com

IBM Press Program Managers: Steven Stansel, Ellice Uffer

Cover design: IBM Corporation

Associate Publisher: Greg Wiegand

Marketing Manager: Kourtnaye Sturgeon

Publicist: Heather Fox

Acquisitions Editor: Katherine Bull

Development Editor: Ginny Bess

Managing Editor: Kristy Hart

Designer: Alan Clements

Project Editor: Chelsey Marti

Copy Editor: Keith Cline

Indexer: Erika Millen

Compositor: Gloria Schurick

Proofreader: Kathy Ruiz

Manufacturing Buyer: Dan Uhrig

Published by Pearson plc

Publishing as IBM Press

IBM Press offers excellent discounts on this book when ordered in quantity for bulk purchases or special sales, which may include electronic versions and/or custom covers and content particular to your business, training goals, marketing focus, and branding interests. For more information, please contact:

U. S. Corporate and Government Sales
1-800-382-3419
corpsales@pearsontechgroup.com.

For sales outside the U. S., please contact:

International Sales
international@pearsoned.com.

Library of Congress Cataloging-in-Publication Data

SOA governance : achieving and sustaining business and IT agility / William Brown ... [et al.].

    p. cm.

  Includes bibliographical references.

  ISBN 978-0-13-714746-5

  1. Web services. 2. Business enterprises—Computer networks—Management. 3. Computer network architectures. I. Brown, William, 1959 Oct. 20- II. Title: Service oriented architecture governance.

  TK5105.88813.S63 2008

  658'.05—dc22

2008042212

ISBN-13: 978-0-13-713084-8

ISBN-10: 0-13-713084-8

Text printed in the United States on recycled paper at Courier Stoughton in Stoughton, Massachusetts.
First printing December 2008

I'd like to dedicate this book to my wife, Rachel, and our children,
Alex, Anthony, and Kelly, whose love and support I can't do without.
To Lureon and Chase Walker, the little Walker to come,
and to Martín Garcia.
Together little ones, anything is possible.
And, to my family and friends.
"Good friends we've had, and good friends we've lost...";
Dad, Pop, Lois, Miriam, Kevin, Kenny, I love and miss you everyday.
—*William Brown*

To my wife, Amy, and my sons, Thomas and Jack; many fine adventures.
To my leadership mentor, Gus Lee, an extraordinary writer in his own right,
who encouraged me to share my insights; thanks for pushing me.
—*Robert G. Laird*

To my very patient wife, Gwen, and to my many friends and colleagues in
both IBM and our clients around the world, who helped make my long career
there a lot of fun and very professionally rewarding. I will miss working
with you guys. Thanks for the happy memories.
—*Clive Gee*

I dedicate this work to my grandfather NarendraNath and grandma
Sovana, whose pedigree is what I am trying to live up to; to my uncle Abhijit
and aunt Mandira, who have been a part of my life and my values;
and to my sister, Tora, with whom I grew up in my formative years.
My wife, Tania, has always been by my side and has inspired me through the
long nocturnal hours of work that has gone into this book. And not the least
to my mom, Manjusree, and dad, Dibakar, for making me what I am today.
—*Tilak Mitra*

Contents

Foreword

Market forces drive the need for change and innovation in many companies. Whether the market force is mergers and acquisitions, changing market composition, regulatory demands, or new technologies, companies are finding that being competitive in demanding markets requires change; and, for many, IT can be an inhibitor to change. New ways of reaching customers and increasing flexibility is paramount where the expected benefit of flexibility is reduced time for system integration, increased asset reuse, and reduced time to market for solutions. Companies are responding in several ways, but overwhelmingly, the strategies that we see organizations adopting across the world means adoption of service-oriented architecture (SOA) in one or more facets.

The expected benefits of applying SOA vary from improved operational efficiency by deploying one or more shared functions across the organization to faster integration of core systems. SOA can reduce cycle times and cost for external business partners, facilitate flexible dealings with business partners, increase revenues, create new routes to market, and create new value from existing systems. SOA can reduce risk and exposure, improve visibility into business operations, or simply provide a more flexible business design by moving to architectures capable of business flexibility and game-changing business models.

These benefits cannot be achieved solely by defining and adopting a new architecture, strategy, or approach—that is, SOA. SOA software and services have quickly become a $1.1 billion market. While line-of-business executives and CTOs are spending the dollars on an SOA, it is up to line-of-business executives, business architects, IT architects, and designers to actually make sense of, construct, and implement an SOA that achieves the desired business goals and benefits. SOA governance is a critical enabler for achieving and sustaining desired business goals and benefits when adopting SOA.

One of the most difficult aspects of defining and implementing a new architecture is the definition and assignment of roles within an organization. SOA is no different; it continues to be viewed and defined depending on perspective and role.

Developers often equate SOA and web services as one and the same, whereas designers view SOA as a set of implementation patterns that should be applied during development. Many IT architects view SOA as another in a long line of architectural style. Executives (business and IT), line-of-business executives, and business stakeholders see SOA as a core underpinning to their IT strategy or as a critical enabler for business process management or key transformation initiatives. The point is that SOA means many things to different practitioners, highlighting the need for a shared vision and definition for SOA to achieve the promised benefits of SOA. So, how does an organization, a company, or line of business achieve the benefits of SOA when there is no common agreement within the organization?

For many organizations, SOA governance is a starting point for addressing this issue. Your first questions might be, "What is SOA governance, how does it help corporations reach this common agreement, and how can it make a difference? Why is SOA governance a critical success factor for both achieving and improvement in time to market for new products and features, reducing costs, improving business process flexibility, and ultimately turning business agility from a platitude to reality?"

The answer is not a short or easy one, but getting to that answer is easier if you read this book. The authors thoroughly address these key questions based on their collective experience of successfully implementing projects at organizations where business agility comes to life with the use of SOA governance. The authors recognize that not every organization is exactly the same, and so they provide the tools and guidance for how to make SOA governance work for any organization's culture.

When I talk to practitioners and executives about SOA governance I often hear in their voices, see in their body language, and see in their eyes that familiar reluctance. I can almost here them thinking, "Here we go again. Why do I need this esoteric thing called SOA governance? Our project does not have time to factor in issues around governance, and more important, it will not result in getting our projects completed faster." I understand where they are coming from and nod affirmatively. Then, I ask a few questions about their reasons for adopting SOA, and I ask what their expectations are for applying SOA principles to their IT architecture. Most of the time, their answers center on reuse and the expected benefits of improved time to market, improved flexibility, and other competitive benefits. Then I ask them how the project will enable these goals and benefits. At this point, the room full of practitioners and executives tends to become very quiet. I go on to ask how flexibility is defined and how will they know when they have met their intended goals? As the discussion continues, the benefits of utilizing SOA governance, whether it be cost reduction, process flexibility, or improved fusion between business and IT, starts to become clear to everyone in the room.

I often tell a story of déjà vu for those who don't know we have been down this road before. During the 1970s, when database technology was being introduced, we had these exact same conversations. Why do I need a data model? Exactly, what is a DBA? Let me understand this, I need a data modeler to do what? You are asking me to create data owners and have data stewards? Now we ask the questions about "services." What is a service model? Why do I need service modeling? What is a service lifecycle? Who are service owners? This book addresses these questions.

If you are a practitioner, manager, or executive tasked with the job of making SOA benefits real in your organization, this book will help you take SOA governance from concept to reality. SOA governance describes both a framework and method for applying SOA governance in your organization and making it work given your organization's idiosyncrasies. More important, the authors provide case study insights for an organization faced with the strain between strategic intent and tactical goals. The authors provide both tools and guidance for making SOA governance both practical and real.

This book is a must read for those who must understand and address all the challenges faced in making a SOA implementation successful. Authors Bill, Clive, Robert, and Tilak are seasoned practitioners with a wealth of experience in SOA deployments, and anyone who is tasked with making the benefits of SOA real will realize a competitive advantage from reading this book. I highly recommend this book and believe it makes an invaluable contribution to the IT industry.

Kerrie Holley
IBM Fellow
San Francisco, California
September 2008

Acknowledgments

We would like to thank Kerrie Holley, an IBM Fellow, who agreed to be the executive sponsor for the book and encouraged us to share our insights about SOA governance. We also want to thank Kerrie for taking the time to write the Foreword to this book and providing his thoughts on SOA and SOA governance.

We thank the people at IBM Press and Pearson Education, the publishers and staff who have helped market and complete the production work that goes into publishing a book like this. At IBM Press, we thank Tara Woodman and her team. At Pearson Education, a huge thank you and acknowledgment to Katherine Bull, who was with us from beginning to end. That's dedication! Katherine supplied great leadership, even agreeing to lead weekly author meetings on the weekend. She patiently gave suggestions, quelled disputes, provided encouragement, and firmly kept the end result in mind. We thank development editor Ginny Bess Munroe for her keen eye on comprehensiveness and synchronization. We could not have possibly created a quality product without Ginny. We thank Sue Outterson for her technical review and her guidance on what worked and what didn't, what was opaque and what was clear. We also thank the production and marketing teams at Pearson who helped make the book real.

Many people have volunteered their time to help with the book. David Hodge, in Singapore, and Levine Naidoo, in Australia, provided timely reviews and keen insight. Randy Langel, from the United States, has continued to be a thought leader on the business aspects of SOA governance and the alignment of the business with IT. Bruce Hawken, in Australia, showed his insightfulness and dedication to making SOA governance real and has inspired many people with his ideas and ability to produce results that matter. We would like to thank Tony Carrato and John Falkl, who encouraged this book to be written, and who have provided sage advice many times.

We want to thank William J. Tegan and Garrison A. Moore for their contribution to the thinking and hard work around the SOA governance space, and Rahgu Varadan for his work on enterprise service bus (ESB) governance. It has been a pleasure and honor to work with you.

We also want to thank Patrick Haren, IBM Executive Architect, with whom we had some very interesting discussions about SOA maturity. Our sincere thanks goes out to Peter Bahrs, IBM Distinguished Engineer, who provided access to some eye-opening research data on the industry's experience with SOA adoption. We would also like to thank Ray Harishankar, IBM Fellow, who encouraged and constantly egged us along to complete our work on this very interesting and important topic.

About the Authors

William A. Brown is a Master Sr. Certified Executive IT Architect with IBM Global Business Services, Enterprise Architecture & Technology Center of Excellence, and the SOA Center of Excellence. He is the SOA Governance SGMM global lead and the lead author of IBM's SOA Governance and Management Method (SGMM), SOA CoE Offering, white papers, presentation, and technique papers on SOA governance. Mr. Brown specializes in SOA governance and enterprise architecture, about which he continues to write articles, provide education, mentor, teach, present, develop assets, and deliver solutions to customers worldwide.

Robert G. Laird is an architect with IBM in the SOA Advanced Technologies group, performing worldwide consulting for IBM customers in the area of SOA governance, SOA architecture, and telco architecture. He has previously coauthored *Executing SOA* for Pearson Publishing, and has also written white papers and articles on SOA and SOA governance. He has more than 30 years of industry and consulting experience. Bob worked at MCI (a U.S. telco) as the chief architect, where he led the Enterprise Architecture group and the creation of an SOA-based single-stack strategy for multiple legacy applications and networks, and led automation projects in network management, provisioning, and restoration. He also consulted nationally for American Management Systems.

Clive Gee, Ph.D., one of IBM's most experienced SOA governance practitioners, recently retired from his post as an Executive Consultant in the SOA Advanced Technologies group. He has worked in IT for more than 30 years, during the last few of which he led many SOA implementation and governance engagements for major clients all around the world, helping them to cope with the complexities of successfully transitioning to SOA. He now lives in Shetland, United Kingdom, but travels widely and does freelance consulting, especially in the area of SOA governance.

Tilak Mitra is a Senior Certified Executive IT Architect with IBM Global Business Services working very closely with the worldwide SOA Center of Excellence group in IBM. He specializes in SOAs, helping IBM in its business strategy and direction, fostering the maturity of SOA in the company. He also works as an SOA subject matter expert and architect, helping clients in their SOA-based business transformation, with a focus on complex and large-scale enterprise architectures. His current focus is on building SOA solutions for the chemicals and petroleum industry to optimize oil drilling and refinery processes. He has coauthored *Executing SOA* for Pearson Publishing, and has written several white papers and articles on SOA and SOA governance. He is a contributing editor of the *Java Developers Journal (JDJ)*.

Introduction

A Services Approach

"A man who does not think for himself does not think at all."

—Oscar Wilde

Service-oriented architecture (SOA) has been around long enough to justify a close examination of the benefits from its adoption, adherence, and usage in any organization. It is about time that the promises of SOA are measured against real-world SOA implementation experiences and that a business be able to learn how to properly govern an SOA program without having to do it the hard way, like through the pain and expense of personal experience. Some of that is inevitable, but this book shows you ahead of time what to do to save your company time and money.

This chapter begins with a discussion of some key benefits of SOA. Based on our real-world experiences with numerous SOA initiatives and implementations, we then explain why so few organizations actualize the full benefits of SOA, why certain dimensions of SOA are not executed correctly, and how other aspects of SOA are implemented to maximize its advantages.

Benefits of SOA

> *"In all affairs, it's a healthy thing now and then to hang a question mark on the things you have long taken for granted."*
>
> —Bertrand Russell

SOA presents a compelling value proposition that addresses a distinct set of business challenges which enterprises face today. The fundamental tenet of SOA is that it demands as much of a priority and commitment from the business stakeholders as it expects from the IT department. SOA demands that for a business to be agile and adaptive, the organization must represent the enterprise's core business processes through flexible business models. Next, one must expose its IT infrastructure, application capabilities along with its business critical information through a set of shared and reusable services so that each such service can participate in the implementation of the flexible business models. By building flexibility into the business models, through their representation as a set of participating services, enterprises can integrate third-party services into their core business processes, and thus reduce the cycle time and cost of integration with external businesses. SOA promises a way for businesses to model and structure their organizations and operations so that they can efficiently leverage individual capabilities, coordinate their efforts to leverage IT profitably, and reduce complexity. The net result is a greater ability for businesses to monitor, react, and adapt to new opportunities and changes.

SOA enforces standardized definitions and consistent implementations of business services, enabling IT transformations aligned with the business imperatives and drivers of the enterprise. The standards-based SOA layers between the digitized business processes and the underlying IT applications and infrastructure enable the business to confidently embrace agility, adaptability, and change through its flexible business processes. It also allows technology maturity, replacement, and modernization to take place without affecting or impeding the agility and adaptability of the enterprise business processes. Deconstruction and modularization of the business into a set of business-aligned services—a fundamental tenet of SOA—make SOA a close reflection of the business operating model.

The benefits of SOA are realized through the ways it tries to bridge the chasm that exists between the current business models and the traditional ones. As an example, a typical traditional business model is linear in structure. Business processes in such a traditional model are typically handled completely by individual departments or lines of business (LoB) in a company without any significant interaction and dependence on other parts of the organization. Today's business model must be nonlinear in nature, with parts of the business process typically being performed by either different departments in the organization or externally through business partners. For example, a customer may place an order through a company portal. Then, shared services in different parts of the organization, such as merchandising or the supply chain, perform different steps in the process. An example of this would be suppliers contributing to vendor-managed inventory or shipping being outsourced to a third party. This kind of desegregation of the business process, requiring a lot of flexibility, is made possible by SOA. The shared services are identified, designed, and implemented in ways such that a service can participate in multiple different business processes—both current and future.

SOA has many other benefits. By creating new value from existing systems, it changes our traditional view of legacy systems. It provides the value proposition of reusing legacy systems that have been the heart of existing enterprises and have been performing brilliantly. Reuse the existing system and applications without replacing them, but expose the capabilities that have been locked inside these proprietary and dated systems. As an example, consider an arcane Customer Relationship Management (CRM) package that stores business-critical customer-profile information. The access to such information typically requires a proprietary access protocol and data format. However, this customer information is increasingly required by businesses to provide, services such as, auto insurance, home insurance, and in the future, health insurance. Such critical data and functionality should be identified and exposed in a way that it can be accessed using a common and standard mechanism. SOA principles, best practices, and guidelines may be followed to achieve this goal. Such standard mechanisms of exposing business-critical information as a set of services enable an enterprise to drive down cost and operating expenses, eliminate duplicate systems through consolidation, and improve the time to market for new or enhanced capabilities. Through the incremental maturity of the enterprise service portfolio, the cost benefits of SOA result in a financial boon to the enterprise. None of this happens by accident though; there needs to be an explicit governance capability—without which, such efforts are doomed to failure.

What Goes Right?

"Honest differences are often a healthy sign of progress."

—Mahatma Ghandi

SOA is at the forefront of many business and IT initiatives. Consulting firms and product vendors have started to support SOA by demonstrating their capabilities, expertise, and maturity in this emerging discipline.

Organizations that have successfully crossed the initial hurdle of SOA have quickly realized that the most practical way to achieve the benefits of SOA's, reusability and flexibility is through standardization. In industries where a common domain model exists, such as ACORD in the insurance industry and eTOM in the telecommunications industry, enterprises have started to use those industry domain models as references. The industry domain model is usually inherited and customized to define an enterprise-level Common Information Model (CIM). The CIM is subsequently leveraged to derive the Common Message Model (CMM), which plays a critical part of the service definitions. The CIM and the CMM form the basis of standardization that can be applied to interfaces and data structures. Such standardization is also reducing the complexity of data-transformation requirements inside the enterprise perimeter—a necessary step to reduce the complexity of service-based integration.

There is now an increasing focus by companies to clearly understand the scope of the SOA transformation and follow well-proven methodologies for SOA.

SOA experts and consultants are keen to enforce a clear understanding of scope by employing a technique called goal-service modeling. The crux of this technique is in using business goals as the basis of defining and constraining the scope. Business goals are clearly articulated, prioritized, and signed off by the business stakeholders. So as to provide the greatest impact, only those services and applications are considered in the scope of the transformation that have a direct traceability back to the realization of the prioritized set of business goals that the business is keen on achieving. Chapter 4 of the book *Executing SOA—A Practical Guide for the Service-Oriented Architect* has a detailed treatment of these techniques. (For more information about the book, see Appendix B, "References.")

To mitigate and contain the risks related to learning this new, business-focused technique, organizations are performing a technical feasibility exploration (TFE). A TFE is performed in cases where the technology is not well proven and has a degree of complexity that is not easy to factor into a project plan based on a pure conjecture. TFEs are usually manifested through a set of proof of concepts (PoCs). These TFEs are identified and scoped ideally during the initial phases of the project, executed, and then their output and results are used to not only gain a better understanding of the technical complexity and nuances of service implementation but also to refine the architecture and design decisions. This added understanding assists in assigning resources (time, personnel, and expertise) commensurate with the complexity of the service implementations.

The industry has faced a nagging problem of how to crisply define the handoff between business and IT. Organizations are now keener to follow a prescriptive technique to document business requirements. Technology has assisted in formalizing this technique. We now have the luxury of using sophisticated business process modeling (BPM) tools that provide tooling and prescriptive guidance on how to capture the "as-is" and "to-be" BPMs. Many organizations have adopted the approach of using BPM tools and techniques to not only trace the lifecycle of the key business entities but also to document the requirements. We believe this is the correct approach to gain consensus and consistency of understanding and also to hand off requirements, in digital form, from the business to the IT departments.

Often, organizations in their early SOA adoption stages face daunting challenges in implementing new methodologies around SOA. These companies frequently face critical architecture decisions that risk large penalties for the wrong choices. These scenarios are addressed by working on a small piece of functionality that has an end-to-end coverage through all the layers of the SOA solution stack. Organizations use the outcome of such implementations to recalibrate the scope and complexity of SOA initiatives.

What Goes Wrong?

"He who has not first laid his foundations may be able with great ability to lay them afterwards, but they will be laid with trouble to the architect and danger to the building."

—*Niccolo Machiavelli*

In the formative years of SOA adoption, which by no means are over, we have frequently seen organizations take their existing business and IT staff and assign them new roles that are required to execute on an SOA initiative. Application architects are assumed to play the role of the SOA architect, and traditional business analysts are assumed to seamlessly pick up the similar role in an SOA project. Such assignments expose a lack of understanding by organizations about the specific requirements of a role in the context of SOA. The decision makers assigned the responsibility to staff SOA projects need to understand and acknowledge that role transition is neither trivial nor simple. For example, you can't just transition an application architect to an SOA architect. The person who does this job needs a deeper knowledge of the new products and technologies that constitute the entire SOA solution. A paradigm shift must occur in the process of architectural thinking, with reusability perceived at a higher level of abstraction, that of a business service. The architect must identify services that have business relevance and traceability; therefore, the architect must soundly understand the organization's business goals and drivers. This transformation from one type of architect to an SOA architect is just one example of the new skills, expertise, and thought processes that need to be mastered to meet one role of an SOA adoption.

Traditional business analysts must transition to operate in an SOA environment. This paradigm shift requires them to use new tools, technologies, and methods to define and develop the business requirements. This helps to transcend traditional organizational boundaries and thinking in terms of reusability of services and business processes at the enterprise level.

Organizations often jump onto the SOA bandwagon without assessing whether the organization has the maturity to adopt SOA as a business and IT imperative. We recommend that organizations first assess their organizational, cultural, technological, infrastructural, and personnel capabilities. Organizations must understand where they are from an SOA maturity standpoint. Then, they can use the maturity indicator metrics to develop a plan that helps them iteratively progress up the SOA maturity ladder.

Organizations also tend to jump onto the SOA bandwagon without assessing their capability to adopt SOA as an enterprise initiative. Commonly, such organizations fail to reap the true benefits of SOA and thus doom their investment. To mitigate this risk, IBM, as one of the leaders in championing SOA, has developed the Capability Assessment Tool (CAT), which enables its customers to perform a self-assessment of their maturity as it pertains to SOA adoption. It is publicly available, and the underpinning of this tool is an IBM technique called the Service Integration Maturity Model (SIMM). SIMM is used to measure the maturity of a company's SOA across seven dimensions. It is used in SOA assessments to identify where a company resides in terms of maturity, what target state of maturity it wants to achieve, and the benefits gained from achieving that target state. (For more information about SIMM, see Appendix B.) We highly recommend organizations to use SIMM as a stepping-stone into the world of SOA to avoid the pitfalls discussed in this section.

Communication between the business stakeholders and the IT department is a key to the success of SOA. It is common to come across SOA projects that fail to develop and execute an effective communication framework that keeps the business stakeholders in the loop from start to finish. The business stakeholders should be the ones to finalize whether a service that is identified by IT makes business sense and is relevant for them. Failure to keep business stakeholders properly informed is a sure way to miss out on the true value proposition of adopting SOA.

In most companies, a major deficit is an efficient governance structure that incorporates and enforces an effective alignment mechanism between the business and IT. The continual fine-tuning of the services, based on business inputs, is a highly recommended approach to demonstrate how business agility can be achieved through IT agility underpinnings. Through continual and effective governance, tangible results and benefits of SOA can be achieved and demonstrated.

SOA projects are often poorly estimated. Currently, no de facto standard technique exists to estimate SOA projects. Therefore, it is advisable to be more conservative than aggressive regarding the estimated timelines for each phase of the SOA project. However, the reality is quite the opposite, especially in organizations where the SOA maturity is still in its infancy. Estimations are frequently fooled by the mantra that SOA reduces the overall latency between requirements and deployed code. Many projects, by falling into this trap, shortchange themselves after overpromising to deliver. The reality is that the advantages of SOA directly correlate with the maturity of the organization in their SOA adoption. For low- to medium-mature firms, project costs for SOA initiatives, for the first couple of projects, will typically be more than that of traditional component-based development. This extra cost—in the form of time, resources, and funding—should be factored into the estimation model.

The scope of SOA adoption must be broadened and considered from the viewpoint of the enterprise of which the business units are part. Executing individual SOA projects that have their own imperatives and are not aligned with or traceable to the business vision and drivers is a recipe for failure. To mitigate such risks, we recommend that an SOA Center of Excellence (CoE) be set up at the enterprise level. The members of the SOA CoE should be adequately represented by both the business and IT wings of the enterprise. One of the primary SOA CoE responsibilities should be to set up an SOA governance model and framework. The SOA governance model works as a central decision rights and management framework and ensures that any SOA project has an enterprisewide and cross-project scope. Coordinating IT project initiatives through a central governing body ensures the correct level of granularity of a service's focus: Each SOA project is a cog in the wheel of an enterprisewide SOA initiative; all cogs need to turn smoothly and in harmony for the wheel of enterprise SOA adoption to gain momentum and move forward.

Conclusion

SOA is an architecture paradigm that enables IT to organize, define, and implement their projects in such a way that their value can be directly correlated with the business goals, vision, and drivers of the enterprise. Success in this endeavor requires SOA Governance. Although the benefits of SOA have far-reaching and positive influence on how an organization can leverage its IT capabilities and assets to prepare for business agility and responsiveness, SOA adoption is a serious undertaking that requires the organization to define a structured, iterative, incremental, and phased approach. The approach should be commensurate with the maturity of the organization across its various disciplines and dimensions.

This book shares our collective experience and knowledge gained from numerous SOA projects in the practice of SOA Governance. As we discussed earlier, successful SOA projects share common "good" practices, whereas other SOA attempts fail to maximize the benefits possible or fail outright. Based on our experience, we believe that SOA attempts fail more often than they succeed at this point. With that in mind, our goal in this book is to teach you how to use SOA Governance to properly govern and manage the SOA journey, increase the return on investment of the results, and decrease the risks.

I

Introduction to Governance

"Don't believe the hype."

—Chuck D., Public Enemy

To address the question *"What is SOA Governance"* we begin by defining and understanding the need for, and types of, governance. Everyone has an opinion about what governance is and isn't. Many think governance is an onerous structure that forces people to do things a certain way. They think it is rigid, inflexible, and unforgiving. They mostly think it just gets in the way. From the way most governance models are built, we can see their point.

Defining Governance

"It is better to lead from behind and to put others in front, especially when you celebrate victory when nice things occur. You take the front line when there is danger. Then people will appreciate your leadership."

—*Nelson Mandela*

Governance addresses the need for a process or set of processes to ensure that where appropriate the laws, policies, standards, and procedures are being adhered to. It also should appropriately distribute the rights and responsibilities under which an organization makes decisions and operates. There are a number of governance categories, including the following:

- Political governance, which includes
  - State and local
  - National
  - International (the United Nations, NATO, the Bank for International Settlements, the World Trade Organization, and so on)
- Enterprise/corporate governance, which includes
  - Compliance (audit and control committees)
  - IT governance
  - SOA governance
  - HR governance
  - Enterprise architecture governance
- Industry governance (industry organizations and associations)
- Nongovernmental organizations (NGOs) (International Red Cross and so on)

There are many other forms of governance that have specific roles associated with the segments of industry that they are responsible for. Examples include central banks, securities and exchange organizations, governing bodies... the list goes on.

Compliance is a key aspect of governance, and it is achieved by higher degrees of communication, comprehension, and buy-in of all the stakeholders. Enterprises conducting business today face a continuously changing business environment and a highly complex set of rules and regulations that require corporations to establish a governance model for the enterprise. For example, organizations must deal with Sarbanes-Oxley, the Patriot Act, and the broad array of industry-specific regulations. This makes governance an essential element of any enterprise.

To be effective, a corporation or enterprise must establish clear *chains of responsibility* to empower people, *measurements* to gauge effectiveness, *policies* to guide the organization to meet its goals, *control mechanisms* to ensure compliance, and *communication* to keep all required parties informed. Thus, we define governance as the following:

- Establishing chains of responsibility, authority, and communication to empower people (in other words, decision rights)
- Establishing measurement, policy, and control mechanisms to enable people to carry out their roles and responsibilities

It is important to clearly understand that there are differences between management and governance. Management, in a corporate context, is charged with directing and controlling people toward accomplishing a goal or goals. In the case of service-oriented architecture (SOA), that goal is the implementation of the processes required for the successful implementation and ongoing maintenance of SOA. This includes providing the required resources—specifically the people, processes, and technologies needed to sustain the SOA—and the associated services. It is these required resources, people, processes, and technologies that are subject to management.

Unlike management, governance is not charged with implementing the SOA; it is charged with providing oversight to see that the SOA is accomplished in a manner that satisfies the principles and policies required to successfully and continually sustain the SOA environment. The governance model, then, specifies the processes, polices, controls, and governance mechanisms required to monitor the SOA throughout the SOA lifecycle. The governance model also provides the organizational structure that defines the roles and responsibilities needed to operate the governance model and to ensure that the SOA is successful.

Corporate Governance

According to the Organization for Economic Cooperation and Development (OECD), Principles of Corporate Governance, 1999 (revised 2004), corporate governance is the system by which business corporations are directed and controlled. The corporate governance structure specifies the distribution of rights and responsibilities among different stakeholders in the corporation, such as the board of directors, managers, employees, and shareholders. It spells out the rules and procedures for making decisions about corporate issues. By doing this, it also provides the structure through which the company objectives are set; and the means of attaining those objectives and monitoring performance are established. The responsibilities of corporate governance include

- Shareholders' rights
- Accountability and disclosures and the integrity of the accounting and financial reporting system, including
  - Independent auditing
  - Controls (financial controls, risk management, and compliance with laws and regulations)
- Adherence to generally accepted standards, such as accounting
- Board roles and responsibilities

The need for corporate governance stems from

- The challenges associated with today's dynamic business environment
- The complexity of conducting business in an Internet-linked world
- Increased regulation by government and its agencies
- The high cost of errors and of remaining competitive
- The ever-increasing security needs and the vulnerability of the networked world
- The level and frequency of technological change
- The need to manage risk

In summary, corporate governance establishes the rules and the manner in which an enterprise conducts business, based on its strategies, the marketplace, and its principles of doing business. It defines for employees and for business partners the processes used to conduct operations and the manner in which people interact.

Enterprise Governance

In many instances, corporate governance and enterprise governance are indistinguishable from each other. However, at times, enterprise governance is assumed to be more focused on the "management of the management process" and on specific aspects of governance, such as operational controls, communications, strategic planning, and alignment with the goals of the enterprise.

For our purposes, the distinction between enterprise and corporate governance is not of consequence. SOA governance is focused on realizing the business benefits of an SOA. These benefits include flexibility, agility, reusability, and improved time to market. SOA governance provides a centralized approach with distributed capabilities that enable delivery of service orientation. SOA governance establishes the necessary environment of consistently facilitating interoperability between potential service consumers and providers. It also enables the company to realize economies of scale. As the approach matures, the resources become more efficient at delivering this functionality and progressively providing opportunities to realize the benefits of SOA. Hence the distinction between enterprise and corporate governance is moot because SOA governance focuses on the realization of business goals whether they are defined from an enterprise or corporate perspective.

IT Governance

IT governance addresses the application of governance to an IT organization and its people, processes, and information to guide the way for those assets to support the needs of the business. IT governance may be characterized by assigning decision rights and measures to processes, including, but not limited to, those defined by COBIT or ITIL. For example, IBM has developed PRM-IT (IBM Process Reference Model for IT) to address the set of processes associated with the operations and governance of the IT organization.

IT governance is an essential element of corporate governance that is embedded in all aspects of the corporate environment and touches all departments in an enterprise. As the Internet era evolves, organizations become increasingly dependent on IT and the quality of the services it provides. IT governance provides the framework and the integration point for the best practices associated with this evolution.

IT governance defines a structure of relationships and processes to direct and control the IT aspects of the enterprise to achieve the enterprise's goals by adding value while balancing risk versus return over IT and its processes. Risk is introduced in any IT environment when there are changes or additions to that environment. Without proper IT governance, these changes or additions can have a crippling effect. IT governance is the control or check and balance that enables responsible changes and additions.

SOA Governance

The Organization for the Advancement of Structured Information Standards (OASIS), www.oasis-open.org/home/index.php, SOA Reference Model defines SOA as follows:

Service Oriented Architecture (SOA) is a paradigm for organizing and using distributed capabilities that may be under the control of different ownership domains. It is natural in such a context to think of one person's needs being met by capabilities offered by someone else; or, in the world of distributed computing, one computer agent's requirements being met by a computer agent belonging to a different owner. There is not necessarily a one-to-one correlation between needs and capabilities; the granularity of needs and capabilities vary from fundamental to complex, and any given need may require the combining of numerous capabilities while any single capability may address more than one need. The perceived value of SOA is that it provides a powerful framework for matching needs and capabilities and for combining capabilities to address those needs.

The primary goal of the SOA is to bind the business world with the world of IT in a way that makes both more efficient. SOA is about creating a bridge that facilitates a symbiotic and synergistic relationship between the two that is more powerful and valuable than anything that we've experienced in the past. It is only partly about that bridge—the technology that binds the two worlds; it is much more so about the results that can be achieved from having that bridge in place. SOA allows for both abstracted and distributed technology to be leveraged, as if centralized, which for many organizations is a very appealing concept.

The trend toward componentization of both business and IT promises to make business more responsive. The use of services for this improved responsiveness and flexibility is seen as a key enabler. Recognizing the importance of shared services in companies with federated models or highly application-siloed environments requires governance and management around the notion of a shared service. The need for governance and management is equally important to govern incentive schemes, funding models, and collaborations that help organizations generate value from implementing service orientation.

Organizations must address many key questions if they are to obtain value from SOA. For example

- What major service-oriented capabilities are needed in the enterprise or line of business?
- What organization change is required? What new organizational roles and structures are required to facilitate service identification, design, and sharing?
- How do you organize the IT function to build and leverage service-oriented capabilities?
- What metrics support investment, maintenance, vitality, and sharing/reuse of services?
- How do you ensure that the benefits of an SOA are being realized and that success is being measured?

SOA governance extends IT governance as enterprises increase their level of service orientation. SOA is a cross-functional initiative involving business and IT in the collective pursuit to deliver on the enterprise's strategy and goals. Hence, SOA governance must bridge any gaps between corporate and IT governance.

SOA governance is specifically focused on the lifecycle of services, metadata, and composite applications in an organization's SOA. SOA governance extends IT governance by assigning decision rights, policies, and measures around the services, processes, and lifecycle to address such concerns as:

- Service registration
- Service versioning
- Service ownership
- Service funding
- Service modeling
- Selection of services to meet business needs and goals
- Service discovery and access
- Deployment of services and composite applications
- Security for services
- Service management

SOA Governance Paradigm

"I have discovered in life that there are ways of getting almost any-where you want to go, if you really want to go."

— Langston Hughes

As SOA governance practitioners, we must take a more structured approach to the art of governing, and turn it, as much as possible, into a science. To do this, we define a paradigm for governance. After the governance paradigm is defined, a number of governance components, including the service development lifecycle, are explained in more detail. You may well have additional governance components beyond the ones described in this chapter. The governance paradigm described here applies equally to those additional components and will help you derive the policies, standards, responsible parties, procedures, mechanisms, and metrics that you need to govern that component.

- **Definition of governed component.** Identifies a specific capability requiring governance.
- **Definition of policy.** A deliberate plan of action to guide decision and actions (per Wikipedia). A policy applies to the governed component.
- **Definition of standard.** A rule or requirement that controls (per Wikipedia). The governed component would need to adhere to the agreed standards.
- **Definition of responsible party.** A person or group of people that is responsible for managing the governed component. It must be clear for each component who this responsible party is.
- **Definition of procedure.** A particular method for performing a task. The procedure identifies how a component will be governed.
- **Definition of mechanism.** A particular method for performing a task. This is where an existing asset, methodology, or best practice will be applied to assist in the governance of this component.
- **Definition of metric.** A measure for something (per Wikipedia). It is important to put in place the measurements for the success of this governance component.
- **Definition of processes.** A process is a naturally occurring or designed sequence of operations or events, possibly taking up time, space, expertise, or other resources, which produces some outcome. A process may be identified by the changes it creates in the properties of one or more objects under its influence.

It is important to have a governance paradigm to assist the governance practitioner in specifying each of the aspects of the governed entity. The governance paradigm described in Figure 1.1 is as described in *Executing SOA* and has proven to be a good one in governance consulting practice. The governed component is the capability requiring governance. That governance is guided by policies, controlled by standards, managed by a responsible party, implemented by some process or procedure, supported by a mechanism or method, and monitored by a set of metrics.

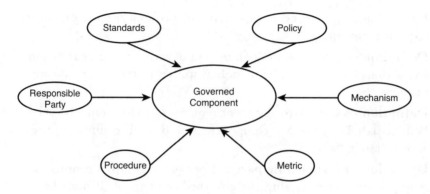

Figure 1.1 SOA Governance Paradigm

As shown in Table 1.1, SOA governance addresses key decisions for service orientation and it extends key IT decisions around the lifecycle of a service that accentuates the SOA aspects required in IT governance. The Key Governance Consideration table matches some areas of IT governance with SOA governance considerations to illustrate how SOA governance extends IT governance.

Table 1.1 Key Governance Considerations

KEY IT GOVERNANCE CONSIDERATION	CORRESPONDING SOA GOVERNANCE CONSIDERATION
Strategic IT Plan	Services Transformation Planning
Information Architecture	Information Transformation Planning
Technology Direction	Technology Transformation Planning
IT Processes, Organization, and Relationships	Service Processes, Organizations, Roles, and Responsibilities
Manage the IT Investment	Manage the Service Investment
Communicate Management Aims and Direction	Service Communication Planning
Manage Human Resources	Procurement of Resources
Manage Quality	Service Development Lifecycle Controls
Assess and Manage IT Risks	Enterprise Program Management

KEY IT GOVERNANCE CONSIDERATION	CORRESPONDING SOA GOVERNANCE CONSIDERATION
Manage Projects	Enterprise Program Management, Change Management
Ensure Systems Security	Technology Transformation Planning
Educate and Train Users	Service Education and Training
Monitor and Evaluate IT Performance	Service Execution Monitoring

See Figure 1.2 for key IT governance decisions.

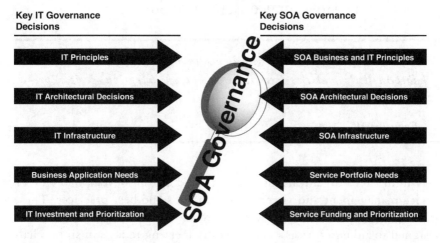

Figure 1.2   Key IT Governance Decisions

An optimal approach to SOA governance is to help SOA governance implementers assess their existing organizational and IT environment, so that they can easily understand what elements they need to consider when defining a governance model. This approach should also help them take these critical inputs and define an SOA governance model that their enterprise will adopt, accept, and embrace with a low learning curve that will lead to a short adoption time frame as opposed to one that the company will just try to circumvent. This approach should also help instantiate and enable the governance model with tooling.

For many organizations, governance is de facto and may not be aligned with corporate governance. For some organizations, SOA governance may not only bridge gaps between business and IT, but over time fix any problems with IT governance. As the enterprise increases its level of *service orientation,* the SOA governance aspect will also increase and eventually SOA governance will merge with IT governance. This is ultimately accomplished when the business and IT gap divide is dissolved.

Successful organizations understand the benefits of IT and use this knowledge to drive their shareholders' value. They recognize the critical dependence of many business processes on IT, the need to comply with increasing regulatory compliance demands, and the benefits of managing risk effectively.

IT Governance Reference Sources

"If you are going to achieve excellence in big things, you develop the habit in little matters. Excellence is not an exception, it is a prevailing attitude."

—Colin Powell

A number of organizations are dedicated to the development of IT service management and governance standards and best practices. These organizations provide a variety of tools, standards, and processes designed to aid enterprises in successfully meeting today's business challenges related to IT governance. Note that the materials referenced here focus on *IT governance,* not SOA governance. However, because much of SOA governance may be viewed as an extension of IT governance, *these materials provide a sound basis for understanding and analysis of the modifications required to establish SOA governance.* We will discuss two of the most widely accepted and implemented frameworks for IT governance:

- IT Information Library (ITIL®)
- IT Governance Institute® (ITGI) version 4.1 of Control Objectives for Information and Related Technology (COBIT®)

ITIL—Information Technology Information Library

ITIL® is an internationally recognized and constantly evolving collection of IT best practices designed to help organizations overcome current and future technology challenges. The focus of ITIL is primarily on IT service management. Originally created by the U.K. government, ITIL® is the result of years of experience contributed by major IT organizations and companies, including IBM. IT departments around the world use ITIL® as a roadmap to help guide efficient and effective implementation of current technology—including the realization of an IT service management strategy. ITIL® is owned by the U.K. government's Office of Government Commerce. For more information, see the OGC ITIL® site and Figure 1.3

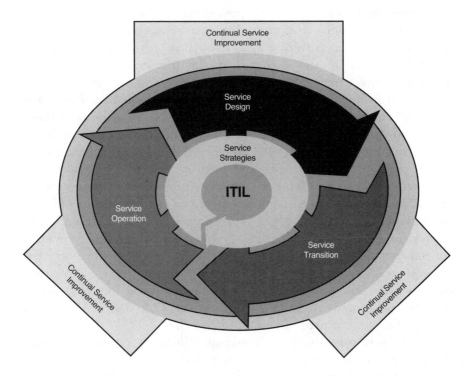

Figure 1.3   Information Technology Information Library (ITIL)

IT Governance Institute® (ITGI) version 4.1 of Control Objectives for Information and Related Technology (COBIT®)

The IT Governance Institute (ITGI) version 4.1 of Control Objectives for Information and Related Technology (COBIT). COBIT is an IT governance framework and supporting toolset that allows managers to bridge the gap between control requirements, technical issues, and business risks. COBIT enables clear policy development and good practice for IT control throughout organizations.

COBIT provides good practices across a domain and process framework and presents activities in a manageable and logical structure. COBIT's good practices represent the consensus of experts. They are strongly focused more on control, less on execution. These practices will help optimize IT-enabled investments, ensure service delivery, and provide a measure against which to judge when things do go wrong. For IT to be successful in delivering against business requirements, management should put an internal control system or framework in place. The COBIT control framework contributes to these needs by making a link to the business requirements, organizing IT activities into a generally accepted process model, identifying the major IT resources to be leveraged, and defining the management control objectives to be considered.

The business orientation of COBIT consists of linking business goals to IT goals, providing metrics and maturity models to measure their achievement, and identifying the associated responsibilities of business and IT process owners. The process focus of COBIT is illustrated by a process model that subdivides IT into 4 domains and 34 processes in line with the responsibility areas of plan, build, run, and monitor, providing an end-to-end view of IT. Enterprise architecture concepts help identify the resources essential for process success (i.e., applications, information, infrastructure, and people). In summary, to provide the information that the enterprise needs to achieve its objectives, IT resources need to be managed by a set of naturally grouped processes.

COBIT is managed by the IT Governance Institute and the Information Systems Audit and Control Foundation® (ISACF). For more information about COBIT, see www.isaca.org/template.cfm?Section=COBIT6.

Many corporations will have developed their IT governance framework from one of, or a combination of, the governance processes defined by these organizations. Note that each of these organizations takes a slightly different approach to IT governance and each defines governance processes in a slightly different way.

The SOA Governance and Management Model

"Those who say it can't be done are usually interrupted by others doing it."

—James A. Baldwin

The SOA Governance and Management Model (SGMM) presents a framework for the definition, design, and implementation of SOA governance and management. The model presented in Figure 1.1 provides a visual representation of the governance and governed processes and the mechanisms and components that are needed to implement and manage them.

To develop the SGMM, the developers will utilize the corporation's SOA vision and the policies and standards to define/refine the processes that will be executed to effectively govern the operation and evolution of the SOA. Each aspect of the governance model has specific processes that may require the definition of new decision rights, policies, and measures, and possibly the modification of some of the existing IT processes.

Figure 1.4 illustrates the key components of the governance and management model. It provides a pictorial example of how the *governed processes,* which are the activities that need to be governed and managed through the services lifecycle, are governed and managed by the four foundational governance processes: compliance, communication, exception and appeals, and vitality. As these governed processes are constructed or modified, metrics and metric collection points are identified, and polices and standards evaluation points are inserted so that compliance or noncompliance can be determined. The model is implemented by the appropriate mechanisms, executed by an organizational structure that possesses the necessary skills. The complete set of components illustrates how a comprehensive governance model can be visualized for SOA governance and management.

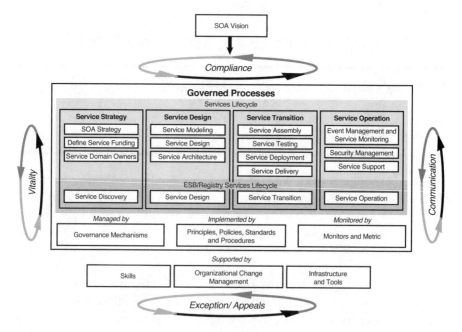

Figure 1.4   SOA Governance and Management Model

SOA Vision

The SOA vision is the starting point for an SOA governance engagement. Optimally, the SOA vision would be the result of activities performed before defining an SOA governance model. The definition of an SOA vision must consider some essential elements that need to be available before an SOA governance engagement can begin. The optimal set of elements would include

- SOA vision and strategy
- High-level business case for SOA
- High-level SOA reference architecture roadmap (which can be done concurrently with the definition of the SOA governance model)

At a minimum, the implementers' governance team would require an SOA vision, strategy, and roadmap to begin an engagement. If these elements are not available, an SOA governance initiative may choose to complete these elements before the start of the governance activities.

Governance Processes

The governance processes (see Figure 1.5) form the building blocks of any SOA governance model.

Governance Processes: High Level View

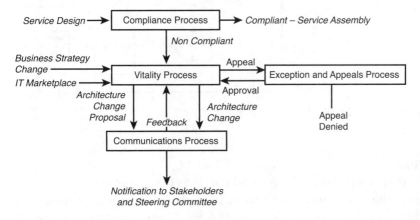

Figure 1.5 Governance Processes

Compliance

Compliance provides the mechanism for review and approval/rejects against the criteria established in the governance framework (i.e., principles, policies, standards, roles, responsibilities, and so on). This process is performed at various points during the SOA governance lifecycle. See Figure 1.6 for more detail.

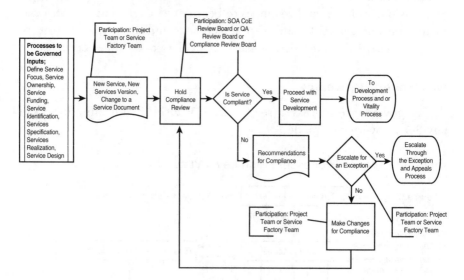

Figure 1.6   Compliance Process

Vitality

Vitality maintains the applicability of the governance model. It requires the governance model to be current, reflecting the business and IT direction and strategy. It must also refine the governance processes and mechanisms composed of organizational entities and supporting roles to ensure ongoing usage and relevance to an implementation. See Figure 1.7 for more detail

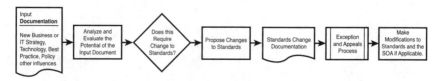

Figure 1.7   Vitality Process

Exceptions and Appeals

The exceptions and appeals process allows a project to appeal for and gain a use exception for a solution, process, policy, investment, or design that is noncompliant with the established governance framework. See Figure 1.8 for more detail.

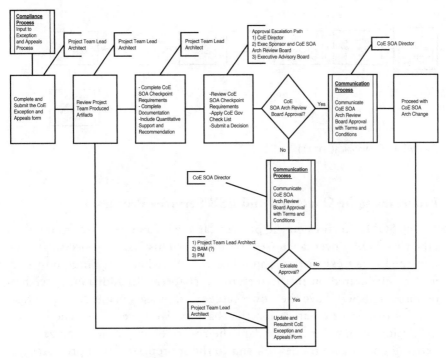

Figure 1.8   Exceptions and Appeals Process

Communications

Communication is aimed at educating and communicating the governance model across the organization. It includes ensuring that governance is acknowledged and understood and setting up environments and tools to allow easy access and use of the governance information. See Figure 1.9 for more detail.

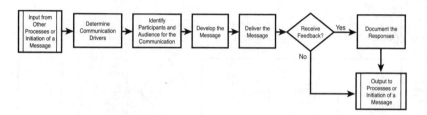

Figure 1.9   Communications Process

Processes to be Governed and ESB Services Processes

The SGMM focuses on the process categories and processes to be governed by SOA governance (see Table 1.2). This list of processes to be governed is not exhaustive, should be considered as a starting point and will be elaborated on in the remaining chapters. In addition, note that organizations will have their own categories, process names, and descriptions within their organization that have evolved over time. The implementation team will need to adapt their work effort to the organization's existing governance framework and to the appropriate set of processes for the initiative.

The scope of the enterprise service bus (ESB) services lifecycle process includes the processes required to identify, design, develop, test, implement, and manage ESB services.

It is *unlikely* that a single engagement would comprise all the processes listed in Table 1.2.

Table 1.2 Processes to Be Governed

Category	Process Name	Process Description
Service Strategy	SOA Strategy	SOA strategy defines the desired degree of service orientation and service maturity. This process provides a mechanism to evaluate initiatives/projects with regard to the corporation's desired degree of service focus.
	Service Funding	This process establishes the rules for service funding for new and enhanced services and for the mechanisms used to provide incentives for service re-use.
	Service Ownership	This process identifies and manages service domains and service ownership.
Service Design	Service Architecture	This process defines the SOA reference architecture, including architectural models, standards and design, development, and infrastructure design techniques.
	Service Modeling	This process defines the key activities required for the analysis to build services and the techniques required for the identification, specification, and realization of services.
	Service Design	Service design addresses the detailed design and specification of services based on design techniques, patterns, and standards.
Service Transition	Service Assembly	Service assembly allows developers to create new services that follow predefined rules and processes based on defined architectural standards.
	Service Testing	Services must be tested at multiple levels to ensure they meet the stated functional and nonfunctional objectives according to the service contract criteria.
	Service Deployment	The service deployment process manages the registration and configuration of services and release into production. Service changes and versioning are also managed by this process.
	Service Delivery	Service delivery manages the realization of service levels, organization satisfaction, and service availability, along with addressing capacity requirements.

Table 1.2 Processes to Be Governed (continued)

Category	Process Name	Process Description
Service Operation	Event Management and Service Monitoring	This process is used to monitor workload and system events that could cause service outages/problems.
	Security Management	This process covers the lifecycle of security concerns, including planning, operational measures, evaluation, and audit.
	Service Support	The service support process manages problems, incidents, and the interaction with service users.
ESB Lifecycle Process Name		
Service Strategy	Service Opportunity Identification	The goal of this process is to evaluate and identify a business need, and to determine whether the business need can be met through the use of ESB shared services.
	Service Discovery	The goal of this process is to complete the discovery phase for a project that has been identified as a potential ESB services candidate project.
Service Design	Service Inception	The goal of this process is to gather the high-level requirements for the ESB shared services that will be developed as part of the potential ESB services candidate project.
	Service Elaboration	The goal of this process is to further define the high-level requirements from the inception phase into detailed requirements for construction to complete the service solution design and to take the necessary steps to prepare for the construction phase.
Service Transition	Service Construction	The goal of this process is to develop the integration components and integrate the ESB shared services components per the design guidelines while meeting/exceeding the necessary quality requirements so that the services can be deployed for general use.

Category	Process Name	Process Description
	Service Transition	The main purpose of this process is to transition the ESB shared services developed in the construction phase to the operations team that will be responsible for ongoing ESB shared service maintenance.
Service Operation	Manage Services	The goal of this process is to manage the ESB shared services after they have been transitioned to the operations team that will be responsible for ongoing ESB shared service maintenance.
	Exception/ Escalation	The purpose of this process is resolve issues that occur during the ESB services lifecycle process in an expedient manner.

Governance Mechanisms

"Great leaders are almost always great simplifiers, who can cut through argument, debate and doubt, to offer a solution everybody can understand."

—Colin Powell

Governance mechanisms provide the structure required to implement and operate SOA governance. The mechanisms specify and describe organizational structures, roles and responsibilities, functions, purpose, and lifecycles. Carefully designed and implemented mechanisms that reflect the organizations culture and principles are essential to effective SOA governance.

Principles, Policies, Standards, and Procedures

In our Governance paradigm earlier in this chapter, we gave brief definitions on some of these governance terms. Let's now elaborate on some of the important governance concepts. The principles, policies, standards, and procedures document the underlying general rules and guidelines that an organization will use to utilize and deploy services across the enterprise.

To be effective, all principles, policies, standards, and procedures should be agreed by both senior business and IT executives:

- A principle defines the underlying general rules that an organization has to use and deploy all business and IT resources and assets, across the enterprise. Principles should always include defined motivation and implication statements.

  Many different types and levels of principles can be defined. In the governance model, we are concerned with the business and IT principles associated with the deployment of the SOA and its governance.

- A policy is a statement of how things will be managed or organized, including management goals, objectives, beliefs, and responsibilities. Policies are normally defined at an overall strategy level and can be related to a specific area (for example, security policies and management policies). In many instances, policies reflect the law and givens, which must be adhered to.

- Standards are defined as something with a predescribed specification, that is measurable, recognized as having authoritative value, and which an organization chooses to implement as a basis for "good practice."

- Procedures are a specification of the series of actions, acts, or operations that have to be executed in the same manner to consistently obtain the same result in the same circumstances (for example, emergency procedures). Less precisely speaking, this word can indicate a sequence of activities, tasks, steps, decisions, calculations, and processes that when undertaken in the sequence laid down produces the described result, product, or outcome.

Monitors and Metrics

The monitors and associated metrics required to measure and report on the performance of the SOA are a key component of the governance model. The model will documents all monitoring metrics associated with the SOA components being implemented.

Skills

An essential element of the governance model is the definition and specification of the skills required to implement and maintain the governance model. Skill requirements include business and IT specialties and the qualifications to implement an effective governance model.

Organizational Change Management

The implementation of an SOA often creates a significant amount of organizational change. This includes changes in the business models, changes in the operating model, and minimization of many "silos." The organization archetype, the way the organization is run, is expected to change to reap the benefits of the SOA. Elements of the organizational change include governance planning, talent management, service ownership, business responsiveness, and organization redesign that must occur to get the agility that stems from an SOA. These changes need to be identified and planned in the organizational change management approach to implementing the governance model and assisting with the implementation of SOA.

Infrastructure and Tools

Underlying all the SOA is an infrastructure that provides security, directory, IT system management, and virtualization functions. The security and directory services include functions involving authentication authorizations required for implementing (for example, single sign-on capabilities across a distributed and heterogeneous system).

Services management includes functions that *relate* to scale and performance. For example, end services, clustering services, and the virtualization capabilities allow efficient use of computing resources based on load patterns and so forth. The ability to leverage grids and grid computing are also included in infrastructural services. While infrastructure and IT service management services perform functions tied directly to hardware or system implementations, others provide functions that interact directly with integration services provided in other elements of the architecture. These interactions also involve services related to the governance model and the associated tools to monitor the performance of the SOA and the governance model.

The SOA architecture is a complete and comprehensive architecture that covers all the integration needs of an enterprise. Its services are well integrated and are delivered in a modular way, allowing SOA implementations to start at a small-project level. As each additional project is addressed, new functions can easily be added, incrementally enhancing the scope of the integration across the enterprise. In addition to supporting SOA strategies and solutions, the architecture itself is designed using principles of service orientation and function isolation.

Case Study Background

> *"Walking is a man's best medicine."*
>
> —*Hippocrates*

We are taking the point of view for this book on SOA governance that a case study approach will help to drive home the points and help you understand and apply the practical aspects of planning and building a governance capability.

At the end of each chapter, the case study will use some of the salient aspects that have been explained to provide an example of the application of those aspects against the governance needs of a fictional company. This company, Ideation Communications, does not really exist, and any resemblance to an existing company is completely coincidental.

Company Background

Ideation Communications started as local, independent communications service provider in the rural areas of the Midwestern portion of the United States, offering Plain Old Telephone Service (POTS) to satisfy the communication needs of a largely agrarian customer base separated by long distances.

Despite its business being initially rural, Ideation has always placed an emphasis on implementing technological innovation as quickly as it makes sense, for the benefit of its customers and workers. Ideation was one of the first communications providers to offer 100% dial service with no manual operators needed. Ideation employed microwave towers in the 1970s in its territory and leased the bandwidth to truckers and local companies. This soon grew into a national footprint that provided a long-distance telephony service that grew profits explosively. Data capabilities with ATM (Asynchronous Transfer Mode) and Frame Relay were added due to corporate demand. Ideation was one of the first companies to see the value of the Internet and chose to purchase a company (Inet) that had created an Internet network capability that both commercial and residential customers use.

Cell (mobile) phone was seen as a strategic differentiator, and Ideation built a strong presence of cell towers and service in its territory and has been trying to expand into a more national presence. There is a repeated emphasis on "the customer comes first," and the company strives to give customers the services that they want at a fair price, while at the same time providing a quality customer service experience at all of their stakeholder touch points.

On the employee side, Ideation has had another point of emphasis on "safety first." For example, in the 1950s, all field personnel involved in truck rolls were equipped with nylon body belts and climber straps when those were first available. Workers have been treated with respect, and their ideas are continuously solicited by management for getting the job done better, faster, and cheaper. As a result of the new markets that Ideation has entered over time, there have continuously been new opportunities for personnel, and this, combined with the progressive treatment by management, has led to a high degree of worker loyalty and commitment.

Ideation is currently experiencing tough times, though. Long distance, a cash cow for several decades, has now been commoditized as a result of deregulation and usage of Voice over IP (VoIP) by many of its former and even current subscribers. Revenue has continued to decrease in this area by 10% a year, and shows no signs of stopping despite repeated marketing campaigns by Ideation's customer service centers. Its ATM and Frame Relay revenue and customers have also atrophied in favor of Internet services such as virtual private network (VPN). Cell phone service has grown about 15% per year, but is now coming under attack from bigger and better capitalized national providers.

Increasingly, management attention has been drawn to the many different systems and operations groups and the various networks that Ideation maintains, as something that is impacting their margins (see Figure 1.10).

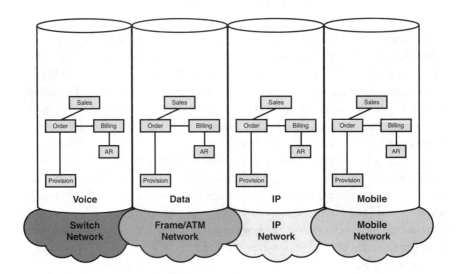

Figure 1.10   Ideation Systems and Networks

There are many different ordering systems, provisioning systems, billing systems, and network management systems. Each of these systems has its own support structure, subject matter experts, business analysts, management structure, and development cycles. Because the business has required products that involve bundles of existing network capabilities, the amount of time to get a new release out has continually increased with missed schedules, project de-scope, budget over runs, or all three.

Business Goals

A year ago, at the direction of the board of directors, Ideation assembled its best and brightest and some industry consultants to analyze the corporate and industry trends and the current situation for Ideation and to come up with the business goals and objectives that would enable it to reverse the negative trends. Some of their conclusions on the current state of Ideation included the following:

■ We built up rapidly because of market opportunities and never took the time to integrate our business well. As a result, we are characterized by many separate lines of business (LoB).

- Our cost structure is too high. We have much duplication of services across our various LoBs, and this is hampering our ability to significantly reduce costs and increase margins.

- Our ability to offer bundles is constrained by the silos that have been built up in our IT infrastructure. Integrating any of our products requires a huge IT effort with a minimum time frame of two years. This is constraining Ideation's ability to react to market opportunities.

- Our ability to gather information about our customers and to exploit our strategic relationship with them to sell new products and services is severely constrained. Customer data is distributed in various LoB databases, each having a different customer ID and name. Ideation is losing out on market opportunities against our current customer base as a result.

- Ideation is too small to survive as an independent entity. It is highly likely that we will be bought in the next three years. Our value will be enhanced to the degree that we are able to integrate our LoBs and operations, decrease costs, improve margins, and improve our business agility. We have 12 months to get this going before we will be constrained by the investment environment.

In consultation with the board, Ideation Communications created the following business goals for the next year:

- Be able to create new product bundles in six months time measured from product marketing ideation to product offering in the marketplace.

- Decrease the operating run rate by 10%.

- Create upsell opportunities with our current customers that result in an increased average revenue per user (ARPU) by 5%.

- Create a common services organization and merge duplicative corporate capabilities into this single organization. This will include finance, HR, and data center support.

- Create and implement a business agility capability that includes a governance organization and linkage to the business so that they can work together. For example, groups such as enterprise architecture, the business, and IT must work together to bring quality to Ideation's business and to achieve the goals Ideation has outlined.

The path ahead is a difficult one for Ideation. Although they still have a positive corporate culture, Ideation experienced its first layoff this year, and the staff is wary of any changes. Rumors about a merger with an acquiring company have been floating around for some time, further inflaming the angst of the staff.

You have been selected by the CIO to lead the governance organization and are working with a highly intelligent and motivated team that has been charged with the task of creating business agility. The first order of business is to do a governance planning assessment. This will be documented in the "Case Study Example" section in Chapter 2, "SOA Governance Assessment and Planning."

Conclusion

"After climbing a great hill, one only finds that there are many more hills to climb."

—Nelson Mandela

In summary, companies that implement an SOA governance model will require a focus in all aspects of SOA governance and management. However, many initiatives will initially be scoped to include only a subset of the elements and components we have presented in this chapter. What is implemented will be determined by the organization's immediate versus long-term needs and plans, and their level of SOA and IT maturity.

2

SOA Governance Assessment and Planning

In Chapter 1, "Introduction to Governance," we introduced the concept of SOA governance and its relationship to IT and corporate governance. In this chapter, we show you how to assess the current status of an SOA and SOA governance initiative for an organization and to identify the most important focus areas and potential inhibitors to success. This assessment then enables you to plan for the definition of SOA governance for the organization. In Chapter 3, "Building the Service Factory," and Chapter 4, "Governing the Service Factory," we begin to develop a treatment plan that addresses the most critical risk areas and introduces some longer-term changes to improve the overall health of the organization's SOA initiatives.

Setting the Vision

> *"The nicest thing about not planning is that failure comes as a complete surprise and is not preceded by a period of anxiety."*
>
> —John Preston, Boston University

There is no single correct checklist for creating effective governance. Tooling can help make governance more effective, but tooling alone is not the answer to something that is so human centric. For example, effective governance can never be achieved through the imposition of a set of rigid authoritarian rules. Humans resent being subjected to dictatorial rules, and if you try this approach, the more creative and inventive members of staff—those who could potentially have most to offer on an effective SOA journey—may well spend most of their energies in finding interesting ways to evade conforming to them. Similarly, letting the "inmates run the asylum" and relying on the IT staff to combine their efforts with little or no supervision is also doomed to failure. The amount of control that is necessary, yet effective, is a matter of the culture of the organization balanced against the risks associated with the failure of the governance function to actually govern.

Excellence can be achieved by encouraging teamwork through the creation of shared goals, and by motivating individuals to contribute toward achieving them. Rules are needed as a final protection against bad behavior, but the emphasis should be on promoting cooperation, professionalism, personal involvement, and commitment, rather than on punishment of misdemeanors. Innovation should be encouraged, provided it performs in support of shared objectives.

Practical governance is all about transparency, which is ensuring that everyone involved in any activity clearly understands his specific roles and responsibilities, what expectations all the contributors have of each other, and how everyone contributes to the overall performance of that activity. People feel more involved when they have a degree of control over their own actions, so empowering staff to make decisions helps to promote individual commitment and responsibility.

We start by looking at what patterns and approaches are common to those organizations that have achieved excellence at SOA, and then we look at some of the more common pitfalls that we have seen in our work with clients who have yet to achieve that status.

What Distinguishes the SOA Winners?

"The important thing to recognize is that it takes a team, and the team ought to get credit for the wins and the losses. Successes have many fathers, failures have none."

–Philip Caldwell

Whatever their size, country of origin, and industry, the organizations that we have seen that are most successful with migration to SOA share some or all of the following characteristics that SOA governance must seek to engender:

- There is a close working relationship between the business units and IT at all levels of the organization. The CIO and CTO are influential members of the board, most or all of the business units see IT as adding value, and the business analysts are regarded by all as the true subject matter experts (SMEs) on how the organization functions. Ideally, the business analysts report to business units, rather than to IT, and are working with a business-facing group from IT.

- For a long time, it was believed that SOA would succeed only when the impetus for SOA was entirely business led. Most SOA professionals now regard this as an unrealistic expectation: Typically, most business operational units have a jaundiced view of the way their IT departments support them, and are skeptical of the value of introducing new technology.

- In practice, most or all SOA implementations are initiatives of the IT department. If the IT department is committed to improving its alignment and image with the rest of the organization, ample opportunity exists for success, even though it might be a lengthy process. Business buy in can be created as IT works with the business and gets it to understand the ability of SOA to provide business agility, but this takes time and effort, principally from the groups responsible for enterprise architecture and SOA governance. A major characteristic of a services approach is that it provides a language that describes units of function that are unambiguous to both the business and IT. Both a business professional and an IT developer would understand exactly what services such as "get customer summary," "process payment," and so on mean, although their contexts would be completely different. For example, the business professional might see them as essential components of a sales process, whereas the developer might think of them in terms of database access or secure communications with a credit card processing service. This provides an opportunity for IT to move up the value chain by communicating with the business in its own language. This makes for more effective communication and is the key to maintaining a healthy relationship between the two.

- The organization has implemented enterprise architecture. IT has adopted and published a set of common standards, architectural decisions, and best practices, together with an organization, such as an architecture board, that enforces their use. The Enterprise Architecture group will have created a cross line-of-business (LoB) vision and plan for the rationalization of the current business, application, information, and technical architectures. "Architectural decisions" is one of the most useful work products of all. It denotes not only what technical decisions have been made, but why those choices were made. They describe the problem being addressed, the alternative solutions that were considered and their respective advantages and disadvantages, the chosen option, and the reasons for that choice. Typical examples include selecting a standard coding language, security infrastructure, operational infrastructure components, and so on.

- The organization has a structured approach to software development; typically, this includes a consistent work-product-based development approach, a common development methodology, common tools to enhance developer and tester productivity, and the existence of an empowered QA department.

- The organization has created a formal set of intermediate work products (for example requirements, a use case model, design documentation, and test plans). These enable continuous quality assessment, helping to detect and correct misunderstandings or errors before the cost of correction becomes excessive.

- No organization should consider outsourcing any portion of its IT activities unless they have a complete set of work products to ensure that their needs are conveyed accurately, completely, and unambiguously to the outsourcers; that there are formal contracts in place that define the vendor's deliverables; their quality and timeliness; and a recognized mechanism to assess compliance to those contracts.

- The organization is committed to use of its common enterprise data model. Some form of a common messaging model, if not an immediate common enterprise data model is an absolute prerequisite to an optimal SOA implementation. Service operations have input and output data, representing business entities. Unless there is a common definition of how to represent these business entities, there is no possibility of creating enterprise-ready reusable services without a significant amount of data transformation for each project. The term operation refers to a specific invocation of a service. The term service has become badly overloaded, and means something completely different to business or IT professionals. Services are really just a collection of operations associated with a specific business entity. (For example, the customer service would include the operations lookupCustomer, getCustomerSummary, and updateCustomer.) Note that services are represented by nouns, and operations by verbs. For those familiar with object orientation, the analogy to methods and classes is obvious.

- Often, a recognized industry data model can be used as the basis for such an enterprise model. Use of such models makes it much easier to share services with business partners (for example, the Association for Retail Technology Standards® Data model; see www.nrf-arts.org/).

- The organization has an effective institutional memory. The best mechanism to enable reuse and avoid duplication is an ability to discover and access all existing assets, be they in the form of knowledge, data, or executables. Leading SOA organizations preserve and catalog assets such as the following:
  - A business term glossary
  - Business rules
  - Requirements (by business entity, as well as by project)
  - Business process model/use case model
  - Services and code fragments that are service components

- Application capability and design documentation
- Application programming interfaces (APIs)
- Data dictionaries

Note that it's the cataloging that is most important. Documents hidden in massive documents for specific projects, on individual's hard drives, or buried in a morass of individual team rooms are completely worthless when it comes to reuse. Data dictionaries are important, too, because they describe how to translate data elements between the standard (canonical) enterprise data model, and whatever form they take in any applications, systems, or databases that do not conform to the canonical format.

- The organization has already instituted effective corporate and IT governance.
- The organization knows which services to create or knows how to go about deciding which services to create in terms of business priority, service granularity (size, complexity, scope), and return on investment. Executives have realized that SOA is beginning to have real impact on the bottom line.

Note that the preceding bullets are not specific to SOA, but are basic tenets of effective IT governance. They are, however, virtually mandatory prerequisites for success at SOA, and if the organization you are supporting does not possess these capabilities, you will have to develop these to some degree before you will have any chance of succeeding in implementing SOA and SOA governance.

Antipatterns: Common SOA Pitfalls

"There is nothing so useless as doing efficiently that which should not be done at all"

—Peter F. Drucker

Here are some of the common antipatterns—destructive chains of behavior by individuals or organizations—that we see regularly when we visit clients who are having problems with managing the transition to SOA:

- Belief in the "silver bullet" or quick fix. This is an astonishingly common antipattern, especially in North America. Almost invariably, taking an overly simplistic solution to a complex problem will create yet more problems. And, if the same approach is taken to solving those problems, you have a chain reaction on your hands. As far as SOA goes, there are no silver bullets we've seen yet, although there are some effective "lead bullet" products on the market that can fix many of the problems if aimed with suitable precision.

- Excessive expediency. The willingness to sacrifice principles, goals, standards, or best practices in the interest of urgency is risky (for example, the insistence on meeting IT project deadlines even if it means sacrificing quality, scope, or reducing testing). Cutting corners is also risky and inefficient. You will almost certainly have to take the effort to achieve the necessary quality eventually, so it is generally less expensive and considerably less embarrassing to get it right the first time. One must understand the risk and overall cost involved (not just the cost now, but the cost later) when making such decisions.

- Reliance on "acts of heroism" rather than streamlined processes. Relying on one or two superior genius individuals to achieve consistently outstanding results, instead of having a formal process with built-in quality controls is a mistake. Heroism has its place when extreme creativity is needed or when a critical deadline has to be met, but it really doesn't scale. For example, what happens if the genius that you rely on most gets a better job offer from a competitor?

  The best way to get value from the heroes is to employ them to help define world-class processes, define best practices, and mentor their colleagues to help them achieve excellence. That doesn't mean to underestimate the value of heroes. The best code developers, for example, are up to ten times as productive as the average programmers, and they have lower error rates, although they certainly don't command ten times their salaries.

- "The code is its own documentation." This is a true recipe for a future maintenance nightmare; it makes future maintenance nearly impossible. In fact, a common and effective use of SOA has been to create flexible services to wrap existing applications whose code cannot be changed, to provide a practical way to modify functionality or to integrate them with new IT components.

- Organizations that take a "mega-projects" approach. Companies that have relatively few IT projects, but those that do occur are large, perhaps 25-person jobs or jobs that take years risk making the management of projects too complex. The complexity increases exponentially with the size of the project. We have seen many projects that remained officially at the status 90 percent complete for months or years, where real progress was almost undetectable. Eventually, management wises up, and the project is often cancelled.

- Often the mega-project approach is further compounded by using a strict sequential waterfall development methodology. No design is commenced before all the requirements have been signed off, no development activity begins before the full design specifications have been signed off, and no testing begins until functional coding is complete. This might sound efficient, but if the full process takes a year or more, what happens when the requirements change because of external forces and what happens if testing discovers a fundamental design error made more than a year ago that invalidates much of the code? This type of sign-off process doesn't scale to mega-projects, which need be more granular to be manageable. A more modular approach where subcomponents of the overall solution are developed as separate mini-projects, and are perhaps even deployed individually is much less risky. It is much easier to govern and perform change management across multiple small projects than it is to govern a single massive one.

- Excessive bureaucracy. Having too much governance is as bad as having too little. Professional employees are neither robots nor slaves, and they resent being treated as such. If you take this approach, the more competent professionals will rapidly find a new employer who treats them better. SOA skills are in high demand.

- Excessive empowerment. Allowing one or two senior staff carte blanche access to override architectural rules, decisions, standards, and best practices, or to approve or disapprove major work products without concurrent personal accountability is a potential disaster, especially if those individuals decided for themselves that they have such authority rather than having it granted officially. You are wasting your efforts in creating processes or rules in the first place if you make it too easy to get around them without a good reason and an impeccable audit trail.

This is a question of personalities, management styles, and abilities. The worst scenario of all is where a senior manager refuses to conform to agreed rules and processes, or refuses to cooperate with the governance team or other stakeholders, typically because they are "control freaks." In such cases, the only recourse is to ask the executive sponsors to correct this behavior. Naturally, if you haven't already established executive commitment to improving governance, this antipattern will inevitably derail your efforts.

- "Everything's a service." An overenthusiastic approach to SOA leads to an enterprise replacing all of its applications with services. For example, every control on each GUI screen invokes a service, also known as the "piano-accordion" style of user interface, instead of being handled by a Model-View-Controller logic. Services proliferate, sometimes into the thousands, but there is little reuse of them, and managing such large numbers of services is difficult and resource intensive. There are unlikely to be any tangible business benefits.

- An "under-the-radar SOA implementation." Often, the IT department decides to experiment with SOA by using it to implement a new project, without involving the business users in the decision or project execution. This presents no issues if the object of the exercise is to evaluate the technology associated with SOA. However, expecting to get any real, measurable business benefits from such a project is naïve, because the real benefits of SOA stem from improving the alignment and minimizing the "impedance mismatch" between service consumer and service provider, business, and IT.

- Creating services that are too fine-grained. There is a significant performance overhead in executing a service, related with marshaling, encrypting, decrypting, and unmarshalling messages. If the overhead exceeds the cost of executing the business function of the service, performance is almost certainly going to be an issue, especially if multiple small services are combined sequentially into more useful composite services. Poor performance will deter potential new service consumers most effectively.

- Creating services that are too coarse-grained. Creating services that mostly perform complex tasks leads to poor reuse, because the more complex and specific the business task, the less likely it is to be duplicated. On the other hand, if the business service is at a granularity that aids business agility, it is appropriate.

- Creating services that are not enterprise ready when it is possible to do so. *Enterprise ready* means the services have been designed to meet requirements of multiple consumers across the enterprise and its business partners, rather than for the first project that needed them.

It will require additional resources and take more time to

- ◆ Determine who the potential future consumers of a proposed new service might be
- ◆ Persuade potential service consumers to define their detailed requirements
- ◆ Design and test the additional function needed

An important value judgment is required here, in determining what are the correct trade-offs between immediate costs and overall generality. The approaches we have seen vary, but there appears to be an increasing trend toward creating the first version of a service for a specific consumer, and then generalizing it for all known consumers the first time it is reused.

SOA Governance Capabilities

"The patient does not care about your science; what he wants to know is, can you cure him?"

—Martin H. Fischer

There are a set of governance capabilities that need to be considered in any good SOA governance implementation. This chapter introduces those capabilities and discusses a maturity or planning assessment for the organization. Chapters 3 and 4 show how to address the governance needs of the organization.

Plan & Organize

This domain covers governance of the strategic planning and enablement of the SOA journey. SOA will probably change the way in which IT and business decisions are made as the enterprise migrates from a silo approach to a cross-LoB capability. Consideration and planning should be performed on the set of common services that need to be created to engender reuse across the LoB while also creating business services that enable agility and fast response to market opportunities. This implies that common patterns, standards, policies, and reference architectures exist and will be governed and used across the SOA effort. The process of aligning the business and IT to identify business and IT strategy and tactics is important to the SOA effort and is one of the more sophisticated capabilities that we must govern. Common message modeling, data schemas, and information services must be considered so that the organization escapes the Tower of Babel syndrome and is actually able to interact. The right infrastructure and tooling must be in place to enable and speed the transformation to business and IT agility.

The Plan & Organize domain is also concerned with the enablement of SOA and SOA governance to perform its day-to-day job of creating and governing business and IT agility. It is charged with answering a set of enablement questions. Is the enterprise organized in the optimum way to implement and govern SOA? Do we have the right balance of skills, and can we implement effective SOA governance without becoming too bureaucratic? Are roles and responsibilities well defined and understood? Are there service ownership and funding guidelines that allow the SOA journey to proceed smoothly? Are there processes to enable the communication of a cross-LoB services approach to both the business and IT to gain buy in and acceleration? Is there a return on investment (ROI) model that takes the cross-LoB benefits into account so that we can guide our investment to maximize value? We want to inform the project portfolio selection process and track common costs and the actual business benefits realized.

The governance activities in this domain need to be performed once, as part of planning, and decisions made reviewed regularly to ensure they remain applicable. This level of governance strategic planning might not be possible initially, because experience and maturity is usually gained first with the service development lifecycle (SDLC) and program management of the SOA services, but this strategic planning is eventually the key to unlocking business agility. It will be necessary for executives to endorse and lead the changes that implementing SOA will require throughout the organization (for example, the development of new skills, changing organizations and roles, and new ways of interacting with other operating units and external partners).

The SOA Governance Plan & Organize Capabilities are as noted in Table 2.1.

Table 2.1   SOA Governance Plan & Organize Capabilities

SOA Governance Capability ID	SOA Governance Capability Name	SOA Governance Capability Description
P01	Service Transformation Planning	Capability to identify and plan for the set of service domains and services, especially business services, that support the to-be agile business process based on the business vision.
P02	Information Transformation Planning	Capability to identify and plan for the set of information domains and information services that supports the need for business and IT agility.
P03	Technology Transformation Planning	Capability to create and maintain the technology plan for standards and policies for hardware, software, development life-cycle, and services reference architectures to have a cost-effective approach to the creation of services and business and IT agility.
P04	Service Processes, Organizations, Roles & Responsibilities	Specification of the processes used for SOA governance of the SOA journey, including the responsibilities of organizations that are enhanced or created as a result of the transition to an SOA approach. This will include the manner in which the organizations interact with each other. The roles and responsibilities of the personnel leading and participating in the SOA journey will be specified.
P05	Manage the Service Investment	Managing the investment of funds within the organization to maximize the ROI for the SOA approach. This includes updating the business case process to take the benefits of service reuse and business agility into account for investment decisions and creating a business case for SOA.
P06	Business Vision & IT Alignment	Capability to create the business vision and goals for the creation of business agility and to align IT goals and strategy in the support of the business vision.
P07	Service Portfolio Management	Capability to manage the process for selection of programs and projects that demonstrates the ability to direct investment resources based on the business case service investment guidelines.

SOA Governance Capability ID	SOA Governance Capability Name	SOA Governance Capability Description
P08	Service Ownership & Funding	Capability to identify and control who funds what services, who owns what services, and how rights and obligations are distributed.
P09	Service Governance Vitality	Capability to inspect and measure results of the SOA program, including SOA governance, and take corrective action as needed.
P10	Service Communication Planning	Capability to plan and execute the communications of both the business and technical aspects of a services approach to all stakeholders. This includes the ability of the business to understand and lead the application of business processes, business services, business rules, and business metrics to create an agile enterprise.
P11	Service Education & Training	Capability to educate and train stakeholders on the SOA approach and provide the necessary training to be knowledgeable and efficient in all aspects of SOA.

Program Management Controls

This domain is concerned with planning and governing the implementation of SOA at the level of an enterprise-wide program that must manage individual development projects. It is concerned with questions that enable the current program management silo approach to be expanded into a true enterprise cross-LoB capability. How do we provide change management across LoB and in such a way that minimizes risk and impact on the overall enterprise program? What is the common method for procuring resources to minimize costs and maximize value? How do we manage vendors so that the same standards, policies, and quality of service (QoS) are created, whether we develop in house or outside? How do we manage project dependencies across a program? How do we identify and allocate shared costs across the enterprise? How do we follow up on a program and identify the real business benefits of an SOA approach? The activities covered in this domain should be repeated for every program where use of an SOA approach is contemplated.

Executives must ensure that the operating units who initiate future development projects understand and support IT SOA initiatives. Both business and IT management will need to consider the impact of SOA when justifying, planning, and running future development projects. Program managers will need to understand how to deliver and manage projects that include the development of services and that span LoB.

The SOA Governance Program Management Controls Capabilities are as noted in Table 2.2.

Table 2.2 SOA Governance Program Management Controls Capabilities

SOA Governance Capability ID	SOA Governance Capability Name	SOA Governance Capability Description
M01	Enterprise Program Management	Capability to effectively provide program management across LoB and departments to ensure the delivery of SOA project results within agreed-upon time frames, budget, and quality
M02	Change Management	Capability to manage the process of program change in responding to changing business requirements
M03	Procurement of Resources	Capability to manage the process of procuring the resources necessary for services in a cost-efficient manner while meeting the need for resource quality
M04	Vendor Management	Capability to manage third-party vendors providing SOA services or resources in such a manner that the same standards and policies are adhered to by vendors as are adhered to within the enterprise
M05	Identify and Allocate Costs	Capability to identify and allocate costs of a common services approach
M06	Monitor Business Benefits of SOA	Capability to monitor and provide a feedback loop on the business benefits for a specific SOA program after the program is operational

Service Development Lifecycle

This domain defines activities that govern the development of individual services and automated business processes. Enterprise models that describe business entities and business processes are critical inputs to service development. Because the eventual portfolio of services will become a major company asset, governance of the service modeling activities is especially important, because the success of the implementation of

SOA is directly dependent on choosing the right set of services and implementing them effectively.

This domain also covers the activities that govern development and unit test phases of the service lifecycle. Governance of these activities is critical to ensuring the functional and technical quality of all services and automated business processes that the organization will produce. Other than oversight, there are no specific executive-level activities for this domain.

IT management needs to ensure that the developers have the right set of tools and training, and ensure that architectural decisions, accepted best practices, and design patterns are being used consistently by all developers via governance control points. Developers and testers need to understand the vital importance of service code quality and exhaustive service testing, and to be actively involved in validation of accuracy and completeness at each stage of the process.

IT management needs to institute formal acceptance procedures that validate that there are no risks involved in deploying each service into the production environment, that the quality of service of each execution can be managed and monitored successfully, and that the service meets the organization's requirements for systems management.

IT operations professionals need to ensure that the services are deployed and managed as efficiently as possible, and that the integrity of the operational environment is maintained through efficient build procedures and configuration management.

The SOA Governance Service Development Lifecycle Capabilities are as noted in Table 2.3.

Table 2.3 SOA Governance Service Development Lifecycle Capabilities

SOA Governance Capability ID	SOA Governance Capability Name	SOA Governance Capability Description
D01	Service Development Lifecycle Controls	Capability to govern the SDLC and ensure QoS by using control points or similar mechanisms
D02	Requirements Gathering & Prioritization	Capability to govern the creation of business requirements to ensure the quality of such requirements and that they are complete and adhere to best practices, standards, and policies
D03	Service Identification	Capability to govern the service identification process to support the quality of the service identification and the correct level of granularity

Table 2.3 SOA Governance Service Development Lifecycle Capabilities (continued)

SOA Governance Capability ID	SOA Governance Capability Name	SOA Governance Capability Description
D04	Service Specification	Capability to govern the service specification process to support the quality of the specification of business services and operations in a manner such that the services are readily built and deployed
D05	Service Realization	Capability to govern the service realization process to support quality in the creation, maintenance, and testing of services
D06	Service Certification	Capability to govern the service certification process to support the certification of business services and operations in a manner such that the services are operationally ready for production

Service Operations

This domain covers activities that govern the QoS delivered to service users, and the ability to monitor and report on the operational aspects.

IT management needs to ensure that the correct set of contractual terms has been negotiated with the operating units and business users that govern the QoS of any services that they consume, and that the infrastructure continues to be able to support those contractual commitments.

IT operations professionals need to monitor the QoS achieved for each service and automated business process and execution, monitor compliance with contractual commitments and security needs, and manage the operational and end-of-life aspects of the service lifecycle.

The SOA Governance Service Operation Capabilities are as noted in Table 2.4.

Table 2.4 SOA Governance Service Operations Capabilities

SOA Governance Capability ID	SOA Governance Capability Name	SOA Governance Capability Description
O01	Service Execution Monitoring	Capability to specify, monitor, and report results of required service level agreements (SLAs) for external services and operational level agreements (OLAs) for internal services, including identifying when there is acceptable and unacceptable service operations.

SOA Governance Capability ID	SOA Governance Capability Name	SOA Governance Capability Description
O02	Service Operational Vitality	Capability to manage the operational vitality of QoS. This includes service latency, service elapsed time, hardware and software quality in support for services, priority of services support, service versioning, and prioritized allocation of customer service support.
O03	Service Support	Capability to effectively manage the analysis and resolution of incidents affecting services quality.

Ultimately, companies that implement an SOA governance model will require a focus in all aspects of SOA governance and management. However, many governance initiatives will initially be scoped to include only a subset based on an organization's immediate versus long-term needs and plans.

Understanding the Patient's History

"In the sick room, ten cents' worth of human understanding equals ten dollars' worth of medical science."

−Martin H. Fischer

The authors have found that the field of medicine provides an interesting model for thinking about governance. We need to apply some human understanding here instead of blindly applying an ossified one-size-fits-all methodology of governance to each organization.

In doing so, we must understand the "patient's history." To do this, you review the patient's symptoms and diagnose the root causes to determine the patient's ability to accept the treatment needed to affect a cure. We must understand the medicines available to us in planning a treatment plan.

In the case of SOA, the "doctor" should have some common approaches in understanding the current organizational style of the business and IT to solve the business problems that are the reason for the existence of IT in the first place. In this case, our doctor, Dr. Governance, will want to include these methods in his repertoire:

- Assess existing company documentation. The idea on this item is to get an unbiased, third-party view of how well the organization currently works without being prejudiced by insider views of what works and what doesn't (that will come later!). This includes, for example, a business vision document, existing project business cases, enterprise architecture documents (including architectural standards and the strategic plan for IT), project plans, development methodology documents, QA documentation, and operational documentation. The governance practitioner would also want to know who owns, reviews, approves, maintains, updates, and who has access to the existing documentation because that will provide important clues on the corporate culture.

- Review existing IT and business organization charts. It is important to comprehend roles and responsibilities in the current organization. How do the lines of business interact? Who controls the financials? Is there a Program Management Office? If so, where does it report? Is there an Enterprise Architecture group, and if so, where does it report? Is the QA group independent or dependent on development? Is there a single or are there multiple QA groups? How are user acceptance tests currently accomplished and by whom?

- How do business and IT interact? Is there a business-facing group within IT? Do special groups exist where IT and the business interact? Where do important decisions affecting the IT mission get made?

- Interview stakeholders. Now that you have gained an initial understanding of the organization via documentation and organization charts, it's time to interview the stakeholders and understand the human element. We have found it best to talk separately to IT and business stakeholders to get the unvarnished truth. The interviews should be a combination of 1:1 meetings with key stakeholders, including senior executives, and group meetings with others. Discussion of the governance items documented in the SOA Governance Maturity Model presented in the next section is a good way to gather input on where the organization stands and attitudes by these stakeholders toward governance. At the end of these sessions, you should have an excellent understanding of the patient's history!

In seeking to then evaluate this patient history, our experience has shown several key questions to be good predictors of an organization's capability to become agile and support a mature level of SOA and SOA governance. Those questions are

- Does a true Enterprise Architecture (EA) group exist, and how well is it being leveraged? Does EA have a strategic plan for making IT more agile, and is it being followed? If not, why not? Is there a set of stakeholders that feels threatened by change? Who are they, and are they powerful enough to block the entire SOA effort? Are there stakeholders paying only lip service to the idea of change and agility but are actually more comfortable left in their silos and have no intention of coming out? Does the CIO have the leadership to force change in IT where it is needed? Is there a transformation officer that is responsible for effecting change?

- How are projects selected and funded? Is a business sponsor required for each project? Are all potential projects considered at an enterprise level, or does each silo receive a bucket of money and get to pick what they want to do? Are projects required to have a business case, and is there any effort to validate that the assumptions of the business case were met upon project completion? Are strategic goals used to help pick the set of projects for funding, or are all funding decisions local and uncoordinated?

- Is there true teamwork across the LoB, or is work optimized within a silo with little or no communication outside? Is there a Program Management Office or equivalent organization that coordinates across the LoB? On projects, is there a collaborative approach involving architects, business stakeholders, IT operations, and support staff?

- What are the patterns of engagement between IT and the business? Is there alignment of the goals of the business and the goals of IT? Do business and IT professionals meet regularly? Does the business review and sign off on the requirements that IT uses? Does the business take part in acceptance testing? Are there individuals on the IT side who are business facing and vice versa?

- What are the means and methods of communication within the organization? Does communication take place mainly via documentation? Are there informal contacts where IT sits down with their business colleagues and really gets to figure out what the business needs? Do different silos within IT regularly meet with and coordinate with each other? Are there means of skip-level communications from the CIO or other management to the staff so that they understand the strategic and tactical direction of the organization? *Skip-level communication* is face-to-face communications that skips levels of the organization hierarchy from time to time for senior levels of management to receive "unfiltered" information from those at the lower levels of the organization who are doing the real work. An example might include the CIO periodically having breakfast with eight to ten programmers, analysts, and testers to find out how the messages they are imparting are actually being received and implemented and to find out what problems the CIO could help rectify.

Understanding the Patient's Symptoms and Diagnosing the Root Causes

"When you are called to a sick man, be sure you know what the matter is—if you do not know, nature can do a great deal better than you can guess."

—Nicholas de Belleville

SOA governance is as much art as science, but there does need to be more science than what SOA governance practitioners have been using in the past. It is instructive to consider existing IT governance models for maturity and then apply a services approach to realize an SOA Governance Maturity Model that we can then use to understand the patient's symptoms and create a worthy governance plan in a more scientific manner.

COBIT (Control Objectives for Information and Related Technology) was created by the Information Systems Audit and Control Association (ISACA) and the IT Governance Institute (ITGI). COBIT provides a set of generally accepted measures, processes, and best practices for maximizing the benefits of information technology and developing IT governance. You can find additional information about COBIT at www.isaca.org/cobit.

A governance maturity model provides a quantitative means to measure specific aspects of governance maturity in an organization. As governance practitioners, we seek an objective way to measure the current health of the organization with respect to SOA governance specifically, although there are aspects of measurement of IT governance and business governance that inevitably creep into our assessment. A structured methodology helps us to understand the governance symptoms of the organization while at the same time diagnosing the root causes of why this patient is in governance ill health. This will give us a place to start, a common set of metrics we can use to measure the "as-is" and "to-be" governance maturity to report on the improvement as the patient's health improves, and a framework for prioritizing the actions we must take to nurse the patient back to health.

COBIT provides an IT Maturity Model (for more information, see "Generic Maturity Model," at www.isaca.org/AMTemplate.cfm?Section= Downloads&Template=/ContentManagement/ContentDisplay.cfm&Con tentID=34172, page 19), which itself derives from the Software Engineering Institute's Capability Maturity Model (CMM). In the case of the CMM, for example, the basis for comparison would be the organization's software development processes. The maturity model uses standard CMM-based maturity level numbers with explanations as modified by COBIT and described in Table 2.5.

Table 2.5 Governance Maturity Levels

Governance Maturity Level	Description
0 - Nonexistent	Complete lack of any processes. The enterprise has not recognized that this is an area to be addressed.
1 - Initial / Ad hoc	There is evidence that the enterprise has recognized that this is an area to be addressed. There are, however, no standardized processes; instead, ad hoc approaches tend to be applied on an individual or case-by-case basis.

Table 2.5 Governance Maturity Levels (continued)

Governance Maturity Level	Description
2 - Repeatable but Intuitive	Governance processes have developed to the stage at which similar procedures are followed by different people undertaking the same task. There is no formal training or communication of standard procedures, and responsibility is left to the individual. There is a high degree of reliance on the knowledge of individuals, and therefore, errors are likely.
3 - Defined Process	Governance procedures have been standardized, documented, and communicated. It is mandated that these processes should be followed; however, it is unlikely that deviations will be detected and corrected.
4 - Managed and Measurable	Governance authorities monitor and measure compliance with governance procedures and take action where processes appear not to be working effectively. Processes are under constant improvement and provide good practice. Automation and tools are used in a limited or fragmented way.
5 - Optimized	Governance processes have been refined to a level of good practice, based on the results of continuous improvement. Governance is used in an integrated way across the enterprise to improve quality and effectiveness, making the enterprise quick to adapt.

As discussed in "SOA Governance Capabilities" section of this chapter, SOA governance is split into domains that we need to assess to gauge the current maturity. Based on our experience, people tend to rate their organizations as having a higher maturity than actually exists (the so called Lake Wobegon effect, where "all the women are strong, all the men are good looking, and all the children are above average").[1]

In the interview process, you should ask enough probing questions to ascertain the real current "as-is" maturity. This is also a good time to understand the desired "to-be" maturity, and here is when the opinions of stakeholders are more valid.

Examples of the types of questions that you should ask for the Plan & Organize domain include the following:

1.   http://en.wikipedia.org/wiki/Lake_Wobegon

Service Transformation Planning

- Is there a business vision and strategy for creation of business agility (for example, to go to market faster or to reduce costs)?
- Is there a business architecture that identifies service domains, business processes, and the optimal set of business services?

Information Transformation Planning

- Are information domains that are important to the business identified?
- Is there an ability to analyze data content and align and correct the data?

Service Processes, Organizations, Roles, and Responsibilities

- Is the interaction between organizations involved in the SOA process defined with clear roles and responsibilities?
- Is there an ability to take action, to provide direction, to resolve issues and conflicts and channel escalations appropriately?

Manage the Service Investment

- Have the critical success factors for SOA been identified, and are these being used to guide the investment of resources at the enterprise?
- Is the business value of a program measured after the program is complete and has had a chance to produce the expected results?

Business Vision & IT Alignment

- Has the business vision been documented, and is it generally known and understood within the enterprise?
- Are the goals of the business and IT aligned, and are there consistency checks to make sure those goals stay aligned?

Service Portfolio Management

- Does SOA guidance exist on the assessment and prioritization of projects and services in the service portfolio management process?

Service Ownership & Funding

- Does a process exist to resolve how common services are funded and owned?

Service Governance Vitality

- Do regular published reports or dashboards exist that identify governance metrics and provide assistance in identifying issues to be resolved?
- Is there a process for submitting recommendations for improving governance, metric benchmarks, checklists, guidance, and training within SOA?

Service Communication Planning

- Does an SOA communications plan exist for each stakeholder, and has it been executed?
- Is the business able to articulate the benefits of a services approach and therefore provide thought leadership on SOA?

Service Education & Training

- Does an education plan exist for each SOA stakeholder, including education materials?
- Is there an ability to support project and solution planners with advice on what SOA is, and how best to develop and exploit it?

Program Management Controls

Examples of the types of questions that you should ask for the Program Management Control domain include the following:

Enterprise Program Management

- Is there an ability to provide scope management, issue management, change management, communications, and coordination among the various project responsibilities for the program?
- How well does the Program Management group work across the LoB and the different organizations within IT?
- Is there an ability to look for systemic issues across projects and ensure lessons learned from previous projects are incorporated into future projects?

Change Management

- Do standards and best practices exist for processing change requests in a professional and responsive manner?
- Are change requests able to be assessed quickly with financial and temporal impacts to the program identified and understood?

Procurement of Resources

- Is procurement aware of and using the technology plan to restrict purchase orders to approved technology vendors?
- Do procurement metrics exist that provide feedback on efficient usage of resources by the enterprise (for example, volume discounts earned)?

Vendor Management

- Are SOA policies and standards used when assessing new products and vendors?
- Are outsourced or offshore vendors subject to the same quality-of-service (QoS) standards and policies as are used when developing in house?

Identify and Allocate Costs

- Is there a cost-identification and allocation scheme for shared services?

Monitor Business Benefits of SOA

- Does the project business case include SOA considerations (using a business case checklist)?
- Is there an ability to follow up on the actual business benefits of a program after it is operational?

Service Development Lifecycle

Examples of the types of questions that you should ask for the Service Development Lifecycle domain include the following:

Service Development Lifecycle Controls

- Does an SDLC exist that defines standards and best practices, tasks, and roles and responsibilities?
- Are governance control points used at each significant lifecycle transition to apply quality to the development process of the services?

Requirements Gathering & Prioritization

- Have standards and best practices been established and used for the creation of business requirements?
- Is a common requirements repository used that helps to drive the rest of development?
- Have standards and best practices been established for the creation of nonfunctional requirements (NFRs)?

Service Identification

- Do standards and best practices exist for service identification?
- Are standards and best practices used for service granularity, visibility (who should be aware of the service), and accessibility (who may use the service)?

Service Specification

- Do standards and best practices exist for service specifications?
- Does automatic tooling exist to validate the standards and best practices for service specifications?

Service Realization

- Do standards and best practices exist for building and testing services?
- Are services able to be traced back to their original business requirements?

Service Certification

- Does a checklist exist for operations to formally accept responsibility for service QoS?
- Is there a registry/repository that allows services to be registered and controlled and made available in a public manner?
- Is there a process to identify production problems to identify deployment issues and update standards?

Service Operations

Examples of the types of questions that you should ask for the Service Operations domain include the following:

Service Execution Monitoring

- Is there a process to define and deliver performance targets and continuously monitor and report the degree of their achievement?
- Is there a process to ensure that adequate data is captured for each service invocation (who invoked it, how long did it take, were there any errors, were SLA conditions maintained)?
- Has trend monitoring to prevent SLA violations due to lack of system resources been implemented?

Service Operational Vitality

- Is there a process to create, maintain, and monitor metrics to measure operational service quality and use these to maintain vitality in the QoS architecture, design, and development?
- Does operations monitor current and proposed system load to ensure adequate resources are always available to meet SLA commitments?

Service Support

- Is there a process to create and maintain standards and policies for service support, including trouble ticketing and a consumer support function?
- Is operations able to identify errors, trigger responses, allocate resources, and monitor results, as appropriate, for the severity of any operational problems?

Determine the Patient's Ability to Accept the Treatment Needed to Effect a Cure

"There is no curing a sick man who believes himself to be in health."

—Henri Amiel

The governance practitioner must consider two main factors when identifying the level of governance that the patient can accept. The first is to understand who has decision or input rights into the IT and business governance process and the attitudes and beliefs that those stakeholders have about governance. The second is to understand the suitability of governance (this is discussed in the more detailed and upcoming "Suitability Considerations" section) given the industry that is being governed and the level of risk that the industry and particular company can accept. This risk tolerance will drive a decision about whether to make tight, loose, or medium levels of governance control for each governance control point.

Organization Type

As described in their groundbreaking book *IT Governance*, professors Peter Weill and Jeanne W. Ross, from the MIT Sloan School of Management, describe the six types of IT governance archetypes to identify the possible "combinations of people who have either decision rights or input to IT decisions...as Business Monarchy, IT Monarchy, Feudal, Federal, IT Duopoly, and Anarchy."

Business Monarchy, a group of business executives leading, is a positive governance archetype for SOA governance. Business or C-level executives make decisions about where to invest and how to proceed with input from both IT and business stakeholders. This implies that there is already some degree of business and IT alignment, and the business considers IT a partner to be worked and consulted with. This type of organization is likely quite eager for the business agility that SOA can bring, and it would make sense to be aggressive in enhancing SOA governance and promoting the Plan & Organize governance domain.

IT Monarchy, a group of IT executives leading, is a typical governance archetype to be dealt with, because many times the SOA journey will start as an IT initiative. Frequently, in this situation, IT will tell you that you "can't talk to the business because it doesn't know what SOA is and it doesn't like IT anyway." This is a somewhat negative governance archetype for SOA governance, because there usually are many different silos and people who consider themselves "in charge" and "know what's best for the organization," even though they only have experience with their own silo. It's best to tread carefully here, and focus initially on governance for the Service Development Lifecycle domain. Likely, IT already has a SDLC and will have some, probably inadequate, controls around the lifecycle. But at least you're not starting from ground zero in this area and it's something that IT is comfortable with.

The Feudal model is challenging for SOA governance. In this model, you have business units or IT departments that receive their own funding and can basically do whatever they want. This implies that the enterprise is not looking for synergies across the units and that a more decentralized governance approach will need to be adopted. You have probably been brought in to help one of the IT departments, and you can help locally optimize what they are doing, including governance for the Service Development Lifecycle domain. Other than that, you'll need to see about working across the governance pods, and try to create synergies where possible; therefore the company progresses with a more strategic business agility initiative.

The Federal model is typically found in government organizations and involves business units, C-level executives, and IT executives who make consensus decisions. The problem with consensus, of course, is that it is difficult to achieve, and is therefore likely to cause delay in whatever you are doing. With respect to SOA governance, the Federal model is a neutral governance archetype. Strong leadership and communication skills are needed on the part of the SOA program and SOA governance. Organizations such as an Executive Steering Committee with weekly meetings are a must, with structured agendas and strict due dates for investigations and decisions. However, it is possible to get things moving with this model.

The IT Duopoly is interesting and has a positive bias for SOA governance. IT is in the middle of the decision making, but is working with a set of decentralized business units. IT is able to add value by having the "big picture" that can help the business units make decisions that are optimized for the enterprise. To the degree that IT contains groups such as Enterprise Architecture and has good IT leadership that can communicate and work with the business, it should add value to what the decentralized business partner would be able to do on its own. If IT does not have these capabilities, you'll need to work more closely with the business groups and see whether they are willing to provide leadership. If both of those are not true, the SOA governance probability of success becomes smaller.

Anarchy, where every group does what it likes, sounds bad because it is. On the other hand, no one is in charge, and there are great opportunities for someone to come in and show leadership and whip this organization into shape! The silent majority will want that, but be afraid of the knife in the back from the bad apples that no doubt abound here. It's best to try to work this top down and see whether you can coach those who are supposed to provide executive leadership to wake up and do the right thing.

Suitability Considerations

Cantor and Sanders describe the suitability principle, which states that "the needs of the organization determine how the level and style of governance will be tailored."[2]

2.   IBM Developerworks, Cantor, M., Sanders, J., 17 May, 2007, "Operational IT Govern-ance," http://www.ibm.com/developerworks/rational/library/may07/cantor_sanders/

One needs to consider the governance needs of the organization being assessed. Some, such as a pharmaceutical firm, have mission-critical products that need formal, auditable governance. Less mission critical, but certainly subject to government regulation, are financial institutions. These organizations have stricter policies and standards that will be closely governed at the various control points. Other organizations can have a more relaxed mode of governance and may pick their processes that are tightly controlled while others are more laissez faire.

Depending on the degree of control of SOA governance you want to exercise, you can choose one of the following levels of quality assurance for each work product:

- **Level 0—No governance.** This approach is suitable only for activities that are completely risk free!

- **Level 1—Train and inform.** This minimalist approach attempts to educate staff in the work products that need to be produced, and their roles in developing, quality assessing, and approving them. It then lets staff get on with it, apart from regular communications and periodic training to maintain the currency of their skills. This level of control may be appropriate after an enterprise has reached a high level of SOA maturity, but would be a recipe for disaster before that point for most work products

- **Level 2—General affirmation.** This level of governance requires all staff, on a yearly basis, to read a conduct guidelines document and sign it to indicate that they understand it and agree to conform to it. This is effective only when the risks are very low, or the intention is to establish who was at fault after an untoward event occurred, rather than avoiding it in the first place. Again, this would be ineffective for governing SOA for nearly all enterprises.

- **Level 3—Self-assessment.** This level requires any member or staff who is accountable for a work product to validate its quality. This is typically achieved by having the person in that position complete and sign a checklist. It should be adequate for most intermediate technical work products.

- **Level 4—Automated review.** This level uses tools to automate the review process and provide near real-time feedback to the authors of the work product. This is an emerging and interesting technology.

- **Level 5— Peer assessment.** Peers of the staff who are responsible and accountable for a work product formally review its quality and document the findings either in a set of minutes or, more formally, in signed checklists. Peer assessment is an effective governance mechanism and an excellent way of performing on-the-job mentoring to less experienced staff.

- **Level 6—Formal quality review.** Conduct a formal review by a suitably appointed board, at a specific stage or stages in the lifecycle of a major artifact, such as a project, where decisions are made to progress, halt, or require rework. This is often called a *decision checkpoint* or *control point.* It is a highly appropriate mechanism for approving significant capital expense items.

- **Level 7—Formal audit.** Typically applied to a small sample set of work products, as a belt-and-braces approach. Nobody *expects* the Spanish Inquisition, but everybody fears it. This process involves a close inspection of both a work product and the approach used to create it. To maintain credibility, it is essential that the team performing the audit has a different reporting structure than the team creating the work product.

- **Level 8—Step-by-step inspection.** This mechanism consists of a formal quality assurance (QA) assessment of the quality of a work product after each step in the development process. Generally, this inspection is carried out by a specialist audit team. This is an onerous and time-consuming approach and is generally justified only when the perceived risk is high.

Given the suitability principle, one should think about a gauge for each governance area or item. Consider, for example, Figure 2.1, which shows an example of the strength of governance to be used for each of the SDLC governance areas.

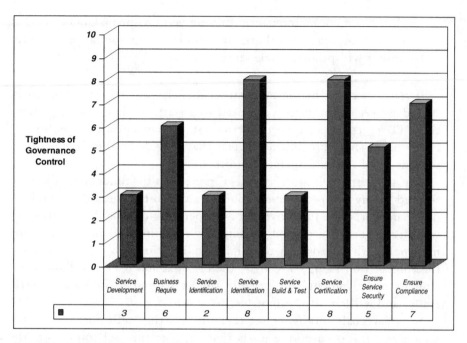

	Service Development	Business Require	Service Identification	Service Identification	Service Build & Test	Service Certification	Ensure Service Security	Ensure Compliance
■	3	6	2	8	3	8	5	7

Figure 2.1 Set the SOA Governance Tightness of Control Based on the Suitability Principle

Determining the Governance Priorities and Near-Term Goals

> *"Pick battles big enough to matter, small enough to win"*
>
> —Jonathan Kozol

In our view, two major inhibitors to more universal adoption of SOA have been

- The name *service oriented architecture. Service, oriented,* and *architecture* are "techie" terms, likely to glaze the eyes of anyone with a business focus. We stick with the acronym SOA. These days, it's a familiar term to nearly all businesspersons.

- For a few years, the mantra of SOA was *reuse.* Now, there's nothing wrong with the idea of reuse; every developer worth his salt frequently reuses code written by himself and a few trusted peers, and pervasive code reuse is certainly a way to reduce complexity and lower the costs of maintenance. But can you imagine a CEO or CIO of a major corporation authorizing a multi-million-dollar project just because it will promote code reuse?

If reuse is not a major business goal in its own right, what goals should we set as the targets we need to govern to? For most organizations, IT represents a support function rather than a profit center, so any IT initiative should be based on goals that provide bottom-line benefits to some or all the core operating units.

The aphorism "sell more, cost less" represents the fundamental way to succeed in any competitive environment, and so this should be the kernel of any corporate initiative, for any operating unit or IT department, whether governance related or not. For governmental bodies or state monopolies, this needs only the slight modification "Do more, cost less"; the competition being, of course, the organization itself. Without continuous improvement, any organization will tend to lose touch with reality and will rapidly become fossilized.

So, what goals might we set that support the "sell more, cost less" strategy? Typical corporate goals that support the "sell more" or "do more" strategy include the following:

- Improve the organization's public image
- Increase sales of existing products or services
- Speedier delivery of existing products or execution of services
- Improve business flexibility and agility—thereby creating new, more innovative products, with a faster time to market

Typical corporate goals that support the "cost less" side of the equation include the following:

- Reduce risk, thereby eliminating the costs of recovery from errors or failures
- Control direct costs
- Improve operational efficiency
- Improve synergy between operating units
- Avoid waste
- Invest wisely to promote innovation

Note that these are universal goals that apply to any organization, and any operating unit or department within that organization, including IT. These do represent the basis for a business case that the CEO and CFO will endorse. Any SOA governance-related initiative should be linked to one or more of these. Naturally, the relative priorities between these goals will differ from organization to organization, but every organization will support most or all of them.

We hope the relative priorities of these goals should be obvious to IT management. If the governance practitioner finds that there are no clear business goals, corporate governance is non-existent, and there is poor alignment between business and IT, then eliciting the business goals and driving the alignment of IT to these goals would be an even more valuable governance function. Free and open discussion of corporate and individual goals among all stakeholders is essential. Transparency is the primary key to effective governance.

So, how do these business-focused goals relate to IT, and specifically to SOA, and to the governance capabilities map introduced in this chapter?

Tables 2.6 through 2.16 should help this process.

Rows in these tables have been grouped by the set of "buy more and cost less" strategic corporate goals described earlier. Look for those sections that match the priorities of your enterprise.

The three columns in the tables represent the following:

- **Column 1.** Sample objectives that support those goals, for a typical business operating unit (under the heading "Operating Unit Objectives").
- **Column 2.** Sample objectives for the IT department, split into two subcategories:
  - Sample objectives that describe how IT should support the operating units (under the heading "IT Support for Business Units")
  - Sample objectives for the IT department, in its own role as a business unit (under the heading "IT Department Internal Objectives")
- **Column 3.** The objectives for which an SOA approach is particularly well-suited are written in italics. The third column (headed "Associated SOA Governance Capabilities") describes the SOA governance capabilities as described in this chapter that you will need to

develop to support your specific business priorities. Note that some of the SOA governance capabilities we describe support multiple business objectives, and so they appear multiple times.

Using these tables should enable you to add the set of SOA capabilities that you need to develop and to prioritize them in terms of the business goals they support. You should also outline how to construct a business case for their development.

Table 2.6 Sell More by Improving the Enterprise's Customer Image

Operating Unit Objectives	IT Support for Business Units	Associated SOA Governance Capabilities
Better responsiveness to customers	Improve efficiency of back-end IT systems, help desks, call centers, and so on	D06—Service Certification
Improve marketing and advertising	Improve ability to monitor system/operator efficiency	O01—Service Execution Monitoring
Reduce complaints and improve complaint handling	Maintain currency, reliability, and efficiency of IT systems	O02—Service Operational Vitality
	Maintain effectiveness of technical support to all IT consumers	O03—Service Support

Table 2.7 Sell More through Increased Sales of Existing Products

Operating Unit Objectives	IT Support for Business Units	Associated SOA Governance Capabilities
Increase number and effectiveness of channels to market	Improve ability to communicate and share information with sales channels and business partners	P06—Business Vision and IT Alignment
Improve product sales presentation material	Improve quality and timeliness of sales data and sales reporting	P10—Service Communication Planning
Improve quality of sales support		P09—Service Governance Vitality
		D02—Requirements Gathering and Prioritization

Table 2.8 Sell More through Enhanced Product Delivery and Production Capacity

Operating Unit Objectives	IT Support for Business Units	Associated SOA Governance Capabilities
Improve supply chain	Improve vitality and currency of IT solutions that support supply chain and distribution, and product manufacture/ assembly	M03—Procurement of Resources
Improve distribution logistics		P07—Service Portfolio Management
		D02—Requirements Gathering and Prioritization

Table 2.9 Sell More through Creating More Innovative Products, with Faster Time to Market

Operating Unit Objectives	IT Support for Business Units	Associated SOA Governance Capabilities
Improve technical research	Provide and maintain currency of tools and services to support research, product design, vendor/business partner communication and exchange of data, testing, and QA	P03—Technology Transformation Planning
Improve market research and analysis and create more agile and flexible operational procedures and processes for speedy product design	Ensure that IT systems are flexible enough to be able to support new/improved products in time to capitalize on new market opportunities	P01—Service Transformation Planning P02—Information Transformation Planning
Improve communications effectiveness	Provide IT-based products directly to customers and business partners, aggregate services to provide value-add products	P10—Service Communication Planning
Improve vendor and business partner relationship management		M04—Vendor Management
Improve component sourcing		D02—Requirements Gathering and Prioritization

Table 2.9   (continued)

Operating Unit Objectives	IT Support for Business Units	Associated SOA Governance Capabilities
Streamline product manufacture/assembly, testing, and QA		D03—Service Identification D01—Service Development Lifecycle Controls

Table 2.10   Sell More by Outgrowing Competitors

Operating Unit Objectives	IT Support for Business Units	Associated SOA Governance Capabilities
Find and board new business partners	Provide componentized IT solutions that can easily be interfaced to business partners/new acquisitions	P01—Service Transformation Planning
Manage mergers and acquisitions (M&A)	Develop the capability to absorb or replace the IT systems of new acquisitions quickly and with low risk	P06—Business Vision & IT Alignment
Outsource noncore activities where it is cost-effective	Maintain continuity of employment during M&A activity	M03—Procurement of resources
		M04—Vendor Management
		M01—Enterprise Program Management
		D01—Service Development Lifecycle Controls
		D03—Service Identification

Table 2.11   Cost Less by Reducing Risk

Operating Unit Objectives	IT Support for Business Units	Associated SOA Governance Capabilities
Ensure compliance with all relevant governmental regulations	Provide and maintain IT solutions that support regulatory compliance, and whose compliance can be easily audited	D02—Requirements Gathering & Prioritization

Operating Unit Objectives	IT Support for Business Units	Associated SOA Governance Capabilities
Maintain financial control	Fund investments that will have a positive ROI	P05—Manage the Service Investment
Improve project estimating, planning, and execution	Ensure that internal IT projects meet quality, completeness, timeliness, and budgetary targets	M05—Identify & Allocate Costs
Maintain rigorous product quality control	Ensure continued reliability, availability, and QoS of all IT solutions	M01—Enterprise Program Management
	Operate within IT development product budgets	D01—Services Development Lifecycle Controls

Table 2.12 Cost Less by Reducing Operating Expenses

Operating Unit Objectives	IT Support for Business Units	Associated SOA Governance Capabilities
Ensure constant ability to monitor true costs of doing business effectively	Ensure that IT provides excellent value to operating units, and that any costs are charged out to the operating units	M03—Procurement of Resources
	IT must stay within budget	M05—Identify & Allocate Costs
Control costs of raw materials, perform audits, outsource noncore activities		
	Maintain financial control within internal IT initiatives	M06—Monitor Business Benefits of SOA
		P05—Manage the Service Investment
	Reduce the proportion of IT resources spent on maintenance	P07—Service Portfolio Management
	Manage costs of providing IT platform, solutions, and support	M01—Enterprise Program Management
		P06—Business Vision & IT Alignment

Table 2.13 Cost Less by Improving Operational Efficiency

Operating Unit Objectives	IT Support for Business Units	Associated SOA Governance Capabilities
Avoid redundancy/ duplication of resources and equipment, reduce complexity	Maintain efficient analysis, design, development, and operational processes	P03—Technology Transformation Planning
Increase consistency	Maximize reuse, avoid duplication or rework	M03—Procurement of Resources
Reduce rework	**IT Department Internal Objectives**	P04—Service Processes, Organizations, Roles and Responsibilities
Improve operational processes and staff skills	Train and motivate staff	P10—Service Communication Planning
		P11—Service Education and Training
Improve quality	Maintain effective catalogs of all IT assets	D06—Service Certification
	Implement continuous process improvement	P08—Service Governance Vitality
		O02—Service Operational Vitality
	Maintain currency and vitality of development approach, estimation metrics, architectural standards and decisions, best practices, lessons learned	D01—Services Development Lifecycle Controls

Table 2.14 Cost Less by Improving the Synergy Among All Operating Units

Operating Unit Objectives	IT Support for Business Units	Associated SOA Governance Capabilities
Ensure overall vitality of the organization	Cross-reference goals, objectives, and targets with all other involved operating units	P06—Business Vision and IT Alignment

Operating Unit Objectives	IT Support for Business Units	Associated SOA Governance Capabilities
Enable active cooperation among operating units through the creation and publication of well-defined, nonoverlapping responsibilities	Monitor performance and share results with other operating units	O01—Service Execution and Monitoring
	Maintain a common set of IT-related roles and responsibilities	P04—Service Processes, Organizations, Roles and Responsibilities
	Define interdependencies between all operating units	M01—Enterprise Program Management
	Create agreements or "contracts" between operating units that define realistic expectations they may have of each other	P04—Service Processes, Organizations, Roles and Responsibilities

Table 2.15 Cost Less by Avoiding Waste

Operating Unit Objectives	IT Support for Business Units	Associated SOA Governance Capabilities
Avoid unnecessary duplication of effort	Reduce the incidence of failed or curtailed projects	P07—Service Portfolio Management
Avoid unnecessary work	Ensure that the majority of projects complete on time, to budget, and meet quality targets	M01—Enterprise Program Management
Eliminate unnecessary bureaucracy	Improve relationship between IT and other operating units	P06—Business and IT Alignment
Encourage cooperation rather than competition between all operating units	Ensure that the degree of governance applied is commensurate with the perceived degree of risk	D01—Service Development Lifecycle Controls M01—Enterprise Program Management
	Ensure that internal IT projects (for example, new infrastructure components, tools) have the same discipline as any other project	P04—Service Processes, Organizations, Roles and Responsibilities

Table 2.16   Cost Less by Making Wise Investment Decisions That Promote Innovation

Operating Unit Objectives	IT Support for Business Units	Associated SOA Governance Capabilities
Choose the correct investment areas and most cost-effective projects	Provide accurate cost and time estimations for new IT projects	P01—Service Transformation Planning P02—Information Transformation Planning
Monitor effectiveness of previous investment decisions	Provide input on new technology-based opportunities	P03—Technology Transformation Planning
Monitor ROI of all business areas, and adjust investment priorities accordingly	Provide metrics on usage and ROI of IT solutions	P06—Business Vision and IT Alignment P05—Manage the Service Investment
	Recommend IT investments that have good ROI	P07—Services Portfolio Management
	Monitor ROI of all IT investments	M05—Identify and Allocate Costs
		P07—Services Portfolio Management
		M06—Monitor Business Benefits of SOA
		D02—Requirements Gathering and Prioritization

SOA Governance can help the SOA program can provide some major benefits to support the IT department specifically, including the following:

- **Enabling reuse by making it easy to find existing assets.** It will be much simpler to locate existing potentially reusable software assets if they are packaged as services, with full searchable descriptions, maintained in a centralized repository tool.

- **Making it easier to align business and IT priorities.** Business services provide a level of granularity of functional unit that makes it possible for all the stakeholders to understand and communicate about effectively. This should also make it easier to manage traceability from the full lifecycle, from requirements to functional solution.

- **Improving the ability to "get it right the first time" and reduce the number of software bugs.** Publishing candidate and planned business services, and deployed services, can allow potential service consumers to identify prospective candidates for reuse in time to register their interest and add any requirements that are specific to them in time for the first service release, thereby reducing need for later re-versioning (with the associated regression testing costs). Well-defined business services create modular units of function that are readily identifiable both to business users and to developers, vendors, or systems integrators.

- **Providing a better approach to vendor management.** There are multiple facets to this:

  - Describing components in terms of services—that is, contracts for both functional and nonfunctional required behavior—represents an unambiguous, level playing field approach to dealing with vendors.

  - The service model can also be used to help determine the ability of vendors and their packages to help qualify their value to the organization.

- **Packaging functional software assets as services** with standardized interfaces defined by a formal contract creates much smaller, more manageable deployments units. This has many benefits, including the following:

  - Decoupling of the development of services from the larger applications that consume them.

  - Enabling more granular testing. After a service has passed acceptance testing and certification, it should only need regression testing if is changed or re-versioned. Making changes to any calling application will require retesting of that application, but there should be no need to specifically regression test any services that it uses.

  - It is much easier to manage multiple parallel small service development projects that incrementally build toward a major solution than to create the major solution in a single "all or nothing" development effort.

Case Study

"Let the young know they will never find a more interesting, more instructive book than the patient himself."

—Giorgio Baglivi

Now that the CIO has assigned you the task of implementing the SOA governance function at Ideation, your first step is to understand all the governance items that you must address. Although you know that you won't be able to attack all of them simultaneously, nevertheless you want to get the big picture first.

SOA Planning Assessment

The first order of business is to use the SOA governance planning assessment that was discussed in this chapter to understand Ideation's current state from an SOA governance and SOA program point of view.

You need to assess not only where the organization is today, but also the areas of greatest program and governance need. Doing so will enable you to establish priorities for the governance transition plan to be created. This not only gives you a structured planning tool, but it also gives you metrics to measure the success of the transition plan at periodic milestones. It also helps you by giving some standard metrics for the necessary discussions that you need to periodically have with the SOA program and governance executive leadership to communicate progress and accept feedback on areas of focus.

Using the SOA governance planning assessment, you will interview various stakeholders from both business and IT. This will consist of some 1:1 sessions so that you can get frank and open comments and some team sessions where you will get information from the right people in a particular area. Topics will include the SOA governance assessment domains of Plan & Organize, Program Management Controls, Service Development Lifecycle, and Service Operations.

At Ideation, the assessment information you are getting is eye opening even though you thought you knew the organization quite well. The development process in the various organizations is haphazard and not well structured. One highly respected SME says to you, "The inmates are running the asylum here. I'm really not sure how we get anything done. It's only because we have heroes who step in at the last second and save the day that we get any releases out. Even then, we've cut so much of the scope that I wonder why we bother at all." Another manager says, "Of course we do everything right, but all of the other groups are idiots. How they keep their jobs, I'll never know." A project manager says to you, "There is no consequence management. The same people screw up, and everyone just shrugs. I'm sick of spending so many hours here to make things work when management doesn't seem to know or care."

Whew! You have to take a step back and think after the interview sessions. The reactions were passionate, and the people involved kept looking at you with a mixture of hope and cynicism. "Nothing around here ever really changes, will it?" one tester questions you. "When the going gets tough, the execs around here will always compromise doing something meaningful and with quality for the sake of looking good to their bosses and meeting their dates." You patiently explain that that's why governance is being assessed and that their leadership, ideas, and passion are needed now more than ever.

Although there are many issues that governance should eventually address at Ideation, a few key ones stand out:

- The lack of a consistent process, repeatability, best practices, and quality controls are obvious. When some of those things have been tried in the past, they usually end up sacrificed upon the altar of project dates. Problems that should have been caught and resolved during business requirement, solution architecture, and design find their way to testing, where it is expensive and time-consuming to fix. Something that must be redesigned, recoded, or reassembled and retested is a long process.

- The company has been thinking about ideas around creating business agility, particularly across LoB. There's a strategy group somewhere in corporate that is alleged to have done some thinking about this, but some quick checking determines that the strategy group is an "ivory tower" organization that is not steeped in the realities of the business. Apparently, no group is really charged with the responsibility of figuring out what business services make sense, and consequently, each project team must figure it out on their own or just write something that works for their LoB. Chances of cross-organizational cooperation and success are low without planning and real thinking in this area. Also, there are some common IT services, but it is unclear what they are and who owns or maintains them. You know that there need to be some ground rules around service ownership and funding, especially when they affect cross-organizational projects that must come together as a program.

- It is not clear how the cross-department organizations should interact with each other. Who makes decisions when the various LoB disagree with each other and the goal is to create a capability that is cross organizational? How does the work get managed across groups? How are common standards and principles set and promulgated across the organization? How are reference architectures created and accepted and architectural decisions made? How does IT interact with the business? All of these must be addressed by governance, and the rules of engagement must be specified.

- Service certification has been a disaster. The rules of engagement are unknown, and operations continually complain that they are not consulted until it is too late and they have to fix things in production. Most of second- and third-level support are burned out after being called in continually on nights and weekends and several have quit.

- There is no vitality in any of the processes that do exist. *Process* is probably too strong a term for what actually happens; organized chaos is probably closer to reality. "If you don't measure it, you can't improve it," one program manager says to you, and you wholeheartedly agree.

You present the results of the survey to the Ideation leadership team from the SOA planning assessment, as noted in Table 2.17 with the values corresponding to the maturity levels noted in this chapter. It is agreed to go forward with the steps necessary to define the first phase of an SOA governance transition plan.

Table 2.17 SOA Governance Planning Assessment Results for Ideation Inc.

SOA Governance Planning Assessment	Ideation Rating	Ideation Desired Rating
Plan & Organize		
Services Transformation Planning	1.67	4.00
Information Transformation Planning	1.00	3.83
Technology Transformation Planning	2.12	4.17
Service Processes, Organizations, Roles & Responsibilities	1.00	4.00
Manage the Service Investment	0.50	4.50
Business Vision & IT Alignment	1.75	3.50
Service Portfolio Management	1.83	4.33
Service Ownership & Funding	2.00	4.00
Service Governance Vitality	0.00	3.00
Service Communication Planning	2.00	4.00
Service Education & Training	1.17	4.00
Plan & Organize Average	1.37	3.94
Program Management Controls		
Enterprise Program Management	1.50	3.50
Change Management	1.00	3.00
Procurement of Resources	1.00	3.00
Vendor Management	1.50	3.00
Identify and Allocate Costs	0.50	2.50
Monitor Business Benefits of SOA	0.50	3.00
Program Management Controls Average	1.00	3.00
Service Development		
Service Development Lifecycle Controls	1.00	4.00
Manage Business Requirements	1.00	4.00
Service Identification	0.50	3.00
Service Specification	1.00	3.00
Service Realization	1.50	3.50
Service Certification	0.33	3.50
Service Development Average	0.89	3.50

SOA Governance Planning Assessment	Ideation Rating	Ideation Desired Rating
Service Operations		
Service Execution Monitoring	2.00	3.00
Service Operational Vitality	1.67	3.00
Service Support	1.33	3.00
Service Operations Average	**1.67**	**3.00**
SOA Governance Planning Average	1.21	3.51

Conclusion

The study of governance has advanced considerably over the years, and the same degree of "science" must be considered and used for SOA governance. This and previous chapters have given you the basis for assessing the current state of SOA governance at the organization that is under consideration. Next, we need to consider creating a specific transition plan for addressing the SOA governance needs of the organization.

3

Building the Service Factory

"Nothing is particularly hard if you divide it into small jobs."

–Henry Ford

In Chapter 2, "SOA Governance Assessment and Planning," we described how to assess an organization's current SOA maturity in terms of its capability to manage the four principal SOA domains of Plan & Organize, Program Management Controls, Service Development Lifecycle, and Service Operations. In this chapter, we discuss a practical approach to achieving the real potential of SOA through applied governance.

How to Succeed with SOA

We believe that there is a pattern or recipe for success that applies to all governance at all levels. This pattern consists of a simple set of governance tasks that can be applied to any repeated process. Repeating the governance cycle each time the process is used leads to incremental improvements in the quality and speed of executing that process.

These governance tasks are as follows:

- Set realistic goals or targets that you want to achieve at the outset. These might include factors such as resource levels, deadlines, quality goals, policies, or rules that should be met. Ideally, these goals should be aligned with other, higher-level enterprise goals, missions, and objectives.

- Define metrics that you can later capture to determine how well those goals are being met. These metrics need to be concrete, quantifiable, and above all, objective; better, faster, cheaper is meaningless unless you can say "better than x," "faster than y," or "cheaper than z." If you can't find an appropriate metric with a specific numeric target, abandon the goal as meaningless. Pass and fail tests and checklists work well to establish metrics.

- Assign roles and responsibilities at suitable times throughout the execution of the process being monitored, to measure progress by capturing the appropriate metrics; this should happen early enough in the process to take cost-effective, remedial action if required.

- Collate and communicate results to obtain an overall picture of the vitality of the process being monitored. If necessary, handle any exceptions, or grant permission to be noncompliant whenever necessary.

- Learn from experience. Based on the metrics you have captured and on feedback from everyone involved in the process, determine how to refine the process to do it better next time.

These tasks are shown graphically in Figure 3.1.

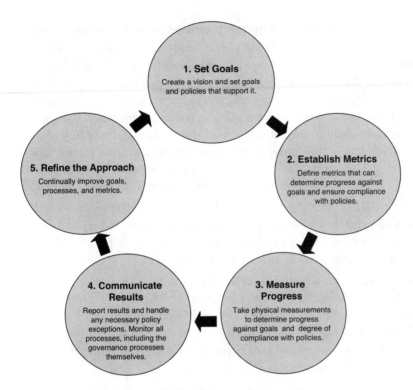

Figure 3.1 A Simple Governance Pattern for Process Improvement

Note that this process is cyclic. Step 5, Refine the Approach, will help improve the quality of the goals in Step 1 the next time the process executes; and each successive execution should be an improvement on the previous one.

A Divide-and-Conquer Approach to Managing Complexity

The main inhibitor to any large endeavor is complexity: The risk of failure increases rapidly as the number of people, tasks, or dependencies involved increases. However, some effective means have been developed for handling complexity through effective coordination and planning, most notably a divide-and-conquer approach that splits large and complex tasks into progressively smaller and simpler tasks and subtasks, until the tasks are simple enough to be performed by a single individual or small team. All tasks need to be associated with specific concrete deliverables, using the following steps:

- Define each task or subtask in terms of *work products* created by that task, subtask, or activity. Work products are intermediate or final physical artifacts (typically models, documents, or code) that provide a record of the results of each activity. Work products may be either *functional* (for example, a use case that defines a business activity or an architectural decision that records a technical approach to solving a common problem) or *governance related* (for example, a policy or a checklist). Every task must create or update at least one work product; any activity that does not produce a related work product is wasted effort. Subsequent sections in this chapter describe the principle SOA-specific work products that should be created.

- Create dependencies between activities so that they correspond to situations where a work product created by one activity is needed as an input for the creation of another work product.

- Apply governance to individual work products as they are produced, to determine their quality, completeness, and fitness for purpose. When work products created by one individual or group are needed by another individual or group, there should be an implied contract about their quality; significant breaches of such contracts should result in visible reprimands.

This work-product approach has major benefits to project management. They provide an objective means to measure progress of any project, if you assume that each intermediate work product you produce is either finished or not.

You measure real progress by the number of work products that are complete, with confidence that the project *will* be finished when 100% of the associated work products are complete. When you have established baseline measurements of the efforts required to complete each work product, you should be able to accurately estimate the remaining effort needed.

Although the work-product approach provides a powerful tool for enabling SOA governance, it is not a cure-all solution, and needs to be applied intelligently. Anything as complex as implementing SOA requires many experienced professionals making decisions and trade-offs. Most of the work products, and certainly those that represent policies, prioritization rules, decision points such as deciding which services will and will not be constructed, quality assessments, or checklists should be accompanied by documentation that gives clear guidance on how they should be used. An example of such guidance documentation is included in Chapter 6, "Managing the Service Lifecycle."

To be fair and even-handed, the same level of governance should apply to all service development in the organization; allowing any part of that organization to opt out is a recipe for anarchy and revolution. In the spirit of transparency, virtually all work products should be made available to anyone who wants to see them; providing additional feedback can help encourage consensus and synergy. Peer review before publication should be the rule, not the exception.

Naturally, it is impossible to define policies, standards, and rules that apply in all cases, and a significant aspect of efficient governance is the recognition that there needs to be a streamlined process for handling disagreements and granting policy exceptions where necessary. Staff should be encouraged to use these processes; they are an essential part of maintaining the vitality of the governance and technical processes, policies, and standards.

As discussed in Chapter 1, "Introduction to Governance," a key aspect of achieving practical governance involves understanding the "style" of the organization, and basing the governance plan accordingly. This includes making maximum use of existing governance bodies, standards, and mechanisms. It is especially important to involve everyone who is a potential governance stakeholder in establishing the SOA governance plan. Unless there is real consensus regarding the need for, approach, and level of strictness of SOA governance, and on the organizational structure that implements that plan, the plan will almost certainly fall short of its objectives. A single dissenting individual, especially if he or she is senior or influential, can sometimes derail the most carefully thought-out plan. Good communication—including the ability to listen to dissenting voices, and effectively handle their doubts or objections—is the key to creating such consensus.

Empowerment of individuals can be managed by assigning everyone to specific roles in developing, testing, and approving individual work products. We generally use the standard project management responsible, accountable, consulted, and informed (RACI) model, where

- *R* denotes the person or people who are *responsible* for the work product—its creators.

- *A* denotes a single individual or recognized authority who is accountable for that work product and takes personal accountability for its accuracy, completeness, and technical quality. This role includes the authority to sign off on work products and to grant exceptions to existing rules when necessary.

- *C* denotes all individuals or roles who need to be *consulted* during the development or approval of the work product.

- *I* denotes those individuals or roles that need to be *informed* when the work product has been completed and approved.

Mapping these relationships to the skills and training needed to perform them enables effective resource management and development of training plans and career paths.

As we describe later in this chapter, defining the work products that will be used, assigning responsibilities for their creation and testing, and determining the appropriate governance mechanism for each of them are important activities in the Plan & Organize SOA governance domain.

The Case for Creating a Service Factory

SOA employs significantly more standardization than traditional application development, and SOA governance must strive to encourage and support this standardization. Services have interfaces defined in a standard way, execute in standardized operating environments, and use a common technical infrastructure. A single common SOA infrastructure provides security, logging, event handling, data transformation, and physical connectivity, which, in traditional application development, each application had to provide independently.

In much the same way that standardization of components led to the industrial revolution, such standardization of components can enable services to be constructed using a manufacturing or assembly approach—a software production line or service factory to create all the necessary work products.

Henry Ford, the author of the quote at the start of this chapter, was the father of the automated production line that revolutionized the automobile production process, and reduced the cost of a car to a level that the average family could afford: Sadly, much current software development still uses a preindustrial "cottage industry" approach to building solutions.

Today's industrial manufacturing processes, like an automotive or aerospace assembly line, are constructed according to the principles of production engineering. Three distinct skill sets are needed for this approach:

- *Product designers* have to create products that are right for the market-place and that can be constructed simply and efficiently from stan-dardized components, ideally using as many existing component parts as possible.

- *Production engineers* spend a considerable amount of effort in creating the most efficient possible production or assembly process, assem-bling the necessary tools, and then defining the skills and resource levels necessary to meet specific production targets. Flexibility of the production line is an important consideration, to minimize any retooling cost when there are product enhancements.

- *Production managers* run and monitor the production or assembly line, creating large amounts of product, to closely specified quality stan-dards, at minimal cost.

There are considerable advantages to using such a production line approach, including the following:

- **Cost.** Due to economies of scale and improved efficiency, the unit cost of producing each product is much lower than using a craft-based or cottage industry manufacturing approach.

- **Consistency and reliability.** Using a standard manufacturing approach ensures items produced meet common functional and quality standards, leading to improved customer satisfaction and more sales.

- **Independence from suppliers.** Using standard commercially avail-able components gives the manufacturer the opportunity to change the source of those components readily, and simplifies and reduces the costs of maintenance or upgrade.

- **Product flexibility and time to market.** Effective production lines ensure that the products they produce are easily customized; for example, an automobile assembly line can easily produce multiple colors, engine, or trim levels.

Assuming that the production line has the necessary level of flexibility so that it can be quickly retooled for a new product, the ability to produce large quantities of a new product quickly can significantly improve the rate at which it begins to gain market share.

Note that all these advantages have a direct dollar value, and all represent goals that can be subject to objective measurements. So, how well does the analogy between the development of software and manufacturing of physical products hold?

Essentially, an effective service production line consists of a series of production cells, manned by skilled individuals or teams that perform a specific set of tasks and then pass their work products to the next team in the production process. Formal or informal contracts determine that each cell performs its tasks to the accepted quality, performs all necessary tests, and completes any required checklists before passing on its work products to the next cell in the process. Depending on the level of governance control you apply, these checklists may need to be signed off by an architect or by QA.

This engineering approach appears to address many of the issues that beleaguer traditional software development:

- **Cost.** Software may be intangible, but it is certainly costly to develop new code, and even more costly to maintain it after it has been created. Despite the focus on methodology and tools over the past two decades or so, most software development still occurs using an approach that is closer to a craft or cottage industry than an assembly line. Because services share much more common infrastructure components and development tools than do traditional applications, it is much easier to apply a production engineering approach to their development.

- **Consistency and reliability.** This is often a major problem with software development. Estimation of total development costs is problematic. Cost or time overruns are common. And, errors, malfunctions, performance, or response time issues are frequent concerns. Using a production line approach can enable incremental quality checks to detect functional or performance issues with services early, before the cost of remedy escalates.

- **Independence from suppliers.** This is a desirable goal for all IT development, as demonstrated by the current widespread adoption of open standards. Use of open standards is embedded in SOA, and because services have a much finer granularity than applications, it is much easier to combine them into compound services than it is to integrate applications. The ability—or inability—to combine or merge IT systems from two organizations is often a make-or-break issue when determining the feasibility of a corporate merger or acquisition. Therefore, the use of open standards and a demonstrable ability to integrate with external IT systems can have a direct effect on a company's value.

- **Product flexibility and time to market.** The purpose of IT systems is to support the ability of each organization to operate successfully, either through automated support of business tasks or by providing functionality that can be sold directly to consumers. Every organization, whatever the industry, has a need for agility of its internal systems and processes to be able to respond to competitive threats or opportunities, or to cope with legislative changes in a timely manner. In many organizations that the authors are familiar with, a perceived inability of the IT systems to change as rapidly as the business environment is a major cause of contention between the rest of the organization and IT; and improving that relationship, through showing an enhanced ability of IT to support business agility, may be the most significant potential benefit of SOA for them.

So, using a production engineering approach to achieve enhancements to the software development process, especially the service development process, is something that virtually all organizations should embrace.

Again, note that these are potential *business benefits,* both for the adoption of a services approach and for the use of a software production line to create them. There should be little or no problem between IT and corporate management in developing shared goals, targets, and priorities based on these.

Populating the Service Factory: Roles and Responsibilities

So, how do we go about creating a service factory to streamline the development of quality services? A number of tool vendors offer promised "silver-bullet" solutions, but the reality is that the people and processes are generally much more important than the tools they use.

Successful adoption of SOA invariably requires changes to development processes and individual roles and responsibilities. It requires everyone involved in IT development to take a cross-project, cross line-of-business (LoB) enterprise approach to defining common requirements and development priorities. This means SOA governance.

Although there is no single "one size fits all," perfect SOA organizational structure to enable such a transformation, we have found that establishing a small group dedicated entirely to achieving the success of SOA works well in practice. Depending on the individual organization, such a group may be called an SOA Center of Excellence (CoE) or SOA enablement team. Alternatively, SOA enablement may be treated as a program and managed under the program management office (PMO) or a team under the control of the enterprise architecture board (EAB). The name and reporting structure is much less important than the skills, analysis, design, development, testing, and operational processes used.

It is absolutely critical that the SOA enablement team includes both senior technical and senior business leaders who are sufficiently empowered to help ensure that business and IT interests are fully aligned. The team also needs to have the necessary authority to make and enforce new standards and working practices. Depending on the style of the organization, these new standards and working practices may have to be endorsed by an authority such as an EAB or PMO.

Although some organizations have succeeded in SOA using multiple or distributed teams, we have found in practice that having one single team of analysts, modelers, designers, and developers who create services for all LoB and IT projects is the preferred approach, for the following reasons:

- Having a single, dedicated services development team helps ensure consistency of quality and methodologies when creating services across the enterprise, especially for the first few services. If different project teams develop their own services, they are likely to create the services that meet only their immediate needs and are less likely to be reusable across the enterprise.
- Having a single team helps to generate synergy between the team members, with the more-experienced team members coaching and mentoring the less-experienced colleagues.
- It's much easier to manage a single, dedicated team than a distributed and geographically diverse group of professionals.

Figure 3.2 represents a logical structure of a dedicated SOA production team. The three layers—Control, Manage, and Perform—represent, respectively, strategic decision making, day-to-day management, and performance of SOA-related activities.

Shadings indicate whether the role is a new SOA-specific role, an existing role, or an existing role that needs to be enhanced for SOA.

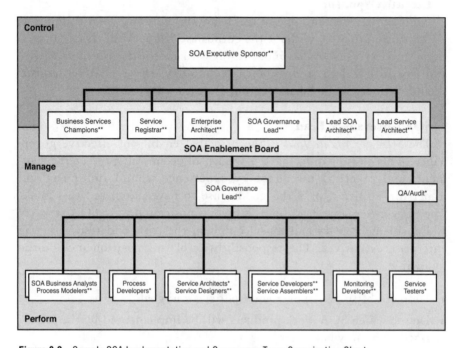

Figure 3.2 Sample SOA Implementation and Governance Team Organization Chart

Roles marked with an asterisk (*) represent existing roles that need to be extended for implementing SOA. A double asterisk (**) suffix represents a completely new SOA-specific role.

Note that Figure 3.2 shows roles rather than individuals. Not all of these roles need to be full time, and it is perfectly possible for individuals to have multiple roles in the SOA enablement team. Five to ten individuals is a typical size of such a team, excluding service assemblers, developers, and testers.

The team assembled to implement SOA does not need to be a permanent reporting structure. Indeed, one measure of the success of an SOA implementation team is that it renders itself obsolete within two years or less, as SOA becomes the normal way of constructing IT solutions. The need for an SOA governance function will, of course, continue indefinitely, as a specialization of the IT governance function.

The principal roles and responsibilities of these team members are discussed in the following sections.

Executive Sponsor

No organization can hope to tackle anything as large and complex as the transition to SOA without the enthusiastic support of its executives. Because effective SOA has more to do with increasing business agility and flexibility than it does with technology, the executive sponsor should come from the business group, not from within IT.

SOA Governance Lead

The *SOA governance lead* is the principal enabler of effective governance. This person must have a wealth of technical, project management, and practical methodology experience, sound judgment and leadership abilities, plus the good sense to have purchased this book! The SOA governance lead holds a pivotal position on the SOA strategy and enablement team and must command the trust and respect of the enterprise executives. The responsibilities of this position include the following:

- Help establish SOA governance policies and goals
- Define which SOA work products will be implemented by the organization and in what order
- Create and publish a formal plan to implement SOA governance across the enterprise
- Establish key SOA governance processes
- Create templates for all SOA governance work products
- Perform successful estimation of service scope and effort

The skills required of this position include the following:

- Have a deep understanding of project management, QA, and development methodology
- Have good interpersonal, communications, and negotiating skills

- Have a keen understanding of all aspects of SOA
- Have a deep understanding of the governance model and compliance measurement
- Manage SOA-related relationships with the other business departments
- Have knowledge of IT best practices

The SOA governance lead works with the following:

- SOA enablement board
- Business service champions
- Service registrar
- The QA team
- The PMO
- Enterprise architects
- SOA architect

Business Service Champions

The *business service champion* is the key player in the transformation to SOA and brings deep understanding of business and IT to the program. The role must be filled by an individual highly respected by both the business and IT organizations. Business service champions hold key positions on the SOA strategy and enablement teams. Responsibilities of this position include the following:

- Ensure business and IT collaboration
- Develop and sell solutions to business and IT
- Balance short-term business improvements with long-term strategic transformation
- Tie together business vision and IT architecture vision
  - Hold together the pure business objectives and IT viewpoints together at the project level
  - Must approve solutions that maintain clear business benefits and adhere to SOA standards

- Facilitate service interface design, implementation, and governance
- Coordinate with functional and technical team members to ensure designs are reached through consensus
- Approve critical SOA work products, attend key reviews, and handle exceptions

The skills required of this position include the following:

- A deep understanding of both business process and IT capabilities
- A focus on business process issues
- Good understanding of project planning and project management
- Knowledge of the organization
- A thorough understanding of SOA and business modeling concepts, activities, and processes
- A deep understanding of governance model and compliance measurements
- Ability to manage SOA-related relationships with the other business departments
- Ability to perform successful estimation of service scope and effort
- Knowledge of the industry's best practices

The business service champion works with the following:

- SOA enablement board
- Enterprise architects
- Business analysts
- Business executives

SOA Business Analysts

There are two specialized business analyst roles involved in SOA: The *business process analyst* models and optimizes complete business processes to reengineer existing business processes or define new business processes; and the *business service analyst* models individual business tasks within processes, at a finer level of detail to capture requirements for business services, and then translates those into potential IT services. Both these analysts can bring requests for business process choreography or new IT services to the rest of the SOA CoE team members to ensure compliance with architecture and service standards. The business analyst's role is typically filled by individuals with experience in multiple business units, with good technical skills, and business expertise. Because of the depth of business knowledge needed, business analysts are typically specialists in a few specific areas of business activity.

The responsibilities of business analysts include the following:

- Create and maintain models of business processes, rules, and requirements
- Run visualizations and simulations of processes to create efficient business processes
- Lead the development of service requirements
- Work with process developers to make sure what is coded for processes is what the business needs and wants
- Provide business process monitoring and reporting requirements
- Provide access (security) requirements for all aspects of business processes, the monitoring dashboard, and reports

The skills of business process analysts include the following:

- Expertise in how one or more significant parts of the business are run and awareness of current IT systems that support it
- A deep understanding of current business processes and ability to model "to be" future business processes
- Proven skills in capturing accurate and detailed business requirements
- An understanding of key performance indicators (KPIs) and other major business requirements
- Familiarity with the enterprise's chosen business modeling tools and conversant with Business Process Execution Language (BPEL)
- Ability to effectively use SOA governance processes for successful reviews and standards compliance

The skills of business service analysts include the following:

- An ability to model individual business tasks in fine detail
- An understanding of the trade-offs in creating IT services of the correct granularity
- An ability to develop business requirements
- The ability to identify and analyze document service requirements
- An ability to translate business requirements to SOA IT requirements
- An ability to effectively use SOA governance processes for successful reviews and standard compliance

The SOA business analysts work with the following:

- Business service champion
- Process modeler
- Service developer
- Process developer
- Service registrar

The Service Registrar

The *service registrar* is the gatekeeper of the organization's service assets, service metadata, and service repositories. The service registrar is responsible for maintaining the service registry and repository with appropriate metadata and keywords to enable search capabilities. He also helps create and assist with enforcing the organizational discipline necessary for populating the repository. The service registrar discourages the creation of redundant services by making it easy for project teams to scan the repository before beginning design and development efforts on a new service. The responsibilities of this position include the following:

- Implement and maintain service repository tools and access interfaces
- Assist with service identification process
- Build consensus around service publication to establish corporate policies and standards

- Enforce the policies and standards for service publication into the repository
- Foster communication between service producers and consumers
- Monitor service usage and reuse

The skills required for the service registrar include the following:

- An understanding of SOA concepts, standards, and best practices
- Skilled in developing service assets and IT operating procedures with an SOA focus
- Expert understanding of metadata, search concepts, and architecture
- Experience in implementing repository control processes with a focus on reusable components and services
- Experience in governance processes—enforcement, service usage, and compliance measurement
- Skilled in services related to asset creation and harvesting and service categorization techniques
- Familiarity with tools that manage services change, version, and usage control
- Skilled in service usage cost estimation and configuration management principles

The service registrar works with the following:

- Business service champion
- Business analysts
- Service designers
- IT operations
- The QA team

The Lead SOA Architect

The lead *SOA architect* provides the technical foundation for the SOA infrastructure, acting as an enterprise architect specializing in SOA technology and creating and maintaining the SOA infrastructure platform. Responsibilities of this post include the following:

- Develop and maintain end state vision for SOA production infrastructure
- Understand and resolve all technical issues with the infrastructure

The skills of the SOA architect include the following:

- An understanding of SOA strategy—management, planning, and vision
- SOA asset management services skills and maintenance skills
- Ability to architect the placement of components and optimize the operational model
- Design and implementation skills for system management functions
- Good communication abilities

The SOA architect works with the following:

- Enterprise architects
- IT operations

The Service Architects and the Lead Service Architect

Service architects provide the technical foundation for services and automated business processes, under guidance from the lead service architect. They develop detailed service design patterns to guide service designers and service developers in the best usage of SOA platform, and work with the business service champion to set vision and strategy for services. Service architects are typically technology specialists that work across multiple projects and business areas. They focus on aspects that apply across multiple services, such as what is the best technology for implementing common adapters, coding and development guidelines, and infrastructure selection and configuration. Responsibilities of this post include the following:

- Develop detailed service design patterns
- Develop and maintain end state SOA vision with SOA enablement team

- Understand and resolve all technical issues with infrastructure and architecture for services
- Define infrastructure services to support implementation of business services
- Define service implementation patterns for each supported application technology environment
- Design strategies and accepted technologies for wrapping legacy transactions as services
- Create and maintain guidance for when (and when not) to deploy function as services

The skills required for a service architect include the following:

- An understanding of SOA strategy, planning, management, and vision
- Ability to develop solutions utilizing SOA architectures and frameworks and patterns
- Ability to develop solutions utilizing SOA services and application products
- Ability to develop integration interfaces and SOA integration protocols
- Ability to develop to design end-to-end services solutions
- Good communication skills
- Experience using the organization's chosen methodologies and tools for developing and supporting solutions

The lead service architect needs leadership and negotiation skills in addition to the above. The service architects work with the following:

- The business service champion
- Service designers
- Security architect
- Database administrator
- Service developers and service assemblers
- Service registrar

The Service Designer

The *service designer* finalizes functional requirements and makes any implementation decisions necessary to make services meet real-world demands such as quality of service (QoS), service level agreements (SLAs), functional requirements, and nonfunctional requirements. The service designer is a solution architect role, and he or she must be experienced in extending an outline functional design of a service to meet deep technical requirements, such as performance, availability, scalability, and recoverability, as well as meeting all adopted standards and best practices. Responsibilities of this role include the following:

- Ensure that all planned services have the optimum granularity or scope
- Create designs for business services
- Finalize functional designs and technical implementations necessary to make services meet demands of QoS
- Ensure final syntax and semantics of service interface design remain useful to any application needing the same functionality

The skills required for this role include the following:

- Strong software architect skills
- Ability to translate business processes into workable service designs
- Ability to collaborate with business analysts to interpret business process context and understand functional requirements
- Ability to analyze, model, design, and iteratively refine service specifications
- Ability to collaborate with service architects to utilize and improve design patterns
- Ability to establish criteria and prove individual service measures up
- Ability to collaborate to establish repeatable processes and best practices for internal use
- Ability to draw from library of prebuilt services and compose complex (composite) services by integrating multiple basic services
- Solid working knowledge of SOA services design techniques, including service analysis and design techniques, and the Unified Modeling Language

- Knowledge of various integration interfaces and protocols
- Demonstrated use of assembly and construction tools and procedures
- Demonstrated ability to build necessary user interfaces and integration points to connect physical business process to services needed

Service designers work with the following roles:

- Business service champion
- Business analysts
- Service architects
- The service registrar
- Service developers and service assemblers
- The QA team

The Service Developer and Service Assembler

The *service developer* is the person who creates executable services (such as web services) based on Web Services Description Language (WSDL) provided by the service designer. The service developer is a strong J2EE or .Net software engineer who codes these services, tests them, and ensures that the services meet both the functional and nonfunctional requirements provided by the service architects, business analysts, and service designer. *Service assemblers* are a subset of service developers, who create composite services that invoke multiple simple services in a single call. Responsibilities of these roles include the following:

- Design and implementation of services
- Ability to reuse existing services and existing frameworks wherever practicable
- Maintain code
- Unit test services for functionality, error conditions, performance, and stability
- Understand the existing mainframe systems functionality and use it to provide services
- Understand and recover from transaction failures when dealing with multiple systems

Service developer skills include the following:

- Strong technical skills and development experience
- Understanding of mainframe connectivity
- Strong software engineering skills
- Expert user of the enterprise's chosen software development kit (SDK)

Service developers work with the following:

- Service designers
- Service architects
- Security architects
- Service designers

Process Modelers

Process modelers are specialists in the technical aspects of process modeling. They work with the business analysts to ensure the creation of consistent, effective, and reusable automated business processes. Responsibilities of process modelers include the following:

- Create and maintain metadata about the business processes
- Ensure the reporting and monitoring requirements are met in the process
- Work with service designers to ensure alignment between the services and the processes that invoke them
- Provide quality input to the business process developers

Process modelers should have the following skills:

- Excellent SOA technology skills and experience
- Proven experience with automated process development

Process modelers work with the following:

- Business process analysts
- Process developers
- Security architects
- Service architects
- The QA team
- Monitoring developers

Process Developers

The *process developer* is a person who takes output generated from business modeling tools and extends it to create executable automated processes, which run in a suitable process execution environment. These executable processes need to cover all known contingencies, enforce security and privacy requirements, and recover or restart if exceptions or problems occur. The process developer binds these automated business process models to services provided by the service developers to create complete working solutions. Responsibilities of this role include the following:

- Implement BPEL-based business processes using the enterprise's chosen tooling
- Test the business processes with emulation and other standard process unit testing
- Enable and produce any necessary events alerts and reports for reporting and monitoring

Skills needed by process developers include the following:

- Strong development skills and coding experience
- Thorough understanding of the business processes being modeled
- Strong skills using the business modeling tools used by the enterprise
- Good communication skills

Business process developers work with the following roles:

- Business process architects
- Business analysts
- Service designers
- Security architects
- The QA team

Service Testers

This is an extension of the existing tester role, the principle differences being that services do not have user interfaces and are typically much finer grained than conventional applications. Service testing includes both functional and nonfunctional testing (for example, performance, throughput, security). A number of useful tools to support service testing are beginning to appear on the market, and the service testers should be thoroughly familiar with any such tools chosen by the organization.

Monitoring Developers

The *monitoring developer* creates the server-side components for monitoring and reporting that are needed for the applications. Monitoring requirements from business analysts, process modelers, and process developers need to be captured and implemented to create the right data access to allow them to be displayed on the process monitoring screen or dashboard. Responsibilities of this role include the following:

- Understand requirements from process modelers and process developers for reporting and monitoring their performance requirements
- Create and implement all required IT components for process monitoring and reporting

Monitoring developer skills include the following:

- Strong technical development skills and experience
- Working knowledge of process monitoring tools and the SDK tools selected by the enterprise

Developers work with the following:

- Business process analysts
- Process modelers
- Process developers
- The QA team
- GUI designers/architects
- Security architects
- IT operations

Security Architects

The *security architect* provides end-to-end security to the application and system to cover aspects such as authentication and authorization and nonrepudiation of service requestors, and ensuring that access to restricted information is to those who have a legitimate right to use it. Responsibilities of this role include the following:

- Provide detailed security requirements for all services and business processes, and assist with their implementation and testing
- Provide requirements for systems at runtime for who can access what

Skills needed for this role include the following:

- Strong security skills
- Expertise in J2EE, Java/.Net development, and any security tools used by the enterprise

Security architects work with all other architects and with the QA and test teams.

The SOA "Plan & Organize" Domain

"A goal without a plan is just a wish."

—Antoine de Saint-Exupery

The SOA Governance Plan & Organize domain is where the major strategic decisions are made to determine the way SOA will be governed across the enterprise. SOA governance can help realize the strategic plans, but needs to be implemented on a secure foundation of existing enterprise and IT governance. Our practical experience is that most large organizations have reasonably effective enterprise-level governance—at least in terms of budgetary controls—but are often lacking effective IT governance, particularly in development and deployment of IT solutions that support more than one line of business.

In Chapter 2, we described this critical domain, and outlined the key capabilities needed to manage it successfully. In this section, we describe a set of work products that support those capabilities and whose creation will provide effective governance to minimize risks, manage issues, and avoid pitfalls.

Tasks in this Plan & Organize domain effectively mirror the initial tasks involved in the production engineering role in planning a factory: establishing the purpose and size of the factory, establishing roles and responsibilities, ensuring that there is sufficient production machinery, and manning the factory with suitably skilled staff.

From an SOA governance perspective, the *SOA governance plan* is the key work product because it describes the action plan for ensuring that the transformation to SOA is smooth and efficient. However, like many other work products, there are some significant dependencies. For example, the SOA governance plan cannot have a strategic component completed without first defining the strategy for how SOA will support the business (using the *services strategic blueprint* work product), that in turn depends on setting a business investment strategy (using the *business and IT financial priorities* work product) and so on.

The critical aspects of planning and organizing for the success of SOA involve selecting which work products to use (ideally prioritize the ones you need sooner and have a plan to ultimately do all of them), what the priority of their development is, the quality of the team that produces them, the style and quality of the work products themselves, and the degree of commitment that the organization has to their use. That is the essence of the art of governance—the applied judgment of how to use the resources on hand to meet the objectives one has been set, or the courage to renegotiate those objectives if they are truly unachievable.

Table 3.1 examines the risks and issues potentially associated with this SOA Plan & Organize domain, and it lists the governance-related work products that can be developed to help avoid them. The table is organized as follows:

- Column 1 lists a capability that the organization needs to display to manage this domain successfully. If the organization lacks this capability to a significant degree, this area should be given focus.

- Column 2 describes the issues and risks that are likely to occur if an organization lacks this capability to the necessary degree. Again, if these risks or issues are already occurring, this area should be given high priority.

- Column 3 is our estimate of the impact that those issues or risks would have on an SOA implementation if they were not addressed. This will obviously vary some from organization to organization. *Critical* issues are ones that left unaddressed may derail the entire SOA transition initiative. *High* risk levels would cause significant waste of resources or loss of important opportunities.

- Column 4 names the work products that can be used to help develop those capabilities and avoid the risks. These work products are deliverables created by performing activities designed to develop those capabilities. For example, the act of creating a *business vision* document and creating consensus about its content with all stakeholder executives helps to establish and communicate a common vision of the organization's future. Interdependencies between these work products are discussed later in this chapter.

- Column 5 contains our estimate of the degree of effort required to address those issues and avoid those risks by implementing those work products and introducing governance mechanisms that control their completeness and quality. Again, the cost of remedy will vary some between organizations. Although the actual levels of effort required will vary widely between different sizes and styles of organization, *low* costs typically relate to a few person-days of effort, *moderate* costs to person-weeks to person-months worth of effort, and *high* costs typically require additional full-time staff.

Table 3.1 Plan & Organize Domain: Capabilities, Risks, and Remedial Work Products

Capability	Associated Issues and Risks	Risk Level	Governance Work Products	Cost of Remedy
1. Service transformation planning	■ SOA can deliver little real value unless there are clear business goals and priorities to guide its implementation. ■ SOA offers the potential for reusable IT assets that are shared across the entire enterprise. This cannot occur if each business operating unit remains a complete silo. ■ SOA must visibly support major business objectives if it is to be championed by the business operating units	High	■ Business vision ■ Strategic business plan ■ Business heat map (high-value business capabilities prioritized across business operating units) ■ Services strategic blueprint ■ *Enterprisewide* glossary of business terms ■ *Enterprisewide* glossary of business rules and requirements	Moderate
2. Information transformation planning	■ Data is a critical corporate asset that needs to be managed carefully. SOA introduces additional demands for data access and sharing. Without an enterprise information strategy and clear rules on data ownership, there is likelihood of data duplication, loss, corruption, or unauthorized access. ■ Services cannot be shared across business operating units unless there is a common enterprise data model that determines how that data will be stored together with a simplified form of that model (a messaging model) to define standard service inputs and outputs.	Critical	■ Information systems strategy blueprint ■ Enterprise data and messaging models	Moderate

Capability	Associated Issues and Risks	Risk Level	Governance Work Products	Cost of Remedy
3. Technology transformation planning	■ Unless there is a well-constructed strategic plan for managing current and future IT systems, there is the potential for a radical new technology such as SOA to cause chaos. ■ Unless there are clear and *enforced* architecture standards, individual designers and developers will generally create incoherent, incompatible, and almost unmaintainable point solutions. ■ There can be delays if infrastructure to support the new SOA projects is not in IT plan. ■ There can be performance problems if capacity estimates and configurations are not adequate to support services and automated business processes.	High	■ Information systems strategy blueprint ■ Architecture standards and design patterns ■ Technology blueprint (extended for SOA) ■ Operational model (extended for SOA) ■ IT capacity management plan (extended for SOA)	High
4. Services processes, organizations, roles, and responsibilities	■ Without clear roles and responsibilities, there will inevitably be duplication of efforts, confusion, misunderstandings, gaps, and omissions that will waste efforts, incur costs, and introduce delays	High	■ SOA organization chart ■ SOA roles and responsibilities ■ SOA Governance Process	Moderate

Table 3.1 Plan & Organize Domain: Capabilities, Risks, and Remedial Work Products (continued)

Capability	Associated Issues and Risks	Risk Level	Governance Work Products	Cost of Remedy
5. Manage the service investment	■ Implementing SOA requires significant investment. Without a good business case, coupled with objective measurements of the real value, it would be impossible to justify investing in SOA.	High	■ SOA reuse and ROI monitoring plan ■ Business agility monitoring plan ■ Business flexibility monitoring plan	High
6. Business vision and IT alignment	■ Unless IT priorities are fully aligned with business priorities, IT cannot provide adequate support for the business. ■ A poor relationship between IT and the business units can lead to business operating units creating their own IT systems. ■ If the business operating units cannot express their needs to IT, and unless IT understands and satisfies those needs, both IT and business resources will inevitably be squandered.	Critical	■ Business heat map ■ Business and IT financial priorities ■ Information systems strategic blueprint (extended for SOA) ■ Services strategic blueprint ■ Business agility monitoring plan ■ Business flexibility monitoring plan ■ Enterprisewide glossary of business terms ■ Enterprisewide glossary of business rules and requirements	Moderate

Capability	Associated Issues and Risks	Risk Level	Governance Work Products	Cost of Remedy
7. Service portfolio management	■ Unless the SOA enablement team has the capability to influence the selection of new projects that will use an SOA approach to create agile business services that support the services strategic blueprint, they will be unable to deliver on it, and the SOA transformation may lose momentum.	High	■ Business heat map ■ Service selection and prioritization policies ■ Service prioritization checklist ■ Service portfolio ■ Other project-related work products described in the next section	Moderate
	■ The whole strategic SOA initiative could be threatened if the owner of a new project involving a strategic area of the business heat map refused to take a services approach.			
8. SOA ownership and funding	■ Without a clear ownership and funding model that provides incentives for creating services that meet the needs of all business operating units, not just the one that identifies it first, there is unlikely to be real reuse.	High	■ Services ownership and funding models	Low
	■ Without such models, it is difficult to determine who should be allowed to access services, or who can approve changes or new versions.			

Table 3.1 Plan & Organize Domain: Capabilities, Risks, and Remedial Work Products (continued)

Capability	Associated Issues and Risks	Risk Level	Governance Work Products	Cost of Remedy
9. Service governance vitality	■ Most enterprises that have experimented with SOA but failed to achieve real business benefits see that ineffective SOA governance was a major contributor to that failure.	High	■ SOA governance plan ■ SOA governance vitality report	Moderate
	■ Achieving a balance between too little governance (anarchy) and too much governance (stifling bureaucracy) is difficult in practice. Like any other business activity, the cost of SOA governance needs to be justified by its results.			
10. Service communication planning	■ Unless a common vision is established, and all stakeholders are kept informed of progress, they are unlikely to develop or maintain enthusiastic commitment to the SOA initiative.	Critical	■ Services strategic blueprint ■ SOA communications plan ■ SOA roles and responsibilities ■ Service portfolio	Low

Capability	Associated Issues and Risks	Risk Level	Governance Work Products	Cost of Remedy
11. Service education and training	■ Successfully implementing SOA requires a high degree of skill. Even if much SOA activity is outsourced, some critical skills (those of business analysts, architects, and so on) need to be maintained within the organization. ■ To attract and retain superior SOA professionals, regular training updates and the existence of a clear SOA-related career path are essential.	High	■ SOA roles and responsibilities ■ SOA education plan ■ SOA career paths	Moderate

SOA Plan & Organize Domain Work-Product Definitions

In the preceding section, we introduced a number of work products that have been proven to be effective in helping to govern and manage successful SOA transformations. For the Plan & Organize domain, most of these work products are either plans, policies, and standards or definitions of an SOA organization or roles. The act of creating these work products should ensure that there are few, if any, missed items of importance in this critical domain.

Most organizations have already produced artifacts that are partially or fully equivalent to these work products, and if so, those should be reused or be extended. Work product names and format are less important than their completeness and quality, which stems directly from how much thought and effort goes into their production.

In this section, we define the content and purpose of each of the work products mentioned in Table 3.1. For convenience of reference, these definitions are in alphabetic order. The actual format of these work products is less important than the degree of effort taken in completing them: If they are well executed and used properly, your SOA governance should be effective and practical.

The Architecture Standards and Design Patterns Work Product

Description: Architecture standards and design patterns represent the foundational policies for implementing IT governance, because they set formal technical constraints on hardware and software infrastructure, application technology and design, the construction and implementation of services, and automated processes that should apply to all future IT solutions unless there are specific individual exemptions. Architecture standards and design patterns represent important IT governance metrics because proposed new solutions must either be compliant with accepted standards or they must have an explicit exemption from them, granted by a suitably empowered IT governance function. The existence of at least an outline set of IT architectural standards and design patterns is an absolute prerequisite for a successful SOA implementation, and there are many specific SOA-related architectural standards and design patterns that are needed to implement SOA (for example, development language, security standards, enterprise service bus [ESB] requirements, service registry requirements, and service monitoring).

Purpose: This work product will have multiple sections, some of which reflect technology or vendor choices, the technical development approach, frameworks, development coding, documentation and testing approach, and so on. Standards that are not followed represent both a major loss of opportunity and a waste of effort on behalf of the senior technical staff who set those standards. Although most organizations manage to define at least some architecture standards, failure of IT governance to effectively enforce those standards is a problem that we regularly face. Governance mechanisms and controls have to be put into place to enforce these, or all future IT solutions, not just services, will be of questionable quality. We recommend a series of checklists, design reviews, code walkthroughs, and a formal acceptance process to ensure conformance. These are described Chapter 4, "Governing the Service Factory."

When needed: Some architectural standards and design patterns should already be in existence, but additional ones will need to be added for SOA. If there are no existing architectural standards and design patterns, this indicates a lack of IT governance that should be rectified immediately.

Responsible: Architects, IT, and SOA governance SMEs, security architect, program/project management office (PMO), and QA.

Accountable: Chief enterprise architect or architecture board.

Consulted: IT staff, business service champions, development leads, and IT operations leads.

Informed: All IT and QA.

The Business Agility Monitoring Plan Work Product

Description: Assuming that improved business agility is a key component of the enterprise's business vision and strategic business plan, there is a need to quantify the current level of agility, define an achievable improvement goal, create a plan to achieve that goal, and create a process to monitor progress as objectively as possible. Agility means different things to different industries, so it is hard to generalize across industries. However, it typically refers to the ability of the organization to make major structural, organizational, or marketplace adjustments. Example metrics include the time and effort taken

- To implement major new business or IT projects
- To outsource a noncore business component
- To fully integrate a new subsidiary that has just been acquired
- To sell off or outsource a noncore part of the business

Purpose: Business agility is hard to measure, but most industries see improved business agility as essential to compete successfully in a market that has an accelerating rate of change. The business agility monitoring plan should look at trends over an extended period, because agility data is likely to be highly variable because of subtle differences in the items being measured

When needed: This is the planning stage of a long-term effort to measure business agility. There may be historical data to help establish an agility baseline; otherwise, you should establish ad hoc metrics and begin taking measurements as soon as possible

Responsible: PMO, organization & methods (O&M) department, if any, possibly with assistance from outside consultants.

Accountable: COO.

Consulted: All C-level execs, business operating unit executives.

Informed: All C-level execs, all business unit and IT executives.

The Business Flexibility Monitoring Plan Work Product

Description: Business flexibility is similar to business agility but on a somewhat smaller scale, because it typically assesses the capability and speed of an organization to respond to external pressures, threats, or opportunities, through maintenance of existing IT solutions or implementation of new IT solutions. Automating business processes allows for very speedy process change.

Purpose: Improve the responsiveness of the organization, in terms of the speed at which it can respond to new legislation, threats, or opportunities. Metrics include the number and scope of new business requirements supported by IT solutions, and the relative proportions of resources devoted to nonbusiness related systems maintenance, business-related systems maintenance, and development of new IT solutions.

When needed: Data capture should start as soon as feasible. Reporting should be around every three months.

Responsible: PMO, O&M department.

Accountable: COO.

Consulted: Business operating unit executives.

Informed: All business unit and IT executives.

The Business Heat Map Work Product

Description: Based on the business vision and strategic business plan, this heat map defines the high-focus aspects of the business to a finer level of detail than contained in the strategic business plan. High-focus aspects are business capabilities, activities, tasks, or processes that are considered to be

- Core aspects of the business
- Critical to meeting the business KPIs
- Areas with high return on investment (ROI)
- Specific areas that the enterprise wants to invest in for strategic reasons

Purpose: This work product provides invaluable input for defining IT investment areas and setting priority business areas that will be supported through creation of services and automated business processes.

When needed: This is an enterprise governance level work product that should be created early in strategic planning for SOA because it forms the basis of many other business-focused strategic work products, such as the business and IT financial priorities.

Responsible: CFO, COO, business unit managers, PMO.

Accountable: COO.

Consulted: All C-level execs, business operating unit executives.

Informed: All business unit and IT executives.

The Business and IT Financial Priorities Work Product

Description: Based on the strategic business plan and business heat map, this defines the investment decision-making strategy and processes for both the business operating units and IT, including investment priorities and financial targets. If this activity is performed well and these priorities are developed in conjunction with each other, it can help establish a secure foundation for alignment of business and IT priorities.

Purpose: Just as for any other business operating unit, management of the process for IT investment decision making should demonstrate the ability to direct investment resources based on achieving the enterprise's fundamental business goals, such as ROI, business flexibility, and business agility. In terms of SOA, this should satisfy the business requirement for IT of continuously and demonstrably improving the cost-efficiency of IT through the creation of reusable and standardized services that are continuously monitored to ensure that they fully satisfy the needs of the business.

When needed: This is an IT governance-level work product that should be created early in strategic planning for SOA because it forms the basis of many other business-focused strategic work products, such as the business and IT financial priorities.

Responsible: Finance business unit, COO, CIO.

Accountable: CFO.

Consulted: Business operating unit executives.

Informed: Business unit and IT executives.

The Business Rules and Requirements Work Product

Description: Most of the client organizations we have worked for capture business requirements and rules in documentation for a specific project, thereby making it difficult to find in the future, no matter how good its quality. Creating an enterprisewide database of requirements and rules, referenced by the business entity that they effect (customer, invoice, and so on) makes it much easier to reuse them across multiple lines of business.

Purpose: Avoid unnecessary work through reusing requirements analysis efforts, rather than repeating the analysis.

When needed: If not already in existence, this should be started immediately and continuously updated. It should be consulted whenever any new business activity is analyzed to look for common reuse opportunities.

Responsible: Business analysts, PMO.

Accountable: Business service champion.

Consulted: All LOB.

Informed: All LOB and IT.

The Business Term Glossary Work Product

Description: The business term glossary defines the meaning of business terms and jargon used throughout the enterprise. This is especially useful for disambiguation—when two different LOB use the same term to mean something different or when they use two different terms to mean the same thing.

Purpose: Maintaining such a document is helpful for maintaining an enterprisewide view of business requirements, and for service definitions.

When needed: If not already in existence, this should be started immediately and continuously updated. It should be consulted whenever any new business activity is analyzed to look for common requirement or confusing terminology.

Responsible: Business analysts, PMO.

Accountable: Business service champion.

Consulted: All business units.

Informed: All business units.

The Business Vision Work Product

Description: The business vision defines the overall strategic goals and priorities of the enterprise for the next two to five years. It is an essential input to developing a strategic business plan.

Purpose: This is a key work product for enabling Enterprise Governance and represents a critical input to enabling effective IT and then SOA Governance.

When needed: This should exist before any widescale implementation of SOA. If not, it's creation should be given high priority before SOA strategic planning is started. Such plans should be reviewed and refreshed at least once a year.

Responsible: The board.

Accountable: Chief executive.

Consulted: All senior executives.

Informed: All.

The Enterprise Data Model and Messaging Model Work Products

Description: Enterprise data model (EDM) and messaging model (MM) work products represent a canonical (standard) business entity model that is an absolute prerequisite for success at SOA.

Many industries have an industry standard model, and any organization within that industry should consider adopting that model, as it can help to simplify business-to-business (B2B) communication and make it easier to implement industry-specific solutions (such as software as a service, where you rent rather than buy software).

The MM is a simplified data model derived directly from the EDM, but it contains fewer business entities and with less rigorous normalization. It is a fit-for-purpose model designed to be the standard message model for service specification and realization in that it defines how business entities and their interrelationships are transmitted as input and output data for service invocation.

The principal characteristics of MM are as follows:

- It is a fit-for-purpose design model that is derived and transformed from EDM.
- It contains the data domains required by services/operations.
- It does not need to reflect how the data is stored.
- It is a representation of data classes related to service messages.
- It is used to derive and compose messaging constructs—request and response pair for each operation.
- It will not contain field validation rules such as mandatory fields, fields length, and enumerations.

It is essential to maintain consistency of the MM and the EDM. Both these models need to be carefully version managed, so that the service developers have a well-defined platform on which to construct and deploy services.

Purpose: The EDM is used to define how data representing physical entities relevant to that business are physically stored. The MM is used to define the inputs and outputs of service invocations.

When needed: Assuming the preexistence of an EDM, work on defining the MM should begin immediately. If there is no existing EDM, implementing SOA will be severely impacted until one is agreed upon, because it is an essential prerequisite for SOA.

Responsible: SOA lead architect service architect, service designer, data architect, database administrator.

Accountable: Business service champion.

Consulted: IT architects, business analysts, data modelers, service developers, QA, testing.

Informed: All IT.

The Information Systems Strategy Blueprint Work Product (Extended for SOA)

Description: This is a work product that belongs in the domain of IT governance, but some extensions and specializations should be applied to support SOA. This is effectively the strategic information plan for IT. It is a critical document for ensuring that IT is well aligned with the business. SOA should be—or should eventually become—a key component of this strategy, and services should eventually receive as much focus as current IT systems.

Purpose: This document describes the policies, processes, and responsibilities that exist to support IT achieving its own goals and objectives and fully aligning with and supporting the business and all business operating units.

When needed: Ideally, this document will already exist, and will just require slight modification to include the use of services to create cross-LOB functionality. If it does not already exist, it should be created and approved as rapidly as possible.

Responsible: IT manager, CTO, CIO, chief enterprise architect, SOA lead architect, SOA architects, business enterprise architects.

Accountable: CIO.

Consulted: Business operating unit executives.

Informed: Business operating unit executives and IT executives.

The IT Capacity Management Plan Work Product (Extended for SOA)

Description: The IT capacity plan work product is the plan that determines that the IT infrastructure has and can maintain the necessary capacity to support the predicted workload. This means using a combination of load balancing and resource planning, including good management of infrastructure component lead and setup times and integrating timings with the infrastructure version management plan.

Purpose: To ensure that the IT infrastructure has and continues to have, the capacity to support the necessary workload and meet all quality of service commitments.

When needed: This is a key IT governance work product that should already be in existence, but that needs to be updated to ensure that the SOA infrastructure is effectively capacity managed and that all service invocations meet their performance commitments.

Responsible: IT architects, systems management leads, IT operations leads, business monitoring developer.

Accountable: Chief enterprise architect.

Consulted: IT staff, business service champions, development leads.

Informed: All IT.

The Operational Model Work Product (Extended for SOA)

Description: The operational model work product is the fine detail level of the design for the IT production-level infrastructure. It contains a description of all the nodes (such as servers, routers, databases, terminals, printers, and firewalls) in the IT network and the software stack (that is, infrastructure software, application components, systems monitoring software, network connectivity, and network addresses).

Purpose: Effectively the operational model is the detailed map of the whole entirety of the IT physical resources, used to plan and define how the IT platform will manage resiliency, systems management, load sharing and capacity, and to assist in systems management and error recovery. Ideally, this model will be held in a software tool that understands the dependencies between components and that maintains the integrity of the operational model rather than a simple generic tool that just draws pictures but has no understanding of their meaning.

When needed: This is a key IT governance work product that should already be in existence, but that needs to be updated (and if need be, created!) to help govern the physical components that comprise the SOA technical infrastructure.

Responsible: Architects, SOA architects, IT operations, network planning, network operations, security architect.

Accountable: Chief enterprise architect.

Consulted: IT staff, business service champions, development leads.

Informed: All IT.

The Services Ownership and Funding Models Work Product

Description: A clear understanding and communication of funding and ownership models is necessary to ensure an optimal adoption rate for SOA. The funding model should be established so as to encourage sharing, reuse, efficient integration, and simplicity. In the absence of clear service ownership and a funding model, ownership may default to silo application and product lines. Ownership and funding are interrelated. For example, persuading a business unit to fund development of an IT asset that belongs to a different business unit can prove problematic.

Consider the example of unifying the user experience across multiple LoB. An SOA-based solution, we believe, is the optimum approach, where we create a set of shared services across all LoB in support of such a uniform user experience, including services that provide unified access to data.

However, creating such services is not just a technical issue. The business operating units need to be involved to answer the following types of questions:

- Who owns the data and is there agreement to allow services access to the data?
- Who should pay for the development of shared services?
- Who should have the authority to approve or deny change requests?
- How is the business going to motivate the separate business operating units to reuse enterprise assets and shared business services?
- Who makes a decision about whether a service can be accessible to other applications?
- What happens if potential users of the service disagree on its content?
- What is the escalation path if these disagreements can't be resolved?

Before making service ownership and funding decisions, the organization should obtain consensus on the service domains and which business operating units own them. Our recommendation is that the domains are delineated according to which business unit owns the corresponding business entities. For example, Human Resources (HR) would own entities such as *Employee,* whereas Order Processing would own entities such as *Order.*

Purpose: Having a well-established and widely published service owning and funding model helps resolve such issues consistently and efficiently.

When needed: This should be produced as soon as the services strategic blueprint has been created and used every time a new service or major new version of a service is proposed. As an organization advances in SOA maturity, workshops among stakeholders such as the IT governance body, architecture review board (ARB), and corporate governance should revisit the appropriate ownership and funding models to determine whether they are still appropriate at their current SOA maturity level.

Responsible: SOA governance lead, business service champions.

Accountable: SOA executive sponsor.

Consulted: Business and IT executives.

Informed: All.

The Service Portfolio Work Product

Description: This is probably the most important work product for SOA enablement, because it represents the totality of services that the enterprise has created or plans to create. The primary function of the service registrar role is to manage and maintain the service portfolio, and we strongly recommended using a commercial service registry product to store and disseminate information about the contents of the service portfolio.

It is important that candidate services are added to the service portfolio and service registry early in the requirements analysis phase, so that any business units that are potential consumers of the new services are informed of their candidacy in time for their requirements to be included.

Purpose: Enable potential consumers to identify services that would provide them with business value.

When needed: As soon as the first service has been planned.

Responsible: Service registrar, business service champions, service designers.

Accountable: Service registrar.

Consulted: Service enablement and service development teams.

Informed: All.

The Service Prioritization Checklist Work Product

Description: Based on the services selection and prioritization policies, this checklist ensures that those policies are applied equitably in practice. The checklist should be completed for all services as part of the service selection checkpoint.

There will inevitably be more candidate services proposed than resources available to design, develop, and deploy them, so some level of triage is essential. Triage and prioritization should be made at the level of individual tasks or operations within a specific business service.

A simple but effective means of prioritizing candidate services is as follows:

- Award a score (0 to 10) for the immediacy of need for the business-level operation, based on the services selection and prioritization policies (0 = no perceived current need, 10 = essential to deploy).

- Award a second score (0 to 10) for potential reuse (0 = no possibility of other additional service consumers ever, 10 = large queue of potential consumers already identified).

- Award a third score (0 to 10) based on the ease/cost of implementation (0 = impossible/too expensive to consider, 10 = trivial to implement).

The overall score is the sum of all these scores. Although this is subjective, and the difference in priority between two candidates that have overall scores that are close may be arguable, this process should make a clear distinction between high-impact/low-cost services and high-cost/low-impact services.

It is important to manage dependencies carefully. If a new automated process relies on some new service operations being deployed, for example, the development of those operations should have the same or higher priority as that new process.

The list of prioritized services should be widely published and regularly reviewed to allow all stakeholders and potential future service consumers a chance to influence it if they believe it is necessary. Publication of this list should form a key component of the communications plan.

Purpose: To ensure that candidate services are given the appropriate priority.

When needed: Should be created as soon as the prerequisite work products have been approved, and then widely published as part of implementing the communications plan.

Responsible: Template created by SOA governance lead and business service champion. Individual work products completed by service designer/service architect.

Accountable: Business service champion.

Consulted: Business analysts.

Informed: SOA enablement team.

The Services Selection and Prioritization Policies Work Product

Description: Almost every IT department receives more demands made upon it than it has resources to deliver. A key attribute of an organization that has high IT and SOA governance maturity is that it has a well-defined and equitable process for deciding the most effective order in which to create software assets such as services.

The policy should define how to prioritize candidate services, in terms of the following:

- Their perceived business benefit (or benefit to IT, in the case of technical services)
- Their impact on KPIs
- The priorities or sequence of the projects that need them
- Their potential for reuse across multiple lines of business
- The needs of business partners

Purpose: To ensure that the enterprise establishes and publishes a policy for which services should be created and in which sequence. Publication and use of this policy should demonstrate even-handedness and the IT department's willingness to work to support the enterprise to the best of its resources.

When needed: Should be created as soon as the prerequisite work products have been approved, and then widely published as part of implementing the communications plan.

Responsible: SOA governance SME, SOA lead architect, lead business analyst.

Accountable: Business service champion.

Consulted: Business analysts and modelers.

Informed: All IT.

The Services Strategic Blueprint Work Product

Description: The services strategic blueprint sets overall priorities for service development, based on the business vision, strategic business plan, business heat map, and technology blueprint. This blueprint should be mapped to a two- to five-year plan that the enterprise is following to create an agile enterprise, and it should ensure that all the prerequisite funding, components, and empowerments for implementing that SOA strategy are available in a timely manner, including the following:

- The ability to establish an organization or team to lead SOA enablement, including development or recruitment of the relevant skills
- The ability to establish a subsidiary organization or team to manage SOA governance.
- The introduction of an approach to establish services requirements gathering to identify potential service consumers, capture their individual requirements, and create a workable set of combined requirements.
- The necessary empowerment to ensure that the EDM, MM, and business process model (BPM) work products that map to the key business heat map components are constructed to sufficient depth in time to develop the required services that need them.

Purpose: To ensure that the enterprise has the capability to create those services that provide the most business value as rapidly as possible.

When needed: This should be created as soon as the prerequisite work products have been approved, and then widely published as part of the communications plan work product.

Responsible: SOA lead architect, SOA governance lead, business service champions.

Accountable: SOA executive champion.

Consulted: IT architects, business analysts, data modelers, service developers, QA, testing.

Informed: All IT.

The SOA Career Paths Work Product

Description: SOA technical skills are a valuable—and scarce—commodity. Creating and publishing formal career path for SOA professionals improves morale and helps to retain the top technical and business talent.

Purpose: Recruitment and retention of key staff.

When needed: Not urgent, but should be available within a few months of the creation of the SOA roles and responsibilities work product.

Responsible: SOA governance lead, HR.

Accountable: SOA executive sponsor.

Consulted: Training department, HR.

Informed: All employees.

The SOA Communications Plan Work Product

Description: Plan and implement the communication of management aims and direction for SOA and SOA governance throughout the enterprise.

Communication is a central part of making the changes needed for SOA implementation. Without a clear set of consistent messages, those affected by the changes will be unlikely to understand their part in effecting them.

There are two forms of communicating information:

- **Dissemination.** This is the provision of information where there is limited or no opportunity to provide feedback, or ask questions of the communicator. An example might be a company magazine or intranet.
- **Consultation.** This is the provision of information in a way that enables the active participation of and feedback from participants. An example of consultation is a workshop.

Both forms of communication are essential. Dissemination is good at informing many people in an efficient manner, whereas consultation reaches fewer people but often more effectively.

Communication about SOA needs to be geared to

- Letting people know how they are affected by the new arrangements
- Allowing them to provide feedback and to offer suggestions for improvements

Specific objectives of the SOA communication are to ensure that people understand the following:

- What SOA is, and what it means to the organization
- How their individual roles and responsibilities might change as a consequence of the new arrangements
- What services are, and how candidate services should be identified and prioritized

The following are the key messages that should be communicated widely:

- General topics to increase awareness of the potential SOA has for the enterprise
- Governance goals and key processes
- The business priority areas and the progress being made to supporting them with services
- Technical topics for the IT audience
- Job opportunities, training and education courses

Each message should be tailored and targeted specifically to the needs of its intended audience. For example, business executives would consider messages about architecture to be spam.

Purpose: Ensure that all members of the organization are informed and remain committed to the SOA transition initiative.

When needed: Immediately.

Responsible: Entire SOA enablement team.

Accountable: SOA executive sponsor.

Consulted: Any interested parties.

Informed: Entire organization.

The SOA Education Plan Work Product

Description: A good education plan is essential, both to develop technical skills and to generate involvement with and commitment to SOA throughout the enterprise.

Most enterprises will already have an education department. This department should be involved early in the SOA migration process. If there are insufficient skills in-house, there are several service organizations that can help "train the trainers."

Purpose: Develop and maintain the high levels of skills needed to excel at SOA.

When needed: As soon as the SOA roles and responsibilities work product has been agreed on.

Responsible: Training department, SOA enablement team, technical leads, business service champion.

Accountable: SOA enablement board.

Consulted: Technical IT staff.

Informed: All IT.

The SOA Governance Plan Work Product (including SOA Governance Process)

Description: This is the principal document that defines how SOA governance will operate throughout the enterprise. It should contain or reference

- SOA governance-related decisions (for example, service ownership and funding model).
- SOA governance policies and rules.
- SOA governance processes. We strongly recommend instituting the following governance check points in the service lifecycle:
  - Regular (for example, weekly or monthly) reviews, where the SOA enablement team assesses and prioritizes new candidate services. New versions of existing services should follow through exactly the same processes as new services.

- An outline approval decision check point for new candidate services or versions, to ensure that ownership has been established and that outline funding exists.

- A service requirements review/decision check point, conducted when requirements gathering is complete, to ensure that all potential consumers are satisfied that their individual requirements have either been met or have been explicitly ruled out of scope in the current planned service release, and to confirm that design can begin.

- A financial approval decision check point to validate the business case for each service before design and development begins.

- Service design walkthrough sessions—relatively informal meetings where service designers discuss tentative design decisions with their peers, helping to improve overall design and mentor less experienced designers.

- A formal service specification review/decision control point (a.k.a. design review quality gate) to ensure that the quality and completeness of a service (or new service version) design is adequate before construction begins. This is especially vital if development is to be outsourced.

- A service acceptance decision control point, where the functional and nonfunctional test results are reviewed, and the operations formally accepts or rejects the service in terms of being able to support it within the terms of the nonfunctional requirements (NFRs) and SLAs.

- A formal certification decision control point process that signifies the SOA enablement team's guarantee that any service about to be deployed operationally meets or exceeds all relevant quality standards, has passed acceptance testing, and has been properly cataloged and deployed.

- A retirement decision control point to ensure that all consumers of a service are prepared to accept the deprecation of obsolete versions of that service, and that they have successfully migrated to the current version before any service version is discontinued.

- SOA governance reporting requirements
- Which SOA governance work products will be implemented and in what sequence
- SOA governance project plan and implementation Gantt chart

The number of reviews/check points we propose may at first seem excessive, but the amount of effort can be kept to a minimum by

- Making extensive use of checklists to reduce the amount of discussion needed
- Conducting these decision check points as agenda items in regular meetings of the SOA governance/enablement team
- Conducting those reviews electronically, with automatic capture and recording of any votes

Purpose: This is an absolutely critical work product to enable SOA governance. Effective SOA transformation is impossible without this work product.

When needed: This should be created immediately after the services strategic blueprint has been agreed on, and then regularly updated as the SOA transformation proceeds.

Responsible: SOA governance lead.

Accountable: SOA executive sponsor.

Consulted: SOA enablement team.

Informed: QA, PMO.

SOA Governance Vitality Monitoring Plan Work Product

Description: The approach to SOA governance, and the degree of control applied need to be monitored continually to ensure that the level of governance is appropriate, that risks are avoided in most cases, and that the governance processes do not detract unnecessarily from development productivity.

A combination of examining the minutes from service development control points, examination of the lessons learned throughout the development process, the number of policy exemptions, the degree that development performance improves over time, and above all, the progress in SOA and SOA governance maturity all provide useful inputs to determine the vitality of the SOA governance processes.

The SOA governance vitality monitoring plan should capture all this feedback and should arrange regular surveys to determine how the SOA development team perceives the efficacy of the SOA governance approach.

Purpose: Ensure that SOA governance continues to provide the maximum balance between overcontrol and overpermissiveness as the level of SOA maturity grows.

When needed: Should be created shortly after the SOA governance plan work product.

Responsible: SOA governance lead, PMO.

Accountable: SOA executive sponsor.

Consulted: QA, enterprise and IT governance teams.

Informed: PMO.

The SOA Governance Vitality Report Work Product

Description: This work product consists of a regular (monthly or quarterly) report that demonstrates the impact that the SOA governance processes and policies are making on the SOA transition. It should include the following:

- Metrics on the governance processes themselves—how many services have passed and failed each of the decision checkpoints, how many exceptions have been granted, and so on
- Details of any major issues (for example, service failures, bugs or outages, security violations, or cases of individual services not meeting their quality of service commitments), the actions that were taken to correct those issues, and the results of those corrective actions
- Growth in the service portfolio, both in terms of the number of services, the number of consumers, and the degree to which the services strategic blueprint has been implemented
- Details of any process improvements that have been made as the result of feedback
- Major governance-related activities and plans for the next reporting cycle
- Information on SOA-related trends (cost per service, average number of executions of services per day, service development resources, and so on)

Purpose: Ensure that there is proper oversight of the governance processes themselves and that SOA governance is itself governed.

When needed: Within three months of creation of the SOA governance plan work product, and then at regular three month intervals.

Responsible: SOA governance lead.

Accountable: SOA governance lead.

Consulted: SOA enablement team.

Informed: IT and business unit executives, PMO.

The SOA Reuse and ROI Monitoring Plan Work Product

Description: An SOA reuse and ROI monitoring plan should be created to ensure that there are mechanisms in place to capture objective data on the effect that SOA has on the enterprise's bottom line.

It is important that the term *reuse* is carefully defined within the context of an individual enterprise. It can include any or all of the following:

- An ROI model to be used for SOA, if one doesn't already exist
- Reuse of an existing service, with or without modification, by each additional business unit or business partner, the benefit being avoidance of the costs of developing their own service from scratch
- Reuse of existing code fragments in the creation of new services, or reusing existing simple services to create new composite services
- Reusing a service across multiple automated business processes
- Reusing and automated business process, with or without modification, to support a new business process or new business operating unit

At a gross level, the direct costs of SOA are relatively easy to calculate—they are the cost of training and maintaining the entire SOA development team, and the rest of the IT resources that the services consume.

Calculating the benefits of SOA is somewhat harder, but here are some guidelines:

- The benefits of automating business processes are simple to calculate. They are the reduction in costs of executing the same processes manually minus the cost of operating the automated versions

- Most IT development involves creating specific IT projects for individual LOB. Estimated or actual benefits of these projects can be allocated to SOA, in proportion to the amount or value of functionality provided by services. If these services are being reused without change, the direct impact of SOA is all benefit with no cost. If the services need rework, the cost of that rework should be added to the business cases.

Purpose: To ensure that the implementation of SOA meets or exceeds the goals contained in the services strategic blueprint.

When needed: The SOA reuse and ROI monitoring plan should be created as soon as the business case for SOA has been agreed on, and it should be implemented as soon as feasible, with continuous monitoring. Confirming the total ROI is likely to take months to years.

Responsible: SOA governance lead, PMO.

Accountable: Business service champion.

Consulted: All IT project leads.

Informed: All business unit and IT executives.

The SOA Roles and Responsibilities Work Product

Description: This is a document that defines the job descriptions of all SOA-related staff. The secret of effective governance is *transparency*—making sure that every stakeholder clearly understands his individual role and responsibilities, who he needs to interact with, and what mutual expectations he should have of others. Creating and publishing clear and unambiguous descriptions of the roles and responsibilities of each stakeholder are critical enablers of such transparency.

Sample role descriptions needed for successful implementation of SOA were listed earlier in this chapter. Each of these should be mapped to the closest role description that already exists in the enterprise, and a gap analysis should be carried out to determine the need for additional training and education or recruitment.

Purpose: Ensure that everyone involved in the SOA transformation understands his or her own roles, empowerments, and limits, and the roles of the colleagues they work with and expectations that each party should reasonably have of each other.

When needed: As soon as the services strategic blueprint has been agreed on.

Responsible: SOA governance lead, SOA enablement board.

Accountable: SOA executive sponsor.

Consulted: Enterprise architect, business service champion.

Informed: HR, PMO.

The Strategic Business Plan Work Product

Description: The strategic business plan defines the plan to achieve the business vision, including investment priorities and financial targets. This document should be the starting point for any business case for SOA. It defines the basic business priorities, drivers, and KPIs of the enterprise that SOA can help achieve.

Purpose: This is a key work product for enabling enterprise governance, and therefore, it represents a critical input to enabling effective IT and SOA governance.

When needed: This should exist before any wide-scale implementation of SOA. If not, its creation should be given high priority before SOA strategic planning is started. Such plans should be reviewed and refreshed at least once a year.

Responsible: Board of directors.

Accountable: CEO.

Consulted: Chief executives.

Informed: Business unit and IT executives.

The Supply Chain and Procurement Processes for SOA Work Product

Description: SOA requires a certain style and usage of standards and policies in the creation of services that are reusable and provide business agility. The standards for technical, application, and information agility will require that these standards be enforced so that rogue departments do not procure resources that violate these standards. In a similar manner, all interaction with the supply chain requires B2B interaction in a standardized fashion that does not compromise the security and integrity of the organization.

Purpose: Create the processes to enforce the necessary standards both for procurement and for all interactions in B2B transactions including the supply chain.

When needed: Existing supply chain and procurement policies should be updated to reflect SOA requirements some time during the initial planning for SOA.

Responsible: SOA governance lead, procurement.

Accountable: Procurement.

Consulted: SOA enablement team.

Informed: PMO.

The Technology Blueprint Work Product (Extended for SOA)

Description: The technology blueprint work product represents the technology plan that describes what hardware and software infrastructure will be provided by the IT department to create a platform to support the IT solutions that the business needs.

Purpose: The technology blueprint should be defined to meet business requirement for having cost-effective, standard application systems, resources, reference architectures, and end-to-end development capabilities that meet current and future business requirements, in the two- to five-year timescale. Effectively, the technology blueprint matches hardware and software infrastructure products to meet the needs of the information systems strategy blueprint and maintain compatibility with the architecture standards and design patterns. SOA aspects within the technology blueprint would include selecting the technology or products for the ESB and service registry, systems management, services testing and monitoring tools, dashboards, governance support, and automated business process execution and monitoring.

When needed: This is a key IT governance work product that should already be in existence, but that needs to be updated (and if need be, created) to help govern the suitability and capability of the SOA technical infrastructure. Because product selection and installation can take a considerable time, this work product should be created and approved as soon as possible.

Responsible: Architects, SOA architects, IT operations, security architect.

Accountable: Chief enterprise architect or architecture board.

Consulted: IT staff, business service champions, development leads, IT operations leads.

Informed: All IT.

Naturally, there are dependencies among many of these work products, because many of the work products need other work products as input. Figures 3.3 and 3.4 should help determine these dependencies, and help the SOA governance lead determine which work products to create in which priority. Figures 3.3 and 3.4 are structured as follows:

■ The four columns represent the first four steps in the simple gover-
    nance pattern described by Figure 3.1. Work products are positioned
    in the column that best describes which step in this pattern they
    apply to.

■ Arrows indicate dependencies: an arrow from a) to b) indicates that
    work product b) needs work product a) as an input.

■ Work products marked with an asterisk (*) are ones that would be
    updated every 6 to 12 months as part of the fifth and last step in
    each iteration of that "Refine the Approach" pattern.

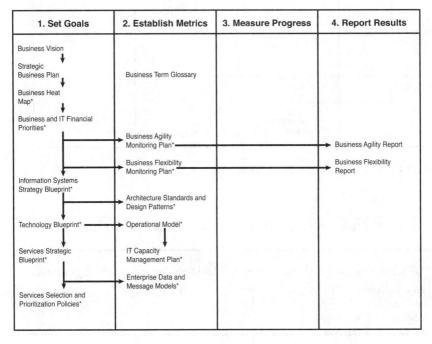

Figure 3.3   Plan & Organize Domain: Work Product Dependencies, Part 1

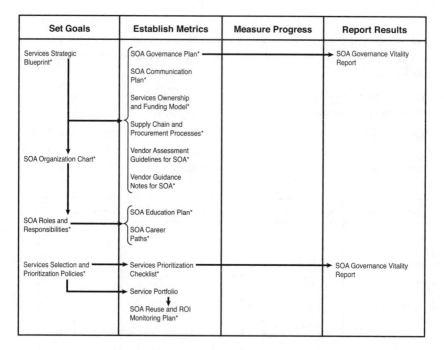

Set Goals	Establish Metrics	Measure Progress	Report Results
Services Strategic Blueprint*	SOA Governance Plan*		SOA Governance Vitality Report
	SOA Communication Plan*		
	Services Ownership and Funding Model*		
	Supply Chain and Procurement Processes*		
SOA Organization Chart*	Vendor Assessment Guidelines for SOA*		
	Vendor Guidance Notes for SOA*		
SOA Roles and Responsibilities*	SOA Education Plan*		
	SOA Career Paths*		
Services Selection and Prioritization Policies*	Services Prioritization Checklist*		SOA Governance Vitality Report
	Service Portfolio		
	SOA Reuse and ROI Monitoring Plan*		

Figure 3.4   Plan & Organize Domain: Work Product Dependencies, Part 2

The SOA Program Management Controls Domain

> *"It's all knowing what to start with. If you start in the right place and follow all the steps, you will get to the right end."*
>
> —Elizabeth Moon

As an organization advances its level of SOA maturity, there will be a natural shift of focus away from large IT projects toward continuous enhancement of IT solutions. However, large development projects will continue to be a key aspect of IT development for the foreseeable future.

Most organizations already have a reasonably mature approach to managing such projects or programs, at least from a financial viewpoint, and implementing SOA governance should be seen as an enhancement of existing program or project governance, and certainly not a replacement for it.

Key factors in ensuring that projects that take an SOA approach are well governed include the following:

- Addressing the risks associated with a proposed program or project, and using the properties of SOA to help lower those risks.

- Adjusting the business case of projects to reflect the benefits of reusing existing services to reduce the implementation costs and timescale of the project.

- Once the service factory is established, it is straightforward to establish benchmarks for the amount of effort required to create services of a given complexity. Because of the repeatable nature of service development, these workload estimates should be reasonably accurate.

- SOA governance needs to extend all projects that adopt an SOA approach; this includes monitoring and reporting SOA resources and SOA-related benefits for all such projects. Good IT governance should extend monitoring resources and ROI of every IT project.

- Because services are, by their very nature, intended to be used across multiple projects, effective SOA project governance requires an increased focus on managing cross-project dependencies.

- Comparing the ability of different projects to complete SOA-related tasks efficiently and using that information to help improve the performance of all future SOA-related projects, and to avoid repeating any mistakes or errors.

Figures 3.5 and 3.6 represent a before and after view of how SOA might affect a typical approach to project governance.

Figure 3.5 shows how IT projects are typically governed throughout their lifecycle. At several control points, a decision made to either continue as planned, change the scope, or cancel the project, generally on the basis of projected costs and benefits.

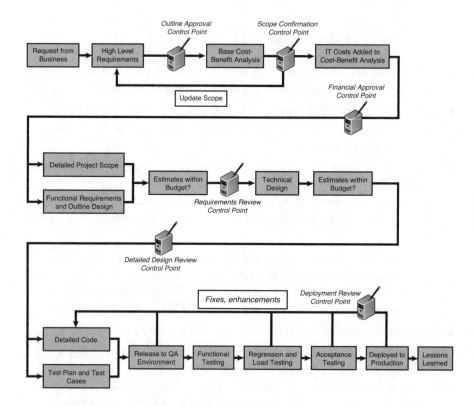

Figure 3.5 Example of an IT Project Governance Lifecycle

Figure 3.6 shows how this basic project governance lifecycle could be modified to include the effects of SOA. In this case, decisions are taken on whether any of the planned functionality can usefully be created as shared services, and these are then passed to the service factory for development. In our experience, a well-established and organized service production line should be capable of producing services well before the projects that need to consume them.

In time, as the service portfolio grows, new projects should find that a significant portion of the functionality they want to deliver already exists as shared services.

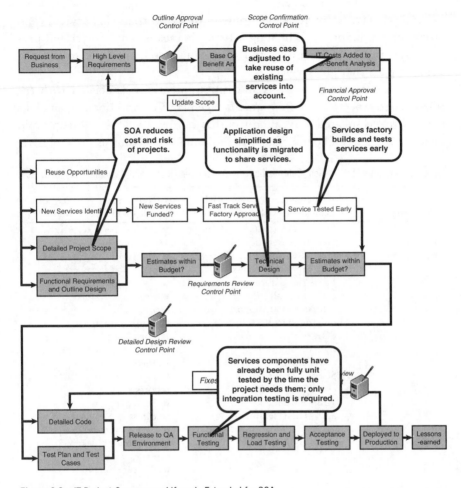

Figure 3.6 IT Project Governance Lifecycle Extended for SOA

As Figure 3.6 shows, successfully implementing SOA can

- Improve the business case for a project or program, especially as the service portfolio grows
- Simplify the design of complex IT solutions, thereby decreasing the risk of failures
- Help in assigning projects priorities and scheduling project development activities
- Enable a more parallel iterative, less of a "waterfall" approach to both development and testing

Projects have a longer development lifecycle than do services, and programs even more so. The longer lifecycle means that project and program governance mechanisms and governance reporting have to occur at a slower pace than for services.

Table 3.2 examines the risks and issues potentially associated with the SOA-related aspects of the Program Management Controls domain, and lists the governance-related work products that can be developed to help avoid them. The layout and definition of the columns is the same as for Table 3.1.

Table 3.2 Program Management Controls Domain: Capabilities, Risks, and Remedial Work Products

Capability	Associated Issues and Risks	Risk Level	Governance Work Products	Cost of Remedy
1. Enterprise program management	Using SOA to take an enterprisewide view of IT solutions that support business needs can reduce the creation of siloed solutions that support only one business unit SOA can reduce risks by reducing project complexity Services are an excellent way to achieve business agility and flexibility	High	■ Project context and scope ■ Project dependencies ■ Project risks ■ Project workload estimates ■ Project execution monitoring plan ■ Project lessons learned ■ Project status reports ■ Project audit findings ■ Requirements and business rules catalog ■ Project control point	High

Capability	Associated Issues and Risks	Risk Level	Governance Work Products	Cost of Remedy
2. Change management	SOA increases the number of dependencies between projects. If projects are responsible for creating their own projects, there is a risk of one project de-scoping a service that is vital to another project.	High	■ Project change request ■ Project context and scope ■ Service portfolio ■ Outline approval control point checklist ■ Project financial approval control point checklist ■ Project benefits and ROI monitoring plan ■ Project actual costs ■ Project benefits and ROI	Moderate
3. Procurement of resources	The procurement process should give preference to SOA-capable vendors. Some useful functionality may be available as a service (that is, rented rather than purchased from some vendors).	High	■ Vendor assessment guidelines for SOA ■ Vendor guidance notes for SOA	Low
4. Vendor management	The current software vendors may not be capable of supplying products that can be wrapped as services, or software as a service.	Moderate	■ Vendor assessment guidelines for SOA	Low
5. Identify and allocate costs	To determine the *real* business value of SOA, it is essential to have accurate costs.	High	■ Financial approval control point checklist ■ Project benefits and ROI monitoring plan ■ Project actual costs	Moderate

Table 3.2   Program Management Controls Domain (continued)

Capability	Associated Issues and Risks	Risk Level	Governance Work Products	Cost of Remedy
6. Monitor business benefits of SOA	Need to have accurate metrics on the real value of SOA to demonstrate its true ROI.	High	■ Project actual costs ■ Project benefits and ROI ■ Business agility monitoring report ■ Business flexibility monitoring report	Moderate

Program Management Controls Domain Work Product Definitions

The following sections include descriptions of the work products whose production can help govern the Program Management Controls domain. Most of the work products referenced are essential for implementing IT governance and should already be in existence, although they will need some extensions to cover SOA-specific issues. If they don't yet exist, good IT governance suggests that they be created urgently.

Some of the work products needed for this domain are also used in the Plan & Organize domain, in which case the descriptions are not repeated.

The Business Agility Monitoring Report Work Product

Description: This report summarizes the metrics captured as a result of implementing the business agility monitoring plan described earlier in this chapter.

Purpose: Monitor changes in the agility of the organization, and determine whether these are attributable to the SOA transformation.

When needed: Every three to six months.

Responsible: PMO, organization and methods department.

Accountable: COO.

Consulted: Business operating unit executives.

Informed: All business unit and IT executives, PMO.

The Business Flexibility Monitoring Report Work Product

Description: This report summarizes the metrics captured as a result of implementing the business flexibility monitoring plan described earlier in this chapter.

Purpose: Determine the extent to which SOA contributes to the organization's business agility, and monitor how that changes over time.

When needed: Every three to six months.

Responsible: PMO, organization and methods department.

Accountable: COO.

Consulted: Business operating unit executives.

Informed: All business unit and IT executives, PMO.

The Project Audit Findings Work Product

Description: All projects should be audited to some degree on completion, to record any lessons learned, be they good or bad.

Purpose: Discover what works well and what doesn't across a range of products, with the intention of improving future projects.

When needed: Immediately when the solution created by a project is deployed to production.

Responsible: PMO, SOA governance lead.

Accountable: PMO.

Consulted: Project managers, project architects.

Informed: Project managers, project architects.

The Project Actual Costs Work Product

Description: Corporate and IT governance should require that all projects continuously monitor actual costs and compare them with the planning estimates. To provide information for the ROI of SOA, projects should be tasked with separately accounting those costs associated with SOA activities.

Purpose: Achieve financial accountability and an accurate measurement of the ROI of SOA.

When needed: Accurate costs should be available as soon as the code produced by the project is deployed to production.

Responsible: PMO, SOA governance lead.

Accountable: PMO.

Consulted: Project managers, project architects.

Informed: PMO.

The Project Benefits and ROI Monitoring Plan Work Product

Description: Part of every project should be a plan to measure and monitor the real costs and business benefits. Without such information, it is impossible for IT to demonstrate what effect they are having on the organization's bottom line, flexibility, and agility. This work product is the plan and associated responsibilities, to capture that data.

Purpose: Achieve financial accountability and an accurate measurement of the ROI of all projects.

When needed: The plan to monitor costs and benefits of any given project should be completed before the project's financial approval control point shown in Figure 3.5.

Responsible: PMO, SOA governance lead.

Accountable: PMO.

Consulted: Project managers, project architects, business service champions, individual business units.

Informed: PMO.

The Project Benefits and ROI Report Work Product

Description: This report should summarize the metrics captured as a result of implementing the project benefits and ROI monitoring plan. As for actual costs, corporate and IT governance should require that all projects monitor their real benefits once they are deployed, and that these are compared with the estimates in the project business case. Again the benefits that accrue specifically through using an SOA approach should be accounted for independently. This is essential data for monitoring the real impact of SOA on the organization.

Purpose: Achieve financial accountability and an accurate measurement of the ROI of SOA.

When needed: Accurate costs should be known as soon as the code produced by the project is deployed to production, and the project business case should provide projected project benefits. However, the real benefits of each project should be measured over a span of months to years, and this report should be updated every 6 to 12 months for each major project.

Responsible: PMO, SOA governance lead.

Accountable: PMO.

Consulted: Project managers, project architects, business service champions, individual business units.

Informed: PMO.

The Project Change Request Work Product

Description: The existing IT governance process to handle project changes may need to be adapted to take account for the shorter development and more frequent deployment of services than for applications, and the project change requests (PCRs) work products will need to be passed to the team that develops services to determine any need for additional service versions.

Purpose: Ensure that any necessary changes to services are handled efficiently and that new service versions are available when projects need them.

When needed: Needed for all projects whenever any new requirements arise or there is a need to change the project's scope.

Responsible: PMO.

Accountable: PMO.

Consulted: Project managers, project architects.

Informed: SOA governance lead.

The Project Context and Scope Work Product

Description: This basic IT governance work product should already exist. Every new IT project context and scope document should reflect any services that the project intends to reuse or create. This provides essential data for establishing the reusability and ROI of services.

Purpose: As the service portfolio expands, there should be a measurable downward trend in the scope and costs of typical IT projects.

When needed: As soon as any project passes the outline approval control point shown in Figure 3.5.

Responsible: PMO, service architects, business analysts, business service champions.

Accountable: PMO.

Consulted: Service registrar.

Informed: Entire project team.

The Project Control Point Minutes Work Product

Description: Minutes from any project control point can provide a useful source for identifying any systemic quality issues and for comparing the relative vitality of different projects.

Purpose: Take a cross-project viewpoint to ensure that all projects learn from the successes and failures of all other projects.

When needed: After any project control point.

Responsible: PMO, SOA governance lead, IT governance lead.

Accountable: PMO.

Consulted: Project managers, project architects.

Informed: PMO.

The Project Dependencies Work Product

Description: Managing dependencies between projects that will share services can be a problem, especially if individual IT projects produce their own services instead of having services created by a single dedicated development team. Managing such dependencies well is a major benefit of having a centralized service factory approach.

Purpose: Projects regularly get de-scoped to fit budgets and deadlines. After they have committed to delivering services that other projects will need, they should not be allowed to remove them from their scope without permission of the owners of those other projects.

When needed: As soon as any project passes the outline planning stage.

Responsible: PMO, business service champions, SOA governance lead.

Accountable: PMO.

Consulted: Project managers, project architects.

Informed: All project teams.

The Project Deployment Control Point Checklist Work Product

Description: If services are deployed when they are ready, rather than with the first project that consumes them, the size of the project deployment unit will be reduced. The existing project deployment control point checklist should be updated to reflect this.

Purpose: Ensure that future projects make optimal use of SOA.

When needed: Needed for the project deployment review control point shown in Figure 3.5.

Responsible: PMO, SOA governance lead.

Accountable: PMO.

Consulted: Project managers, project architects.

Informed: PMO.

The Project Execution Monitoring Plan Work Product

Description: This is a plan to monitor real costs and resource levels for each project and to account the proportions of costs that are associated with SOA activities explicitly. This information forms an input for calculating the ROI for each project and providing input to the business agility report and the business flexibility report.

Purpose: Ensure that data needed to establish the ROI for SOA is captured.

When needed: Needed for any project as soon as it has successfully passed the outline approval control point shown in Figure 3.5.

Responsible: PMO, project managers.

Accountable: PMO.

Consulted: Project managers, project architects.

Informed: PMO.

The Project Financial Approval Control Point Checklist Work Product

Description: This existing governance should be updated to reflect the business value of lowering costs through service reuse. Most organizations have defined, as part of their enterprise and IT governance, a series of signoff levels required for projects, dependent on their projected costs. Often, a minimum threshold is set, where a business unit or IT can approve a small project directly from their own budget.

Purpose: Ensure that future projects reflect the potential costs and benefits of SOA.

When needed: Needed for all projects once the cost-benefit case has been completed and before the financial approval control point shown in Figure 3.5.

Responsible: PMO, project managers.

Accountable: PMO.

Consulted: Project managers, project architects.

Informed: PMO.

The Project Lessons Learned Work Product

Description: As for any other human activity, lessons learned in project and program execution should be recorded to improve future efforts and avoid repeating expensive mistakes.

Purpose: Learning lessons from good and bad experiences on current projects to ensure improved performance on future projects.

When needed: This work product should be produced at the end of all projects.

Responsible: PMO, SOA governance lead.

Accountable: PMO.

Consulted: All project team members.

Informed: PMO.

The Project Outline Approval Control Point Checklist Work Product

Description: This preexisting IT governance work product should be updated to include the benefits each project will gain from reusing existing services, or the value they will add in expanding the service portfolio with strategically important new services.

Purpose: Ensure that future projects handle SOA considerations equitably.

When needed: Needed for the projects outline approval control point shown on Figure 3.5.

Responsible: PMO, SOA governance lead.

Accountable: PMO.

Consulted: SOA enablement team.

Informed: PMO.

The Project Requirements and Scope Control Point Checklist Work Product

Description: This existing governance should be updated for all projects regardless of whether they are using an SOA approach to ensure that existing known requirements and rules contained in the requirements and business rules catalog work product are followed, and those new rules and requirements are added to that catalog. If services or automated processes that embody those requirements or rules already exist, the requirements and scope control point checklist should ensure that their suitability for reuse is assessed.

Purpose: Ensure that future projects reflect the potential costs and benefits of SOA.

When needed: Needed for the scope confirmation control point shown on Figure 3.5.

Responsible: PMO, SOA governance lead.

Accountable: PMO.

Consulted: SOA enablement board.

Informed: PMO.

The Project Status Report Work Product

Description: These provide valuable information for the project execution monitoring plan, and for providing feedback on the project execution process.

Purpose: Maintain an enterprisewide, cross-project view.

When needed: Needed for all projects, on a weekly or monthly basis.

Responsible: PMO, SOA governance lead.

Accountable: PMO.

Consulted: Project managers, project architects.

Informed: PMO.

The Project Workloads Estimate Work Product

Description: An IT governance work product that should already exist. Because of the nature of the service factory, it should be possible to monitor the true status of services as they pass through each successive stage in their lifecycle, to provide accurate estimates of the resources and time that will be required to complete them.

Purpose: A service factory approach should produce more consistent and accurate workload estimates. Feeding these back into projects should improve the accuracy of each project's resource estimates.

When needed: Before the requirements review control point and again used before the detailed design review control point as shown in Figure 3.5.

Responsible: PMO, project managers.

Accountable: PMO.

Consulted: Project architects.

Informed: PMO, SOA governance lead.

The Vendor Assessment Guidelines for SOA Work Product

Description: Most enterprises will already have policies and processes for approving new vendors. These should be amended to give preference to vendors and business partners that can actively assist the enterprise's adoption of SOA.

Purpose: Ensure that preference is given to software vendors that package their products in a way that makes wrapping them as services as simple as possible or that deliver software as a service.

When needed: Existing vendor assessment policies and guidelines should be updated to reflect SOA requirements some time during the initial planning for SOA.

Responsible: SOA governance lead.

Accountable: Current process owner.

Consulted: SOA enablement board, procurement.

Informed: Procurement.

The Vendor Guidance Notes for SOA Work Product

Description: To help develop synergy with vendors and business partners, the organization may publish specific guidance to vendors, as to how their ability to support the enterprise's SOA initiative. This information could be delivered with any Request for Information (RFI) or Request for Proposal (RFP) documentation.

Purpose: Assist vendors to understand how best to support the enterprise's SOA initiative.

When needed: Whenever new SOA-related RFIs and RFPs are issued.

Responsible: SOA governance lead.

Accountable: Current process owner.

Consulted: SOA enablement board, procurement.

Informed: Procurement, vendors.

Naturally, there are dependencies among many of these work products, because many of the work products need other work products as input. Figure 3.7 should help determine these dependencies. The format is the same as for Figures 3.3 and 3.4.

Set Goals	Establish Metrics	Measure Progress	Report Results
Strategic Business Plan Business Heat Map* Business and IT Financial Priorities*	→ Project Context and Scope ↓ Project Dependencies ↓ Project Risks Vendor Assessment Guidelines for SOA* Service Construction Estimation Metrics* ↓ Project Workload Estimates* ↓ Project Execution Monitoring Plan* Project ROI Monitoring Plan Business Agility Monitoring Plan* Business Flexibility Monitoring Plan*	Outline Approval Control Point Checklist* Requirements and Scope Control Point Checklist* Financial Approval Control Point Checklist* Design Control Point Checklist* Deployment Control Point Checklist* Project Change Requests Actual Costs Project Benefits	Control Point Review Minutes Lessons Learned Project Status Reports Project Audit Findings → Project Benefits and ROI → Business Agility Report → Business Flexibility Report

Figure 3.7 Program Management Controls Domain: Work Product Dependencies

Case Study

> *"In all planning you make a list and you set priorities."*
>
> —Alan Lakein

Now that you have successfully completed the SOA governance planning assessment, you are keen to consider the various SOA governance capabilities and figure out where you should be focusing your limited resources.

Service Transformation Planning

You have agreed with the stakeholders about the immediate areas that need to be addressed in phase one of the SOA governance definition and enablement. A heat map has been created to show the results (see Figure 3.8).

SOA Governance Capabilities Map

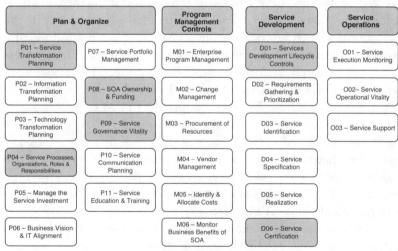

Figure 3.8   SOA Governance Capabilities Heat Map for Ideation

Service transformation planning is an area that many of the most important stakeholders are concerned about. Business agility is one of the main drivers for SOA adoption, and creation of a service transformation plan is important in leading the organization to that goal. SOA governance must ensure that the right resources are engaged in this task.

The Enterprise Architecture (EA) group at Ideation has been studying this and has decided to use a standard industry business function map that can be used to map the enterprise's current business processes. They want to use this map to identify the current business groups and map their business responsibilities to standard business functions to understand how business opportunities can be grouped together. The EA group will use a gap and overlap analysis to identify areas of strength and areas of opportunity for business agility.

Ideation chose to use the TeleManagement Forum (TMF) Next Generation Operating System Support and its standard business process framework called enhanced Telecommunications Operations Map (eTOM; www.tmforum.org/browse.aspx? catID=1648). Figure 3.9 shows some of the standard Level 2 business functions that a typical telecommunications firm would be using, as per the industry TeleManagement Forum.

For Ideation, the enterprise architecture group uses their industry function map in interviews with the business units and identifies that four separate business groups perform the business function of "2.5 Instance & Service-Specific Rating." In some cases, different pricing is available on the same service from a different sales group within the company. Consequently, it is a business goal to create a single rating function for all Ideation Communication products, and an SOA business service has been created with the name Create Rating. This service then consists of a set of subservices—Mediate Usage Records, Rate Usage Records, and Analyze Usage Records—as per the eTOM Level 3 business functional map.

In this manner, an industry business process map drives both a business discussion that results in measurable benefit to the business and the planning of the SOA business services creation strategy. In addition, the business agility discussion is a good time to establish KPIs. In the example on rating, an obvious KPI created might be "single source of pricing for all products by the end of the year." A more business-focused KPI in this case might be "DSL product margin increase 2% due to elimination of pricing mistakes."

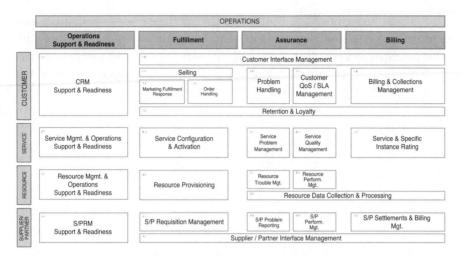

Figure 3.9 Use an Industry Functional Component Model to Guide the Business Agility Discussion

As a result of this analysis, the EA group creates a business architecture that identifies service domains, business processes, and an optimal set of business services that are prioritized as to usefulness to Ideation. The SOA governance function ensures that this standard is used in areas such as investment decision making and opportunities for service creation, to inform and expedite the creation of these business services.

Conclusion

> *"In theory, there is no difference between theory and practice; in practice, there is."*
>
> **–Chuck Reid**

This chapter is intended to lay the foundation for achieving *practical* SOA governance. It introduces the idea of creating and reviewing formal work products as intermediate deliverables at many stages in planning for SOA and for the IT projects that will use an SOA approach. Reviewing these work products as soon as they are produced should allow errors and omissions to be discovered early, before the cost of correction becomes too high.

We also introduced the concept of the service factory—an automated production line for the development of services—and described the skills needed to operate it. The next chapter contains an in-depth discussion about how to run this factory, and what governance mechanisms and work products we can use to govern it.

4

Governing the Service Factory

"Programming today is a race between software engineers striving to build bigger and better idiot-proof programs, and the Universe trying to produce bigger and better idiots. So far, the Universe is winning"

—Rick Cook

Chapter 3, "Building the Service Factory," discussed the value of establishing a service production line to automate SOA development activities, and outlined the tasks, roles, and responsibilities needed to establish such a service factory. Chapter 3 also described a set of work products whose adoption can implement practical SOA governance for the Plan & Organize and Program Management Controls domains introduced in Chapter 2, "SOA Governance Assessment and Planning."

This chapter covers a practical approach for governing both the operation of the service factory and the management of services after they have been deployed to production.

Essential Competencies for Succeeding with SOA

An organization needs certain core technical competencies if it is to succeed with SOA. Good SOA governance is all about developing these competencies and creating governance mechanisms that ensure the service factory runs as smoothly and as efficiently as possible. The following subsections define these core competencies.

Effective Requirements Collection

The old adage "garbage in, garbage out" perfectly expresses the importance of capturing requirements correctly. It is simply impossible to build good software without precise functional and nonfunctional (i.e., technical) requirements. SOA has the major advantage that services should represent some clear agreement or contract between the consumers and developers. As long as good naming standards are used, the purpose of each service invocation (operation) should be instantly clear to both business and IT staff.

There is an important degree of judgment to be made in terms of the effort made in capturing and reconciling requirements from all prospective consumers of a new candidate service. In an ideal world, all potential consumers of each service will be canvassed for their specific requirements, and a service designed that accommodates the full set of needs expressed:

- This has the theoretical advantage of reducing any need for future reversioning of the service, and encouraging maximum reuse (both major positive goals).
- Unfortunately, it has the practical disadvantage of consuming a significant amount of analyst resources, and potentially adding complexity and cost to the development of the first version of the service.

The current balance of opinion is that some kind of 80/20 rule applies: 80% of potential consumer requirements can probably be decided by a skilled analyst with 20% of the effort of an exhaustive study. Defining optimum service granularity, service design, and quality of documentation is as important an enabler of future reuse as an exhaustive initial consumer and requirements analysis.

Creating and publishing a catalog of requirements is critical to encouraging reuse and avoiding unnecessary duplication. Creating a high-level business process model and a common glossary of business terms is a critical precondition to creating a requirements catalog.

An excellent practice is to define the nonfunctional requirements, together with criteria for testing and acceptance of the service, at the same time as the requirements are being captured.

Competency in Service Design

Although service architecture and technical details beyond the scope of this book, we need to make some comments in terms of governing the service design process:

- It is essential to have a formal set of critical architectural work products to guide service designers. These include architectural principles that must be followed, architectural decisions that need to be complied with, recommended design patterns, and a formal target production. A best practice followed by many large organizations is to create an architecture review board (ARB) that is responsible for maintaining the vitality of such architectural assets.

- A strongly recommended best practice is to encourage (ideally mandate) regular service design reviews that include as wide a range of technical talent as possible. This has the joint advantages of optimizing the design of each service, promoting consistency, ensuring compliance with standards and best practices, and, not least, helping to grow the architectural skills of the more junior team members through on-the-job mentoring.

Competency in Service Development

Modern software development kits (SDKs) or tools make the physical SOA development processes relatively straightforward, and using them promotes consistency of technical approach and high quality. In this chapter, we discuss some work products that can help to monitor and assist service development.

Competency in Service Testing and Deployment

A reputation for quality is hard to gain and easy to lose. Thorough testing and an efficient and error-free deployment process are essential to gaining and maintaining a reputation for quality. Again, we describe some work products to help govern these processes.

Competency in Operational Management and Monitoring of Services

One of the easiest ways to lose a reputation for quality is to have products that perform badly or that keep breaking down, so we also address this important area from a governance perspective.

Service Development Lifecycle Control Points

Most organizations already have some type of system development lifecycle (SDLC) and a methodology that is used to perform development, although we often see in practice a lack of enforcement of that approach across different business units, and even if a set of best practices, standards, policies, and patterns has been defined, they are not always enforced.

Effectively enforcing best practices and a consistent SDLC provides a reasonable entry point for real governance, while not being a huge stretch from what is already being performed via the SDLC. At the same time, if the governance maturity level of the organization can be increased to the degree that it is able to govern the SDLC, the organization is then in a much better position to proceed to the next phase of the SOA governance cycle and create program and organization governance.

The danger here for even initial attempts at SOA governance is that often some key individuals view the imposition of any process or governance as being something that might apply to other people but not to them personally. For them, it's an overengineered, useless exercise that just gets in the way of meeting their own deadlines. So, many governance processes are simply bypassed, or they're followed in a less than an enthusiastic manner. The main reason for this is that governance is imposed from the outside and the execution is onerous.

What would happen if governance were mostly automated, easy, and added value to the development process and actually helped with project deadlines? Would the skeptics be more willing to take the medicine if it genuinely eased their pain?

To adequately govern the SDLC, there is a need to establish measurements, policy, standards, and control mechanisms to enable people to carry out their governance roles and responsibilities as efficiently as possible, without introducing overly bureaucratic procedures.

Governance of the SDLC may be characterized by the sorts of decisions that need to be made at certain "control points" within the process of services development. A control point is a decision checkpoint that provides an opportunity to measure adherence to the established processes, whether you are on track to meet the targets and goals you have established, and then decide whether the way the processes are executed or managed needs adjusting. Knowing what decisions involved in the process are critical, when to make them, and understanding what measurements are needed to monitor those processes are all essential aspects of governance.

Certain activities within a process may be associated with a control point. At the end of each identified activity, there is a control point at which the governance function decides whether the program is ready to move to the next activity. Each of these milestones is a control point.

At its essence, the governance of the SDLC provides a way to identify control points and to define the governance rules. At each control point, it is necessary to identify the following:

- The roles for who does what at the control point
- The policies to be applied at the control point
- Measurements at each control point that should be applied and collected for later governance vitality actions
- The proof of compliance records to be created and archived

A control point will be created where there is a demonstrated advantage weighing the standardization and efficiency provided versus the time, effort, and possible project delay. The control point enables SOA governance the opportunity to ascertain progress, to communicate this progress, to forecast efforts for subsequent phases of the SDLC based on scope and issues found, to review and report compliance, and to facilitate the injection of expertise and qualified review of the artifacts, process, or decisions made by the development team.

Control points don't have to consist of huge formal meetings. Services and most automated business processes are smaller entities than projects, and there are many more of them. Therefore, the existing governance approach has to be streamlined or it might grind to a halt. We've found in practice that effective control point reviews can be made during regular—typically weekly—sessions of a subset of the SOA enablement. A real productivity aid in performing these control point reviews is the use of previously completed *checklists,* signed off by one or more senior professionals as certification that one or more tasks has been completed successfully, and that the service, process, or other work product is fit for purpose and ready in all respects for the next task in the development process. These checklists should be viewed as contracts between different experts in the service development process. The most important part of the checklist is the signature block to show who exercised approval authority; people tend to be careful about the quality of anything that carries their personal reputation with it.

Another productivity aid is the use of automated tooling. As much of the governance control point as possible should be automated. This aids in better near real-time feedback to the developers and provides an easy method to recheck work that has been updated. In addition, human beings are busy and will tend to apply governance in an inconsistent manner. Machines are consistent but not usually as flexible as needed. The combination of the two provides an optimal governance mix.

Let's look at the control points needed to govern a generic development lifecycle, at least at a high level. Figure 4.1 represents a "governance dashboard" monitoring a typical SDLC with an eye toward the key concepts and the points where they must be addressed by SOA governance.

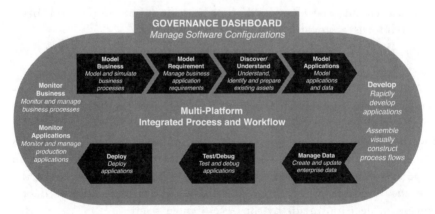

Figure 4.1 Software Development Lifecycle Governance Dashboard

As mentioned previously, we need a streamlined process that can handle the large number of services and automated processes that we need to implement to have real impact on business agility and flexibility. However, that streamlined process must not sacrifice the *quality* of governance just because of the need for extra speed. That would be an unacceptable trade-off.

Some organizations deal with highly regulated processes that have mission-critical or life-critical products and need to apply highly formal, auditable governance to manage the risks involved. Other organizations have processes with lower associated risks that can be more lightly regulated. We have found in practice that the same governance process can handle both these extremes perfectly well. If there is a need for stricter governance, it can be met with tighter policies at the control points together with more stringent policy enforcement and compliance measurement. If less-strict governance is more appropriate, the same process can be used with less restrictive policies, fewer audits, and lower levels of checklist signoff required.

Even within a single organization, different processes may require different styles of governance. Some processes, such as service certification, require stricter governance than other processes, such as solution architecture. Different organizational cultures require different levels of autonomy in decision making. Good governance requires good judgment.

First, let's update our Figure 4.1 with the location of these control points so that you have a visual representation in mind as you read their descriptions. Figure 4.2 shows where the control points occur in that development cycle.

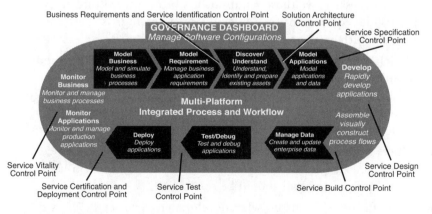

Figure 4.2 Software Development Lifecycle with SOA Control Points

Here are descriptions of these control points.

Business Requirements and Service Identification Control Point

For an SOA approach, there is an emphasis on creating services that provide agility and reuse for the business. This first business requirements and service identification control point consists of a high-level review to determine that services are being identified in accordance with the services selection and prioritization policies that were described in Chapter 3, "Building the Service Factory."

This first business requirements and service identification control point should address the following types of questions:

- Business goals. What are the business goals that the business seeks to attain and how do we measure the benefits or progress toward the business goals via key performance indicators (KPIs)?

- Do the requirements as we currently understand them clearly support those goals, and do they align with the business heat map described in Chapter 3?

- Are those requirements sufficiently understood and agreed to? Are they presented in a form such as use cases, business process models, sequence diagrams, or class diagrams that are consistent with the SOA development approach?

- How do we provide traceability of the requirements so that we can ascertain that those requirements have been met during the development process? Have those requirements been entered into an enterprisewide requirements and business rules catalog? Is there any conflict with existing entries in that catalog?

- Which of those requirements could be translated into good candidate services, either because they represent functionality that may be needed by multiple consumers or that might be needed for process automation? Which requirements could be better supported by deploying applications, automated processes, or manual processes?

- Where we have identified candidate services, have we identified potential consumers, and determined whether any of them have specific requirements that should be considered?

- Given finite IT resources, what development priority should we assign? Is ownership of any new candidate IT asset defined, and is outline funding available for its development?

Solution Architecture Control Point

Different IT developers and groups, if left to make all design decisions on their own, would invariably use completely different platforms, coding languages, tools, styles, methods, and techniques. This variation adds cost and complexity to the ability of the business to make future changes, and makes future maintenance very hard and costly. Further, it reduces the reliability, stability, and interoperability of the organization's IT assets. We have seen this problem at many organizations that we have visited. Simply put, the purpose of the solution architecture control point is to prevent that expensive multiplicity of approaches from occurring ever again.

Essentially, any proposed IT artifact that makes it past this control point is part of the IT build plan. For the area of solution architecture, the governance should control for a series of criteria the following:

- Do the proposed standards, policies, and reference architectures—the solution architecture—identify the standards, policies, and design patterns to be followed in the service implementation? This will include reference architectures, platform standards for hardware, and software-usage standards.

- Have any reusable assets been identified and assessed for suitability? Has the service sourcing policy been followed?

- Have the nonfunctional requirements been identified and assessed? This includes the number of transactions per time unit, a busy hour analysis, the service performance required, presentation access to the service functionality, data managed by the service, space required for the installation of the service, and any dependency and configuration requirements. Governance must validate that all these are considered and addressed.

- Governance must validate that all security policies are being considered and addressed.

- Governance must validate that all legal and regulatory policies are considered and addressed.

- By this stage in the development of IT assets such as services or automated processes, the technical IT staff involved should have a pretty good idea about the complexity of the tasks involved, and the probable level of resources required to complete development. Should development of the asset be confirmed, the scope reduced, or the asset abandoned?

Service Specification Control Point

A service specification should be created for each service whose development has been approved. Best practices for service design must integrate both an IT and business perspective for the design of the interface and the responsibilities of each service. Because the service specification is, in effect, the organization's face to business partners, customers, and other stakeholders, the *service externals*—those details of a service that are to be made public—become an important part of the overall business design. The design should take into account the requirements of all potential service consumers (within reason), and be created at a granularity that maximizes business value. For the area of service identification and specification, the governance should control for a series of criteria the following:

- Does the service identified make sense, is at the right granularity, and is not duplicating an existing service?
- Does the service specification follow all SOA standards and policies?
- Does the service specification follow the messaging model? If not, should an exception be granted?

Service Design Control Point

After the service solution architecture has been turned over to the design team, a number of design elaboration decisions must be made. Collectively, these form the *service internals*—a set of design models, notes, and advice that will guide the service developers as they create and test the service code. For the area of service design, the governance should control for a series of criteria the following:

- Has a service architect confirmed that the design should be able to meet the nonfunctional and functional requirements for this service?
- Have the service designer and data architect agreed that the service can be made to conform to the signature (that is, inputs and outputs) described in the service externals?
- If a service is wrapping an existing or planned application, are the necessary interfaces to that application well defined and stable (that is, won't change if a new version of that application is installed)?

- Have the monitoring metrics (for example, usage, quality of service [QoS] levels) been established?
- In the case of automated processes, have the monitoring requirements been defined and planned?
- In the case of long-running automated processes, have all the necessary actions to handle recovery from process errors or technical failures been addressed?
- Is the overall quality and level of completeness of the service specification package good enough that the service developers or process developers can complete development without further input?

Service Build Control Point

After the service design has been turned over to the service build team, a number of implementation decisions need to be made before development of the code or executable model. In the interests of consistency and quality, we strongly recommend the use of code walkthrough reviews, where peers (that is, other service developers or process developers) review the work in progress and offer constructive criticism.

The service build control point is effectively the last of these code walkthroughs, and should be performed with slightly more formality than the others. Questions that should be addressed include the following:

- Was the asset coded in accordance with the design?
- Does the code follow the accepted coding standards?
- Have all the associated artifacts (for example, load libraries, metadata files, resources) been defined to create a transportable build? Have the versions of each of those artifacts been checked to see that there are no version conflicts with services already in production?

Service Test Control Point

Service testing is different from testing complete IT solutions or applications. Because services and automated processes do not have their own user interface, it is not possible to perform user acceptance testing directly on services or automated processes. Code frameworks or specialized tools are needed to exhaustively test services and automated processes thoroughly to avoid uncovering problems during later formal user acceptance testing when the rest of the IT solution that uses those services or processes has been completed.

SOA governance must ascertain that the services test is being performed in a manner conducive to a services approach, and that exhaustive functional and nonfunctional tests have been passed before releasing any SOA asset to production. The service test team must create and use the right service test environment with tools and data to affect a comprehensive test. This should include the following:

- Using the optimum set of service test tools and frameworks.
- The use of an automated build and test environment that can enable fast changes of the tested software and regression testing. This environment must closely resemble the production environment.
- A load/stress test tool to test nonfunctional requirements, specification, creation, and loading of realistic but artificial test data.
- A test management reporting tool to keep management apprised of the testing status.
- Trace the test case to the original user requirements.

Service Certification and Deployment Control Point

The objectives of the deployment are to migrate the services to the production environment while minimizing client downtime and impact on the business. This process is subject to many errors if performed manually. It is vital that the correct version of the services be deployed and that any deployment binding with other services and applications be performed quickly and correctly. Areas for governance to validate include the following:

- The use of a tool that automates the deployment and back-out process.
- Final certification checks have been made against the services to verify compliance with all policies and standards and being able to demonstrate that what was tested matches not only the requirements but what was delivered, and that no corrective changes made during testing have invalidated other test results.

- IT operations have completed acceptance testing and have formally accepted the asset, signifying their confidence in being able to operate it within the terms of the QoS specified for it.
- The service registrar and business service champion have reviewed the service description in the service registry and approved it.

Certification of a service or automated process is a formal "passing out" ceremony, and granting of certification should signify that the SOA enablement team is happy for their reputation to be associated with the performance of the new asset.

Service Vitality Control Point

Service vitality takes place periodically as part of SOA governance to check up on and update the governance processes, procedures, policies, and standards in reaction to the results of the real world. This involves examining any and all lessons learned in any of the SOA planning, program control, development, or operations activities. It also includes such things as comments and feedback from all stakeholders and an examination of any common patterns (for example, common exemption requests or common reasons for failure to pass one or more control points) that need remedial action. Metrics in the efforts required for each stage of the development process can show trends that indicate improvements or declines in their vitality.

A formal service vitality control point review should be conducted every three to six months to determine whether the SOA transition remains on track, and whether the level and style of governance is optimal.

Individual service or automated processes should be reviewed every 6 to 12 months. Usage data of all versions of each service can determine any "stale" versions that can be deprecated or deleted, and whether the deployment options taken and decisions on who should own and who should access each service are optimal.

The Service Development Domain

"Another flaw in the human character is that everybody wants to build and nobody wants to do maintenance."

—Kurt Vonnegut

The Service Development domain covers the lifetime of services or automated processes from an original concept through to deployment into production. This section covers advice on governance of this development domain. Chapter 6, "Managing the Service Lifecycle," looks in a little more detail at governing specific steps with the service lifecycle.

Most IT departments we have visited currently spend the majority of their resources on system maintenance. One reason for this is that most IT systems consist of applications where there is generally no clear separation between business logic, graphical user interface (GUI) management, and workflow. Any change to an application of this type risks damaging all of these three aspects, and maintenance becomes labor intensive without good design documentation—which is more often than not a major issue.

SOA makes a clear distinction between business logic and workflow. SOA is all about packaging pure business logic as reusable transactional services, and using executable models to manage workflow. SOA does not become involved with any particular style or fashion of GUI or GUI control. In a fully SOA-aligned world, humans will make requests to IT systems to perform tasks, make decisions, or initiate business processes using whatever GUI is best suited to that job; automated business processes can in turn initiate tasks by invoking services or by requesting human intervention or involvement.

In this world, IT solutions grow incrementally as new business processes become automated, and interactions with third parties are increasingly performed using service executions without direct human intervention. Whenever new business initiatives, market forces, or governmental regulations require changes to operating procedures, new or revised automated business processes can be constructed rapidly by reworking or extending existing automated processes. We can expect technology to continue to change rapidly, so the users can interact with the IT systems in radically different ways in the future. Because the SOA approach insulates the user interface from the physical implementation of business function, we can expect that most of the services we create now will probably still exist in some form for the next 20 years or more, whatever interface is used to access them.

End-to-end service development is a complex process. Planning and governance has to be meticulous because there are many complex tasks with many interdependencies. There are critical tasks for governing service development that the governance specialist needs to address in the form of a transition plan that is created and worked just like any other project plan.

Key Capabilities Needed to Govern Service Development

The Service Development domain is highly complex and involves technology that is changing rapidly. Governing such complexity requires a high level of organizational and political skills, together with good knowledge, not just of the SOA technology itself, but how to use it optimally. Few individuals can combine those skills at a world-class level, so practical governance relies on close cooperation between some key technical and nontechnical roles. Close collaboration, and complete trust, among the SOA governance lead, the business service champions, the lead SOA architect, and the lead service architect is critical to success.

Table 4.1 describes the capabilities that the organization needs to govern service development, and recommends some key work products that can assist this complex activity. It is organized in the same way as Table 3.1 in Chapter 3.

Table 4.1   Service Development Domain—Capabilities, Risks, and Remedial Work Ducts

Capability	Associated Issues and Risks	Risk Level	Governance Work Products	Cost of Remedy
1. Services development lifecycle controls	Need to have a streamlined reliable end-to-end development process that finds issues and problems early and corrects them immediately. IT resources should be used as efficiently as possible.	Critical	■ SOA development approach ■ Service build plan ■ Service construction estimation metrics ■ Service construction monitoring plan ■ SOA development performance report ■ SOA reuse and ROI report ■ SOA development lessons learned ■ Control point minutes ■ SOA governance policy exemption ■ Service design walkthrough notes	High

Capability	Associated Issues and Risks	Risk Level	Governance Work Products	Cost of Remedy
2. Requirements gathering and prioritization	■ No IT solution will be of any value unless the requirements are accurate; need to keep requirements as simple as possible, and avoid unnecessary embellishments ■ There is a risk of embarrassment/ punitive fines if governmental regulations are ignored. ■ Business process models should be incrementally developed into executable models. ■ There must be no security violations that threaten data integrity or confidentiality.	Critical	■ Functional and nonfunctional requirements ■ Enterprisewide requirements and business rules catalog ■ Functional and nonfunctional requirements checklist ■ Regulatory compliance approach ■ Regulatory compliance checklist ■ Executable modeling approach	High
3. Service identification	■ Different potential consumers may have incompatible requirements. ■ Resources will be wasted if incorrect choices are made between delivering services or applications. ■ Functionality should be sourced in the most cost-effective way; sometimes this will be using a commercial package that meets most of the requirements, some-times it is necessary to develop solutions in-house. ■ Need to define services of correct granularity to maximize their reuse.	Critical	■ Service granularity, visibility, and accessibility checklist ■ Service reusability guidelines ■ Service sourcing policy	Moderate

Table 4.1 Service Development Domain—Capabilities, Risks, and Remedial Work Ducts (continued)

Capability	Associated Issues and Risks	Risk Level	Governance Work Products	Cost of Remedy
4. Service specification	■ Need to ensure QoS designs and documentation to avoid costly rework after flawed development. ■ Good service design can minimize the need for managing multiple service versions.	Critical	■ Service specification ■ Service specification checklist ■ Service design checklist ■ Service security approach ■ Service security checklist	Moderate
5. Service realization	■ Effective software development tools can markedly increase productivity and accuracy. ■ Services should be exhaustively tested to ensure they meet all functional and nonfunctional requirements. ■ Bugs are costly to correct and embarrassing; zero errors is not an impossible target if testing is thorough. ■ An efficient configuration management/build process is vital to efficiently transfer code between development, functional testing, performance testing, preproduction, and production environments.	Critical	■ SOA development tools ■ Service build management approach ■ Service security checklist ■ Service version management approach ■ Service test plan	High

Capability	Associated Issues and Risks	Risk Level	Governance Work Products	Cost of Remedy
6. Service certification	■ Testing services may require connectivity to systems and data that closely mimic operational systems, such as servers, mainframes, and realistic but artificial test data. ■ Any problems that occur after deployment will damage the reputation of the SOA enablement team. ■ Instituting a formal certification process helps to establish the enterprise's commitment to quality and value.	Critical	■ Service acceptance checklist ■ Service deployment approach ■ Service deployment checklist ■ Service level agreement ■ Service version management approach ■ Service test results	Moderate

Service Development Domain Work Product Definitions

In the preceding section, we introduced a number of work products that have been proven to be effective in helping to govern successful SOA transformations. Although we will describe them as if they are individual text documents or diagrams, in practice, many of the technical work products are best managed as models within tools specifically designed for manipulating them. Models of service internals, for example, should be edited and distributed using a specialized tool that can visualize and validate the interactions between the service components, and then generate most of the service code. No text document or simple picture can do that.

Documenting requirements involves many subtleties and creates multiple opportunities for misunderstandings to occur. A process model contained in a specifically designed process modeling tool that ensures logical continuity, and that requires all possible logical branches to be handled, is much more likely to be interpreted correctly than a use case written as a textual document. Better still if the modeling tool supports full emulation of the process steps.

Many of these work products represent intermediate deliverables that are passed from one professional to another on the service production line. These artifacts must be seen as representing a formal contract between the work product producer and the work product consumer. Delivery of the work product should formally signify that it is of the necessary quality and degree of completeness, and delivery of a substandard work product should be seen as a serious breach of contract. The control points described earlier in this chapter represent checkpoints to assess the quality of the key work products.

Some of the work products that can help govern the Service Development domain have already been described in Chapter 3, where, in addition, the roles of those involved in their production were defined. When creating the SOA governance plan, the SOA governance lead will need to select and create the work products that best manage SOA development service development activities without detracting from the ability to get projects done on time. Some of these work products have already been defined in the preceding chapter. Here are the descriptions of those new work products you should consider adopting, in alphabetic order.

Control Point Minutes

Description: These serve as a record of the results of the key SOA governance reviews, and can provide useful input to any systemic issues and the vitality of the SOA governance approach. The SOA governance lead or program management office (PMO) should examine these minutes to look for any common patterns of issues that need to be addressed by the creation of additional architectural decisions, design standards, best practices, or additional training.

Purpose: Ensure continued vitality of the SOA development approach.

When needed: Should be completed immediately after any service control point.

Responsible: Control point reviewers, PMO.

Accountable: SOA governance lead or PMO.

Consulted: Control point reviewers.

Informed: SOA enablement team.

Executable Modeling Approach Work Product

Description: This defines standards and best practices for developing executable business models, helping to ensure their consistency and quality.

Purpose: Define how automated business processes will be created.

When needed: Create this as soon as the SOA development approach work product has been approved.

Responsible: Service architects, process modelers, process developers, business analysts, monitoring developer.

Accountable: Lead SOA architect or lead service architect.

Consulted: SOA enablement team.

Informed: Process modelers, process developers, monitoring developer.

Functional and Nonfunctional Requirements Work Products

Description: For each service, these define exactly what each operation does, and how well it is expected to do it. Nonfunctional requirements include such factors as performance, availability, systems management, and security. There will generally be a fairly standard set of nonfunctional requirements that apply to most services, and individual services should have to define only additions and exceptions to them. Targets such as latency should be defined in measurable terms; for example, "95% of individual executions of this operation should have a latency of less than 1 second, to the glass on a portal screen, and 90% of executions should complete in less than 1.5 seconds."

As already stated, a good practice for cataloging functional requirements is to maintain a requirements and business rules catalog in a database, indexed by the corresponding business entity in the enterprise data model (EDM) or messaging model (MM). This can avoid wasted effort in duplicating requirements analysis. Requirements should be classified into Mandatory, Valuable, and Optional. In the case where requirements are specific to a single line of business (LoB), this should be made clear in the text describing the requirement.

Purpose: Good management of requirements can avoid duplication of effort and help enable reuse.

When needed: A standard set of nonfunctional requirements should be created as soon as the SOA development approach work product has been approved; functional requirements should be assessed at the business requirements and service identification control point, and nonfunctional requirements should be assessed at both solution architecture and service design control points.

Responsible: Service architects and business analysts (for nonfunctional requirements), business analysts and process modelers (for functional requirements).

Accountable: Business service champion.

Consulted: All service architects, business analysts, process developers, service developers.

Informed: SOA enablement team, QA, testing team.

Functional and Nonfunctional Requirements Checklist Work Product

Description: This checklist is used at the business requirements and service identification point, and nonfunctional requirements should be assessed at both solution architecture and service design control points to ensure that all potential consumers are satisfied that their individual requirements have either been met or have been explicitly ruled out of scope in the current planned service release, and that the design approach for this service should be able to satisfy the NFRs and SLA terms and conditions.

Purpose: Ensure the highest possible quality of services.

When needed: Functional requirements should be assessed at the business requirements and service identification control point, and nonfunctional requirements should be assessed at both solution architecture and service design control points.

Responsible: SOA governance lead creates the template, lead business analysts and service designers complete the checklist for individual services.

Accountable: Business service champion.

Consulted: Business analysts.

Informed: SOA enablement team.

Regulatory Compliance Approach Work Product

Description: Specifies what regulations apply under which circumstances (for example, the country in which the service requestor is based), together with the processes that will be followed to ensure compliance.

Purpose: Avoid the embarrassment and potential punitive consequences of disobeying applicable regulations.

When needed: Should be created as SOA development approach work product has been approved.

Responsible: SOA lead architect, PMO, business service champion, security architect.

Accountable: SOA executive sponsor or existing IT governance function.

Consulted: SOA enablement team.

Informed: PMO.

Regulatory Compliance Checklist Work Product

Description: The template for this document is created by the security architect and any existing IT governance group, and then approved by the lead SOA architect. Individual instances of this checklist are completed by the service designer and approved by the security architect. The regulatory compliance checklist for a given service should be endorsed at multiple control points to ensure that no changes have been made to the service that might invalidate the integrity of its security.

Purpose: Avoid the embarrassment and potential punitive consequences of disobeying applicable regulations.

When needed: Should initially be prepared in time for the service specification control point, then re-reviewed at the service build, service test, and service certification and deployment control points.

Responsible: SOA lead architect, PMO, service designer, service architect.

Accountable: Security architect.

Consulted: SOA enablement team.

Informed: PMO.

Service Acceptance Checklist Work Product

Description: A checklist used to confirm that IT operations agree that it can successfully operate and manage a specific service within the terms of its SLA.

Purpose: Ensure the highest possible QoS.

When needed: Should be completed before the service certification and deployment control point, for which it is a prerequisite.

Responsible: IT operations.

Accountable: IT operations.

Consulted: Service architect, service designers, service testers.

Informed: SOA enablement team.

Service Build Management Approach Work Product

Description: The approach to build management must ensure that SOA components can be migrated easily among development, testing, preproduction, and production environments repeatedly, without error or omission.

Purpose: To maintain continuity of operation, it is essential that the approach to build management is error free, and that it is always possible to re-create any given build configuration.

When needed: Should be created as SOA development approach work product has been approved.

Responsible: SOA lead architect, existing build manager.

Accountable: SOA lead architect.

Consulted: IT operations.

Informed: Service developers, process developers.

Service Build Plan Work Product

Description: This is the set of candidate service operations and automated business processes that comprise the formal SOA asset construction plan. This work product is an essential tool for managing SOA development in that

- It defines the results of the service prioritization.
- It's a key control document for service development project management.
- It communicates the SOA development plan and status to the rest of the organization.

Note that services, in general, have multiple operations—for example, a Customer service may have such operations as lookupCustomer and modifyCustomer. Not all operations will have the same development priority; there is no need to create all operations of each service at the same time.

Purpose: Manage the service development priorities and communicate those priorities to the stakeholders.

When needed: Should be created as soon as any services are planned, and it should be updated weekly.

Responsible: Lead service architect, service registrar, SOA business analysts.

Accountable: Business service champion.

Consulted: PMO, service architect, service developer service designer, process modelers, process developers.

Informed: SOA enablement team, PMO.

Service Construction Estimation Metrics Work Product

Description: These are the resource metrics captured as a result of the service construction monitoring plan. They provide invaluable input to the project management of new services and SOA projects. A steady improvement in these metrics is a sign of growing SOA maturity and effective SOA governance.

Purpose: These are important metrics to enable effective governance of the service factory.

When needed: Should be created as soon as any services are planned and data is captured for every service that is created.

Responsible: Lead service architect, SOA governance lead, PMO.

Accountable: Lead service architect.

Consulted: SOA enablement team, PMO.

Informed: PMO.

Service Construction Monitoring Plan Work Product

Description: This is the plan to capture and continuously update metrics on the resource efforts needed to complete each step in the service and automated business process lifecycle. Typically, resource estimates for each construction step are grouped into complex, intermediate, and simple services/processes.

Purpose: These are essential metrics to enable effective governance of the service factory.

When needed: Should be created as soon as any services are planned and data is captured for every service that is created.

Responsible: Lead service architect, lead SOA architect, SOA governance lead, PMO.

Accountable: Lead service architect.

Consulted: SOA enablement team.

Informed: SOA enablement team, PMO.

Service Deployment Approach Work Product

Description: The current IT deployment approach should be adjusted to allow for the characteristics of services. Typically, the number of deployments cycles in a traditional IT development approach is limited to a small number of major increments each year, to maintain stability of the operational systems, whereas the deployment of services can be almost an everyday occurrence.

Purpose: Ensure that services are deployed in the optimum fashion at the most advantageous times.

When needed: Should be created as SOA development approach work product has been approved.

Responsible: IT operations.

Accountable: Lead service architect.

Consulted: IT operations.

Informed: Service developers.

Service Design Checklist Work Product

Description: This checklist is used to ensure that the service internals contained in the service specification work product are high standard, complete, and unambiguous.

Purpose: Ensures the highest possible quality of services and reduces the need for rework.

When needed: A checklist template should be completed as soon as the SOA development approach has been approved. Instances of this checklist should be completed for each service before the service design control point.

Responsible: Service architect, QA, security architect create the template; service developers complete individual checklists.

Accountable: Service architect.

Consulted: Service designer, service developer.

Informed: SOA enablement team.

Service Design Walkthrough Notes

Description: These are relatively informal notes that describe the results of service design walkthrough sessions (for example, "chalk and talk" working sessions where service architects, designers, and developers meet to discuss the design of individual services, both to optimize that design and to mentor the less experienced staff members).

Purpose: Ensure continued vitality of the SOA development approach by identifying any common concerns that might require the creation of additional architectural decisions, design standards, best practices, or additional training.

When needed: Should be completed after every service design walk-through session.

Responsible: Service designers, service developers.

Accountable: Service architect.

Consulted: Lead SOA architect.

Informed: SOA governance lead.

Service Deployment Checklist Work Product

Description: This is a checklist used to ensure that services are deployed in the fashion described in the service deployment approach, based on a template created as part of the service deployment approach. It should take into account the fact that some services may have multiple instances, multiple access channels, and different QoS levels for different categories of consumer, according to the requirements specified by the service architect or service designer.

Purpose: Ensures that services are deployed in the optimum fashion.

When needed: The service deployment checklist should be completed before the acceptance process.

Responsible: IT operations creates the checklist template with assistance from service architects. Service developers and service architects fill in a checklist for each individual service.

Accountable: Service architect.

Consulted: IT operations.

Informed: Service developers, service registrar.

Service Granularity, Visibility and Accessibility Checklist Work Product

Description: This checklist is used to ensure that services have the optimum scope and are visible and available to any potential consumer that may need to access them.

Purpose: Ensures the highest possible QoS, with maximum business value and reuse potential.

When needed: Complete this before the solution architecture control point and revalidate it at the service design control point.

Responsible: SOA governance lead creates the template, and lead business analysts and service designers complete an individual checklist for each service.

Accountable: Business service champion.

Consulted: Business analysts, service registrar, service designers.

Informed: SOA enablement team, PMO.

Service Level Agreement Work Product

Description: SLAs represent the terms and conditions of a contract among service consumers and service providers. IT operations is responsible for monitoring that both parties comply with all their terms and conditions. SLAs should include the following:

- Guaranteed QoS levels, based on the corresponding service nonfunctional requirements
- Technical support terms and conditions (hours of operation of the help desk, incident response times by problem urgency, and so on)
- Constraints on the service consumer (specifying, for example, that QoS cannot be guaranteed if the service consumer exceeds a given threshold in the rate of service requests)
- For any services that are being offered for a fee, either internally or externally, the pricing structure of service requests
- How version management will affect consumers such as how many versions of services will be supported, length of time support will be available for deprecated services, how much warning service consumers will have of changes, or service retirement

Purpose: Define contractual terms for service usage.

When needed: Standard SLA terms and conditions should be established by the SOA governance lead as soon as practicable.

Responsible: SOA governance lead, business service champion.

Accountable: Business service champion.

Consulted: SOA enablement team, PMO.

Informed: Service owners, service consumers, PMO.

Service Reusability Guidelines Work Product

Description: Based on the SOA development approach, this work product contains guidance to service designers on how to design services with maximum reusability.

Purpose: Ensures that services are designed so as to maximize their reuse potential.

When needed: Should be created as soon as the SOA development approach work product has been approved.

Responsible: SOA lead architect, service architect, SOA governance lead.

Accountable: Business service champion.

Consulted: Business analysts, process modelers.

Informed: SOA enablement team, QA.

Service Security Approach Work Product

Description: The optimum approach for implementing SOA security to enforce the following:

- Authentication and authorization of all service consumers
- Nonrepudiation of service execution requests
- Protection of enterprise data assets
- Encryption of all data transmitted over channels such as the Internet

Purpose: Create and maintain a secure SOA production environment.

When needed: Should be created as SOA development approach work product has been approved.

Responsible: Security architect, lead service architect.

Accountable: Security architect.

Consulted: Operations management.

Informed: SOA enablement team.

Service Security Checklist Work Product

Description: Individual instances of this checklist are completed by the service designer and approved by the security architect. The service security checklist for a given service should be endorsed at multiple control points to ensure that no changes have been made to the service that might invalidate the integrity of its security.

Purpose: Ensure that services that do not comply with the requirements of the service security approach are never deployed into production.

When needed: Should initially be prepared in time for the service specification control point, then re-reviewed at the service build, service test, and service certification and deployment control points.

Responsible: The template for this document is created by the security architect and approved by the lead service architect; individual checklists are completed by a service developer and service tester, and then approved by a security architect.

Accountable: Security architect.

Consulted: IT operations.

Informed: SOA enablement team.

Service Sourcing Policy Work Product

Description: Based on the SOA development approach, the service sourcing policy describes how, once the need for a specific service or service operation has been established, the organization should choose between the options:

- Develop the service functionality from scratch.
- Use an existing IT asset or application, wrapped as a service.
- Buy a commercial, off-the-shelf (COTS) product that is or can be wrapped to be exposed as a service.
- Subscribe to an external software as a service vendor who performs that activity.

Purpose: Ensure consistency of approach in buy versus build decisions.

When needed: As soon as the SOA development approach has been approved.

Responsible: SOA governance lead.

Accountable: Procurement.

Consulted: Business service champion.

Informed: SOA enablement team, PMO.

Service Specification Work Product

Description: The service specification is not a single document, but rather a package that contains all necessary information needed to use, build, test, and certify that service or automated process. It should include the following:

- The service externals and service internals discussed earlier.
- Details of any interfaces to existing IT assets that the service will need to access.

- Functional and nonfunctional requirements for the service.
- Security information for the service (who can access it, authentication, encryption, nonrepudiation).
- Deployment options (for example, need for geographic diversity; "platinum," "gold," "silver" levels of service support)
- Monitoring and systems management requirements.
- Test plan and test data.
- The acid test of the level of completeness and accuracy of a service specification package is that it contains no ambiguity and that it provides a reasonably skilled offshore developer with all the information necessary to develop a high-quality code deliverable without the need for asking any questions to clarify any item it contains. For this purpose, models contained in sophisticated tools are much more valuable than words and pictures in most cases.

Purpose: Ensure the highest possible QoS.

When needed: Service externals need to be completed before the solution specification control point and the whole service specification completed before the service design control point.

Responsible: Lead service architect, QA, SOA governance lead create the templates; the service designer and service architect complete each service specification package.

Accountable: Business service champion.

Consulted: SOA enablement team.

Informed: Service consumers have access to the service externals, and only the SOA enablement team (specifically service developers and service testers) should be given access to service internals.

Service Specification Checklist Work Product

Description: This checklist is used to ensure that all service specification packages are created to the highest possible standards, contain all the information needed, and are clear and unambiguous.

Purpose: Ensure the highest possible QoS.

When needed: Should be completed before the solution specification control point.

Responsible: Service designer, QA, and service registrar.

Accountable: Business service champion.

Consulted: SOA enablement team.

Informed: SOA governance lead.

Service Test Plan Work Product

Description: Thorough functional and nonfunctional testing of services is vital to ensuring their quality. For each service, this plan should describe all the tests that need to be carried out, and what the expected result should be.

Purpose: Ensure the highest possible QoS.

When needed: Should be completed immediately after the service design control point.

Responsible: Service test manager, business analysts.

Accountable: Business service champion.

Consulted: Service architect, service designer, and business analysts.

Informed: Service testers.

Service Test Results Work Product

Description: These document the results of executing the service test plan, and cover both functional and nonfunctional testing. All tests must have been successfully completed before a service can pass through the service test control point.

Purpose: Ensure the highest possible QoS.

When needed: Should be completed after testing is completed successfully and before the service acceptance control point. These test results should be examined regularly to look for any systemic issues that need to be addressed, for example, by additional training or by changing standards or best practices.

Responsible: Service testers, QA.

Accountable: Service test manager or QA.

Consulted: Service architect, service designer, and business analysts.

Informed: SOA governance lead, PMO.

Service Version Management Approach Work Product

Description: This defines how services and automated business processes will be version managed, and assigns responsibility for performing and verifying that this approach is followed in practice. It should include advice on designing services that are as forward compatible as possible—that is, that can be incrementally extended without impact to existing consumers. Chapter 6, discusses service version management in more detail.

Purpose: Define how services will be version managed.

When needed: Should be created as soon as the SOA development approach work product has been approved.

Responsible: Lead SOA architect, service architects, SOA governance lead.

Accountable: Business service champion.

Consulted: IT operations.

Informed: IT operations, service consumers.

SOA Development Performance Report Work Product

Description: These reports are based on continuously monitoring the actual analysis, design, construction, and testing efforts associated with constructing services or automating business processes.

These reports should show actual resources, explain any discrepancies with established service construction estimation metrics, and show trends. In the best case scenario, they reveal a continuous improvement in productivity and decline in rework!

Purpose: Ensure continued vitality of the SOA development approach and the vitality of SOA governance.

When needed: Should be completed and distributed every one to three months.

Responsible: Lead SOA architect, PMO, SOA governance lead.

Accountable: Lead service architect.

Consulted: Service testers.

Informed: SOA enablement team, PMO.

SOA Development Tools Work Product

Description: There are many fine software tools to assist in the development and testing of services and automated business processes, and any organization embarking on a transition to SOA should select a set of tools to improve their productivity. The most effective tools support the principle of model-driven development—that is, the creation of models of services or automated processes that are progressively refined until they are considered complete, at which time the code is generated automatically. Chapter 6 describes this in more detail.

Purpose: Create and maintain a productive development and test environment.

When needed: Should be created as soon as the SOA development approach work product has been created.

Responsible: SOA lead architect, service architects.

Accountable: SOA lead architect.

Consulted: Service developers, service assemblers, SOA business analysts, process modelers, process developers, monitoring developer, enterprise architects.

Informed: SOA enablement team.

SOA Development Lessons Learned Work Product

Description: At the end of any significant task in the service or process automation lifecycle, it is valuable to hold a relatively informal session to discuss any lessons learned from the exercise. Lessons learned should cover areas such as the SOA development process, work products, governance approach and level of governance rigor, and tools and techniques. Whether the lessons learned are positive of negative, they provide valuable insight into the vitality of the SOA development and governance process vitality.

Purpose: Ensure continued vitality of the SOA development approach and the vitality of SOA governance.

When needed: Should be completed and distributed once every four months.

Responsible: All control point reviewers.

Accountable: SOA governance lead or PMO.

Consulted: SOA enablement team.

Informed: SOA enablement team, PMO.

SOA Governance Policy Exemption Work Product

Description: The ability to grant exceptions to having to conform to common standards, best practices, or policies in case of established business need is important, and the exemptions process must be defined in the SOA governance plan, along with a definition of who is empowered to grant such exemptions. The level and type of exemptions and the reasons they were granted or refused are important measures of the SOA governance vitality:

- If there are few exemptions requested, it is possible that either the standards are too lax, the degree of governance applied is inappropriate, or that some developers are ignoring the governance approach or rules altogether.

- If there are too many exemptions requested or granted, the standards might be too restrictive.

Purpose: Record the granting or refusal of requests for exemptions from compliance with standards or best practices.

When needed: Should be completed whenever a request is received for exemption from a policy or standard.

Responsible: SOA lead architect, SOA governance lead, QA, PMO.

Accountable: Lead service architect or enterprise architect.

Consulted: Service architects.

Informed: Exemption requestor (typically a service architect or service designer).

SOA Reuse and ROI Report Work Product

Description: Based on the SOA reuse and ROI monitoring plan, this regular report should assess, as objectively as possible, the real levels of reuse and ROI that have been achieved. Some of the data to produce this report will be obtained from IT projects, through the medium of the project benefits and ROI work product.

Purpose: Measure and report the real business value of the SOA transformation initiative.

When needed: Every one to four months, or alternatively displayed on a real-time governance dashboard.

Responsible: SOA governance lead, lead service architect, PMO.

Accountable: Business service champion.

Consulted: SOA enablement team, service consumers, IT operations.

Informed: Chief executives, PMO, SOA enablement team.

The dependencies among these work products are depicted in Figure 4.3. The format is the same as for Table 3.3 in Chapter 3. Again, those work products marked with an asterisk (*) should be revised every 6 to 12 months to ensure continued vitality.

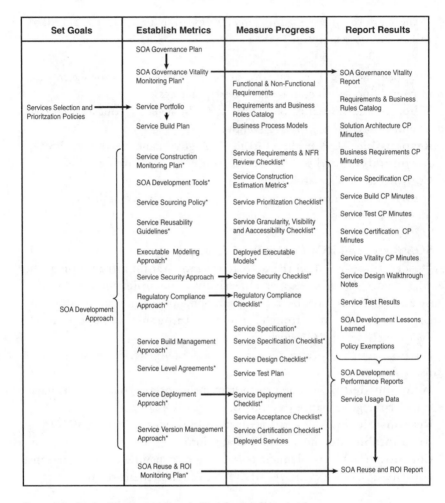

Figure 4.3   Service Development Domain: Work Product Dependencies

The Service Operations Domain

"Civilization advances by extending the number of important operations which we can perform without thinking about them"

—Alfred North Whitehead

This section covers governance of services and automated business processes in a production environment. SOA offers both benefits and challenges to IT operations. The benefits include the following:

- It's much easier to monitor the usage and QoS provided by services, and there are some excellent commercial products that support this activity, some of which even provide real-time "dashboards" to display items such as QoS and usage statistics.
- Services offer much richer deployment opportunities and much more information about who uses them than do applications.
- A generic security mechanism can protect all services from security exposures or malicious threats.

The challenges include the following:

- SLAs need to be continuously monitored, and SLA violations need to be recorded.
- Frequent deployment of individual services can represent a threat to the stability of the production environments unless the service quality, build management, and deployment processes are highly effective.

Key SOA Governance Tasks Involved in Operating Services

Key tasks in ensuring that SOA operations are governed effectively include the following:

- Providing effective technical support for services and resolving software quality incidents efficiently and rapidly

- Monitoring the execution of services and automated business processes, most especially in terms of monitoring their compliance with the terms of their SLAs
- Maintaining the vitality, reliability, availability, and performance of the operational systems

Most organizations have a separate IT operations organization to manage the production IT systems. Table 4.2 describes the key capabilities that an IT operations organization needs to enable effective governance of services.

Table 4.2   Service Operations Domain: Capabilities, Risks, and Remedial Work Products

Capability	Associated Issues and Risks	Risk Level	Governance Work Products	Cost of Remedy
O01. Service execution monitoring	Service consumers expect high availability and good QoS—and the SLAs guarantee that they will receive them.	Critical	■ SLAs ■ QoS goals ■ QoS monitoring plan ■ QoS report ■ Service usage data ■ IT capacity management plan ■ SLA compliance report ■ SLA monitoring plan	Fairly high
O02. Service operational vitality	Service consumers do not want to have to modify their applications every time new service versions appear, unless those versions contain changes that they need.	Critical	■ Service operational vitality report ■ Deprecated or decommissioned services	Moderate
O03. Service support	Service consumers may need technical support if there are any bugs or other problems with services.	Critical	■ Technical support approach and targets ■ Problem incident log	Fairly high

Service Operations Domain Work Product Definitions

This sections contains a list of descriptions of the work products whose production can help govern the Service Operations domain. Most of these work products should exist in any moderately well-governed IT production environment, but some of these need additional extensions for SOA. Again, they are organized in alphabetic order, and work products that have already been defined in Chapter 3 are not repeated. The roles involved in creating these products were also defined in that chapter.

Deprecated or Decommissioned Services Work Product

Description: This is just a list of obsolete services that have been or will eventually be discontinued. Deprecated service should continue to be supported, but no new consumers should be able to access them. The number of such obsolete or obsolescent service versions should help determine the efficacy of the service version management approach—in an ideal world there would be few if any of these.

Purpose: Monitor SOA operational vitality.

When needed: Every four to six months.

Responsible: Service registrar

Accountable: Business service champions.

Consulted: Service consumers, PMO.

Informed: SOA enablement team, PMO, service consumers, IT operations.

Problem Incident Log Work Product

Description: This is a basic IT governance work product that should be updated to reflect the specific needs of service consumers and users of automated business processes. It records details of any technical problems that have occurred and how they were resolved.

Purpose: Used to provide invaluable information about the quality of deployed services. The SOA governance lead and lead SOA architect should look for any system quality issues and correct them as a matter of urgency.

When needed: Should be completed before any SLAs are published, and the SLAs should contain clauses that reflect the level of technical support that will be provided.

Responsible: Help desk / technical support staff.

Accountable: IT operations manager, technical support manager.

Consulted: SOA governance lead.

Informed: Problem reporter, PMO.

Quality of Service Goals Work Product

Description: QoS goals set explicit targets for performance and operational efficiency that services and automated processes will be measured against. The goals should exceed those specified in individual service nonfunctional requirements and SLAs by a small increment to ensure that those contractual conditions are more secure than the QoS goals themselves.

Purpose: Monitor performance of service operations.

When needed: Created as the first services are deployed, then updated every six months or so.

Responsible: Lead service architect, lead SOA architect, SOA governance lead.

Accountable: IT operations manager.

Consulted: Business service champions, PMO, individual business units.

Informed: IT operations, SOA enablement team, PMO.

QoS Monitoring Plan Work Product

Description: This is the plan to monitor execution of services and automated business processes against the QoS goals. This plan should include monitoring the business impact of any SOA infrastructure problem. The breakdown of a single network element might seem relatively insignificant, but if it represents a single point of failure in a major service or function of the SOA infrastructure, it may have significant business impact, unless the operational model includes full redundancy.

Purpose: Ensure that QoS goals are met.

When needed: Created as the first services are deployed, and then updated every six months or so.

Responsible: Lead service architect, lead SOA architect, SOA governance lead, monitoring developer.

Accountable: IT operations.

Consulted: Business service champions, QA, PMO.

Informed: SOA enablement team.

QoS Report Work Product

Description: This a regular report (or ideally a component on a real-time governance dashboard) that compares actual QoS with the QoS goals on a service-by-service basis.

Purpose: Ensure that QoS goals are met.

When needed: At least monthly, ideally updated online in real time.

Responsible: Lead service architect, SOA architect, SOA governance lead, monitoring developer, IT operations.

Accountable: SOA governance lead or IT operations manager.

Consulted: IT operations.

Informed: SOA enablement team, SOA executive sponsor.

Service Operational Vitality Report Work Product

Description: This is a regular summary report that provides an overview of the status of SOA operational vitality, including growth in service usage (both in terms of new service consumers and growth in service execution requests), QoS reporting, and new services deployed during each reporting period. It draws from several sources, such as the QoS report, *SLA* compliance report, and deployed services and service usage data provided by IT operations.

Purpose: Communicate SOA operational vitality.

Responsible: SOA governance lead, monitoring developer, and PMO define the structure and layout of the report; IT operations and service registrar provide the data.

Accountable: IT operations manager or SOA governance lead.

Consulted: Business service champions, IT operations.

Informed: SOA enablement team, SOA executive sponsor.

Service Usage Data Work Product

Description: One of the major advantages of SOA over more traditional software development styles is that it is possible to capture a great deal of operational information about usage of services and automated processes. In fact, it is impossible to govern the Service Operations domain, or to bill third parties for service usage, unless this information is captured and recorded.

It is impossible to capture usage statistics manually, so it is essential that the SOA infrastructure itself automates this task. Data that should be captured for both services and automated processes include the following:

- Who invoked each service operation or automated process?

- Were there any attempts to invoke a service or process by unauthorized requesters?

- What was the total time taken to execute the request, and was it within the SLA and QoS targets?

- What were the overall transaction rates for each service, hour by hour?

In the case of automated processes, additional data needs to be recorded:

- Which of the several possible logical branches were taken in each execution?

- When an automated process invoked a manual task, how long before that task completed?

- Are any manual tasks "hung up"—that is, not completed within the QoS thresholds for that task?

The volume of data this represents will be formidable, and it will need to be summarized in a report or dashboard display.

Purpose: Capture and summarize essential data on performance and utilization of services and automated processes.

Responsible: SOA governance lead, monitoring developer, and PMO define the structure and layout of the report or dashboard display; IT operations provides the raw data.

Accountable: IT operations manager or SOA governance lead.

Consulted: Business service champions, IT operations.

Informed: SOA enablement team, SOA executive sponsor.

SLA Compliance Report Work Product

Description: There are two types of SLA compliance report:

- Regular SLA compliance confirmation. Most, and ideally all, SLA compliance monitoring reposts should show actual QoS numbers achieved that are well within the SLA terms.

■ The more important—but rare, we hope—SLA compliance failure reports. In the event of SLA compliance failures, notifications should be sent urgently to the service consumers, the lead SOA architect, business service champions, and the SOA governance lead, apprising them of the situation and the actions taken to prevent recurrence.

Purpose: Monitor SLA compliance and handle incidents.

When needed: Regular SLA compliance reporting should be performed monthly, in support of the SLA monitoring plan described next. In the event of a SLA violation, immediate corrective action should be taken, and all effected service consumers informed as soon as possible.

Responsible: IT operations, monitoring developer, SOA architect, service architects.

Accountable: IT operations manager.

Consulted: Service architect, service designer, QA in the event of SLA violations.

Informed: PMO, SOA enablement team, help desk / technical support staff, service consumers.

SLA Monitoring Plan Work Product

Description: This is the plan to monitor all service and process executions, consumer by consumer, to ensure that they are executed with the terms of the SLAs appropriate to that individual consumer. SLA monitoring needs to be performed using a formal systems management tool or framework; it is not a task that can be performed manually.

Purpose: There is no point in having SLAs if you don't know whether you are meeting them. There is little value in SOA governance without formal SLAs being in place and enforced.

When needed: At the same time as the SLAs are defined.

Responsible: PMO, lead service architect, lead SOA architect, IT operations, SOA governance lead, monitoring developer.

Accountable: SOA governance lead or PMO.

Consulted: Business service champions, IT operations.

Informed: IT operations, QA, PMO, SOA enablement team.

Technical Support Approach and Targets Work Product

Description: This is a basic IT governance work product that should be updated to reflect the specific needs of service consumers and users of automated business processes. It defines the level and speed of technical support that internal and external service consumers can expect. Enhanced levels of support should be provided for high-severity problems, and for high-value services. Assured levels of technical support should be included in service and automated process SLAs.

Purpose: Ensure that and SLAs honored and that service consumers receive adequate technical support.

When needed: Should be completed before any SLAs are published, and the SLAs should contain clauses that reflect the level of technical support that will be provided.

Responsible: Lead service architect, SOA governance lead, PMO.

Accountable: IT operations manager.

Consulted: Business service champions.

Informed: Help desk / technical support manager, QA, PMO.

The dependencies among work products are shown in Figure 4.4. Again, the format is the same as for Figure 3.3 (in Chapter 3) and Figure 4.3.

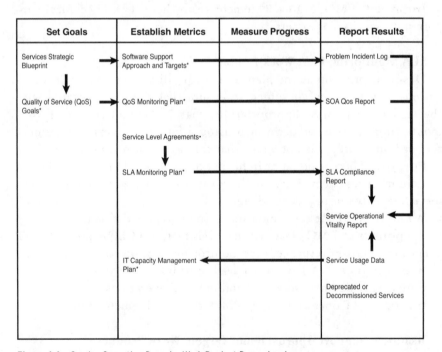

Figure 4.4 Service Operation Domain: Work Product Dependencies

Case Study

> *"To regret one's own experiences is to arrest one's own development. To deny one's own experiences is to put a lie into the lips of one's life. It is no less than a denial of the soul."*
>
> —Oscar Wilde

Service transformation planning was one of the capability priorities that SOA governance needed so that it could work with the EA group and help govern the resultant business service priorities. Service development lifecycle controls (SDLCs) represent another area of great concern. After all, the adherence to best practices and a consistency of approach across the development organizations are needed, especially to help enforce the results of the service transformation planning.

Service Development Lifecycle Controls

Ideation has known for some time that it needs a common and structured development process. Some groups perform peer reviews from time to time on their code, but the reviews tend to be haphazardly completed.

Another group at Ideation is considering a standardized development approach. Your SOA governance team has been asked to propose governance control gates for the service development lifecycle of

- Business requirements
- Solution architecture
- Service identification and specification
- Service build
- Service test
- Service certification

Control Gates for Ideation

In consultation with the development stakeholders, you decide to create the following control gates for the Ideation SDLC:

- Business Requirements control gate
- Solution Architecture control gate
- Service Design control gate
- Service Build control gate
- Service Test control gate
- Service Certification and Deployment control gate

As a first step, you create the template for the Business Requirements control gate and elicit feedback, as shown in Table 4.3.

Table 4.3 Ideation Business Requirements Control Gate

Section	Contains	Definition
Motivation	The justification for this control gate.	We must have a consistent and well-formed set of business requirements to create services that give us the greatest amount of agility and reuse. This requires that we have a consistent and repeatable approach to the specification of requirements and that this specification gives the required information for the rest of the development lifecycle.
Objective	The output objective	Ensure that the business requirements have a sufficient level of content regardless of form so that development can deliver on the requirement; IT will have a true specification of the business need and objective. This better enables IT to size and estimate this project. Enables the alignment of cross-functional teams on the delivery of the business requirement.
Trigger	Triggering event	Complete business requirements are delivered by the business to the project manager.

Section	Contains	Definition
Scale / Applicability Guidance	Indication of what scale/ style of review is appropriate for the circumstance	Perform if project is > $100K in size.
Review type	General classification of review types: ■ Peer review ■ Submission to approver ■ Workshop ■ Formal meeting	A workshop to review the requirements artifact and identify that the correct level of detail per the executive design authority standard for business requirements specification has been followed. The following roles are represented at the workshop: Application architect Process analyst Business architecture Business analyst Requirements analyst Solution designer Project manager
Concept/approach	Description of how the review is conducted and how it supports the objective	The project manager schedules and leads the workshop. The application architect, business analyst, requirements analyst, and solution designer must validate the requirements while meeting the needs of the next steps of the development lifecycle. That is, they have the information they need to do a good job and the requirements are understood. The business architecture must validate the requirements by following the architecture review board (ARB) requirements standard. Needed updates to requirements are noted and assigned for follow up, or requirements are approved or disapproved (with updates required).
	Governing authority	Business architecture is the governing authority responsible for validating form and that all standards for business requirements are followed.
	Responsible/manages	The project manager schedules and leads the workshop.
	Accountable - approves/ conditional approval/rejects	The head of line of business (LoB) must be accountable and approve the business requirements with a final signoff.

Table 4.3   Ideation Business Requirements Control Gate (continued)

Section	Contains	Definition
	Consults/supports/performs	The application architect understands the requirements and ensures all the requirements information needed for the high-level solution architecture (the architecture solution document) is there. The process analyst answers queries about the business process and ensures that the rest of the requirements conform to the applicable processes. The business analyst is responsible for delivering the requirements and is available to answer questions about the requirements or to follow up with any updates needed. The requirements analyst understands the requirements, creates the specification, and identifies the specifications applicable to each development group (to understand which areas are impacted). The solution designer understands the requirements and will take the architecture solution document from the application architect and create the solution design (end-to-end solution). The solution designer also oversees the components of the solution design. Test/QA—Is this requirement sufficiently articulated to be validated?
	Informed	All participants, governance specialist.
Artifacts to be made available	The input that is required	Business requirements should be circulated before the workshop to all participants. (A customer service level agreement [SLA] needs to be considered and agreed to.) Opinions must be sought from the application architect, business analyst, requirements analyst, and solution designer to validate the requirements.

Section	Contains	Definition
	What opinions to be sought	The application architect, business analyst, requirements analyst, and solution designer must validate that the requirements meet the needs of the next steps of the development lifecycle. That is, they have the information they need to do a good job, and the requirements are understood.
Key review criteria	Highlights the key criteria	The business requirements standard must be adhered to, including the following: ■ Consistency of requirements within the business requirements package ■ Adherence of business requirements to business processes ■ Adherence of business requirements to regulatory and organization compliances and standards
Key work product acceptance criteria	Key acceptance criteria to be met for successful review of work product	Consistency and completeness of the business requirements must be followed. Any inconsistencies or gaps or opportunities for improvement or rework of the business requirements must be specified. Record next steps, work assigned, and schedule agreed. Any follow up agreed.
Checklist	Sets a suggested process for the review. Provides objective support for recommendations, rework requests, and signoffs.	Business requirements checklist will be used.
Escalation process	Name of escalation process to be used to request an exception to the control gate result.	Escalates a decision to the program management office (PMO) to drive the business requirements process to conclusion.
Measurements	Metrics to be captured during or at the end of this control gate.	Governance metrics on this gate, including incrementing the number of times this gate has been implemented, incrementing the number of times this business unit has been through this gate, and the results (pass, fail, pass with conditions), and the checklist score.
Outcomes	Who is responsible for final signoff, who gets notified, and who are the results delivered to?	Final signoff—Head of the LoB. Notification—All on the informed list and service registrar. Delivery—The PMO will be the official owner of the results.

As a next step, you need to create and get feedback on the control gate for the Solution Architecture control gate, as shown in Table 4.4.

Table 4.4   Ideation Solution Architecture Control Gate

Section	Contains	Definition
Name	Control gate name	Solution Architecture
Motivation	The justification for this control gate	Approval to proceed with proposed solutions presented in conformance to technology standards and principles: ■ To confirm deliverables are encompassing and "fit for purpose" ■ To promote deliverable integration and support ■ To proactively understand impacts before further investment
Objective	The output objective	To assess deliverable's impact on member domains and resulting consideration: ■ To agree on integration, interfaces, and support of deliverables ■ To ensure alternative approaches and solutions ■ To approve new IT solutions presented.
Trigger	Triggering event	Project manager receives completed solution architecture document.
Scale / applicability guidance	Indication of what scale/ style of review is appropriate for the circumstance	Perform if project size > $100K.
Review type	General classification of review types: ■ Peer review ■ Submission to approver ■ Workshop ■ Formal meeting	A workshop to review the requirements artifact and identify that the correct level of detail per the guidelines has been specified. The following roles are needed: Application architect Process analyst Business architecture Business analyst Requirements analyst Solution designer Head of line of business

Section	Contains	Definition
Concept/approach	Description of how the review is conducted and how it supports the objective	The business analyst must validate the requirements as meeting the standards for requirements, and must then trigger the business requirement review workshop to be scheduled and completed.
Participants, roles, and interests	Governing authority	ARB.
	Responsible/manages	Project manager—Trigger the meeting and provide follow up and results.
	Accountable - approves/ conditional approval/ rejects	Lead architect—Responsible for presenting and answering question on the architecture solution document.
	Consults/supports/ performs	Solution designer—Responsible for representing the technical expertise of standards and policies and evaluating the architecture solution document end-to-end solution as being feasible. Business analyst—Responsible for representing the business client and validates that the solution meets needs of the business and accepts or declines proposed trade-offs. Architecture executives—Provide guidance, review output, and ensure governance. Infrastructure architect (if heavy infrastructure in solution)—Have provided infrastructure architecture in the architecture solution document and answer questions as needed. Infrastructure designer—Validate the solution architecture for structural feasibility. Requirements analyst—Review and understand the high-level solution architecture and context of downstream requirements and analyst comments. Data architect—Provided data architecture in the architecture solution document and answers questions as needed.
	Informed	All participants, Center of Excellence (CoE).

Table 4.4   Ideation Solution Architecture Control Gate (continued)

Section	Contains	Definition
Artifacts to be made	The input that is required	Architecture solution document available.
	What opinions to be sought	The solution designer, solution architect, infrastructure designer, and the requirements analyst must validate the architecture solution document as meeting the needs of the next steps of the development lifecycle. That is, they have the information they need to do a good job, and the high-level design is understood.
Key review criteria	Highlights the key criteria	The architecture solution document must comply with architectural standards, policies, and patterns. The architecture solution document conforms to existing application future views where those views exist. The architecture solution document highlights key infrastructure impacts and requirements. Have services been identified and classified, and are they at the correct level of granularity (services litmus tests)?
Key work product acceptance criteria	Key acceptance criteria to be met for successful review of work product	Consistency and completeness of the high-level design must be followed. Any inconsistencies or gaps or opportunities for improvement or rework of the high-level design must be specified. Record next steps, work assigned, and schedule agreed. Any follow up agreed.
Checklist	Sets a suggested process for the review. Provides objective support for recommendations, rework requests, and signoffs.	Follow the architecture solution document checklist.
Escalation process	Name of escalation process to be used to request an exception to the control gate result	Exceptions to demands for rework can be approved by the ARB. Where the issue is a dispute on service identification, the ARB shall send that issue to the CoE for resolution.

Section	Contains	Definition
Measurements	Metrics to be captured during or at the end of this control gate	Governance metrics on this gate, including incrementing the number of times this gate has been implemented, incrementing the number of times this lead architect has been through this gate, and the results (pass, fail, pass with conditions), and the checklist score
Outcomes	Who is responsible for final signoff, who gets notified, and who are the results delivered to?	Final signoff—ARB lead. Notification—All participants are notified and service registrar. Handoff—The PMO will be the official owner of the results.

Conclusion

> *"Every kind of peaceful cooperation among men is primarily based on mutual trust and only secondarily on institutions such as courts of justice and police"*
>
> —Albert Einstein

This chapter described a practical work-product approach to governing an efficient service factory—a software engineering-based approach to defining, developing, testing, deploying, and operating functional services and automated business processes.

The work-product approach helps to manage the complexity and interdependencies of the tasks involved, by introducing several intermediate deliverables, documenting the transitions between the various states of service and project lifecycles, and creating a set of control points to act as a governance mechanism to ensure that those deliverables have been constructed to the quality needed. Governance is enabled by formal or informal contracts between work-product creators and work-product consumers; such an arrangement enables early detection and resolution of any quality issues, instead of relying on the imposition of rigid centralized controls.

Our approach is not authoritarian—such an approach simply doesn't work in managing anything nearly as complex as migration to SOA. Instead, our approach uses work products and short, efficient control point reviews to act as a collaborative set of checks and balances to apply continuous feedback to improve the quality and completeness of the SOA assets that the enterprise deploys.

In Chapter 6, we revisit the service factory to look a little more closely at the how the production line operates, and how governance is applied to individual transitions in the life of each service or automated process.

5

Implementing the SOA Governance Model

"I don't need a dream. I have a plan."

–Spike Lee

Now that we have discussed the concept of a service factory and defined the details of the various SOA Governance capabilities, it is time to define the holistic governance model that those capabilities will fit into. Many SOA governance implementations start with the good intentions of governing and managing their SOA environment, but fall short in their execution. Some organizations think they can use their existing IT governance model without any modifications or additions to accomplish building an SOA governance model successfully. Generally, these efforts fail because of an initial lack of understanding that governing an SOA requires a different approach. The approach cannot be a rip-and-replace approach; the approach must address the differences SOA introduces.

We discussed the SOA differences in the previous chapters where we outlined the challenges that an SOA introduces. In this chapter, we present a method to construct a comprehensive plan to implement a governance model that will increase the likelihood of achieving the benefits SOA can provide.

This plan starts by identifying reusable elements of the existing IT governance model, prioritizing the elements that need to be added in each iteration, enabling this newly defined model, and measuring the successes, the shortcomings, and increased maturity of the evolving SOA so that the next iteration can mature the SOA governance model in step with the maturing business needs and goals. In this chapter, we lay out a plan and provide a sample work breakdown structure (WBS). Keep this in mind: "If we fail to plan, we plan to fail."

A Model for SOA Governance

"Give me six hours to chop down a tree and I will spend the first four sharpening the axe."

—Abraham Lincoln

The place to start in any complex task is to build a plan. IBM uses a four-phase structure to define the approach to establishing SOA governance, as shown in Figure 5.1. These phases are described in detail in the remainder of this chapter. Each phase is repeated cyclically, and each cycle provides an opportunity for improving the governance approach. This is an iterative and flexible approach, not necessarily a waterfall approach. It doesn't require you to start at task one and continue executing every task in sequence until you reach the end. You decide your priorities and do what makes sense for your business's circumstances during each iteration.

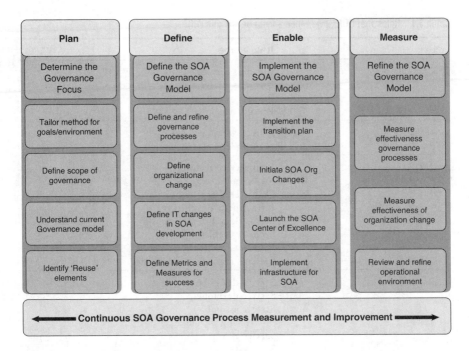

Figure 5.1   SOA Governance Lifecycle

SOA Governance Staffing

In Chapter 3, "Building the Service Factory," we discussed various roles that are relevant to the SOA Governance function. The primary determinant of the staffing for an implementation is the scope that has been defined and agreed to. Depending on that scope, some combination of the roles defined previously, as well as standard IT staffing, will combine to create roles that are relevant for SOA Governance staffing decisions. Those roles identified in Table 5.1 would be used to conduct the engagement. These roles can be in one organizational structure like a Center of Excellence (CoE) or like structure or spread and matrixed back to the CoE.

Table 5.1   Roles That SOA Governance Should Be Working With

Area	Role Name
Business	Business service champion Business analyst Process modelers Process developers
Governance	SOA governance lead SOA governance specialists
Architecture	Lead service architect Service architect Data architect Infrastructure architect Network architect Security architect Solution architect Systems management architect
Technical team	Service designer Service developer Service assembler Monitoring developer Service tester Service registrar
Project management	Program/project manager

These combined roles represent the *SOA governance team*, which performs the tasks and activities described in this chapter. The roles defined here are for illustration purposes, and the names for these roles may differ from organization to organization. Each engagement is unique, and the staffing will vary based on the defined scope. These are roles, not jobs done by a single individual. In addition, with an implementation as complex as SOA governance, it is important to have expert resources that have solid experience in both SOA and SOA governance.

SOA Governance Implementation Timeline

The time required to complete an SOA governance implementation is directly related to the scope of the project and the number of skilled resources that can be deployed. The timeline for the project will be proportional to the number of SOA processes to be governed and capabilities that are in scope for this iteration and level of governance maturity of the organization.

In addition, the development and deployment of an SOA CoE or the selection and deployment of SOA governance tools should have a measurable impact on the project scope, level of effort, and timeline. Let's walk through the activities and tasked needs to build an SOA governance model end to end.

The Plan Phase

"A dream doesn't become reality through magic; it takes sweat, determination and hard work."

—Colin Powell

The plan phase, as shown in Figure 5.2, starts the construction of an SOA Governance Model. In the plan phase, we will understand the current governance model and maturity, the existing organizational structure, and the tools used. We will prepare the team involved with building the new model and set expectations for what we will do and how we will do it. We will look for reusable elements of the exiting governance model and repurpose them for our new SOA Governance Model.

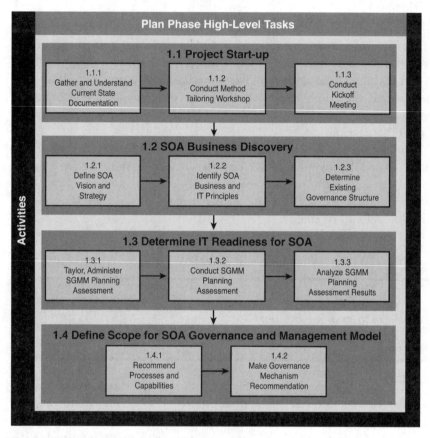

Figure 5.2   The Plan Phase

Activity 1.1: Project Startup

Project startup activities are the activities that help the enablement team get familiar with the existing environment, the future vision, and the ability of the organization to change. During this activity, the SOA governance team will

- Gather artifacts about the existing environment
- Develop questionnaires to gain additional undocumented information
- Prepare and schedule a kick off meeting with the key stakeholders

Task 1.1.1: Gather and Understand Current State Documentation

The purpose of gathering and understanding current state documentation is to collect artifacts about the existing environment from a governance, organizational, business, and operational perspective.

A number of useful artifacts will probably already exist when the SOA architect or consultant starts work. These can come from an existing enterprise architecture or process documentation effort. These existing artifacts are used by the SOA governance team to get a base understanding of the "as-is" environment from an architectural, cultural, policy, organizational, goal, business, and IT governance perspective.

When gathering and understanding the current state of documentation, follow these steps:

1. Prepare a list of documents needed from the organization. Use the list described below in the "Work Product" section as a template.
2. Send a request to the organization for the documents. This request should include the following:
   - A description of why the documents are needed
   - What the SOA governance team hopes to accomplish with them
   - A request for SMEs to address follow-up questions about the documents

The work products and documents that result from these steps include the following:

- Business vision
- SOA vision
- SOA reference architecture
- Current organizational description
- Current organization
- Job roles: responsibilities and competencies
- Operational model
- Current IT environment (from an organizational perspective)
- Application functional model
- Enterprise technology framework

- Principles, policies, and guidelines
- Standards
- Architecture metrics
- Business goals and drivers
- Business context
- Business direction
- Service usage data (if any)
- Service ownership and funding model (if any)
- Business service model (if any)
- IT governance documentation

Task 1.1.2: Conduct a Method-Tailoring Workshop

The purpose of the method-tailoring workshop is to gain consensus on the SOA governance approach to meet the solution design, delivery, and operational requirements. It provides the framework, process, and tools to enable the SOA governance team to select the required tasks from all the tasks and work products available in the SOA governance and management methodology and establish the WBS to meet the requirements of the project. The governance planning workshop approach educates the entire SOA enablement team and other stakeholders involved with the project.

When conducting a governance planning workshop, follow these steps:

1. Present the workshop overview, including objectives and expected results.
2. Review the scope and expectations.
3. Tailor the SOA governance approach.
4. Revise the project plan.

Work products that result from these steps include the following:

- The project plan (input)
- The project plan (output)

Task 1.1.3: Conduct a Kickoff Meeting

The kickoff meeting is used to verify the project scope, verify deliverables, identify the key stakeholders, orient the SOA enablement team, and set expectations with all involved. The meeting is conducted with the SOA enablement team and key stakeholders to develop an understanding of the project domain, scope, deliverables, stakeholders, and their associated organizations.

When conducting a kickoff meeting, follow these steps:

1. Identify key governance stakeholders.
2. Define and verify delivery signoff criteria.
3. Present the plan and verify the project schedule.
4. Agree to and verify the deliverables.
5. Identify and schedule interviews.
6. Plan and schedule workshops.

The work products that result from these steps include the following:

- The interview guide template
- Interview guides

Activity 1.2: SOA Business Discovery

The SOA business discovery activity helps the SOA governance team understand where the organization is in relation to service orientation. During this activity, the SOA governance team will

- Understand the existing governance structure
- Understand how decisions are made today
- Understand the existing SOA business principles
- Determine the organization's existing governance baseline and maturity level

Task 1.2.1: Define SOA Vision and Strategy

This task is used to help an organization formulate a complete SOA strategy, and high-level roadmap to transform organization and systems toward a service-oriented model. Define the SOA vision and strategy if it hasn't been done already.

When defining an SOA vision and strategy, follow these steps:

1. Define guiding principles for SOA strategy formulation and execution.
2. Review business and technology trends.
3. Derive opportunities from business and technology drivers.
4. Develop a vision of SOA.
5. Identify potential benefits from SOA.
6. Establish an SOA vision.

The work products that result from these steps include the following:

- SOA vision and strategy

Task 1.2.2: Identify SOA Business and IT Principles

Business principles are the underlying construct that ensures IT aligns with business. It is essential for the success of an SOA initiative that the alignment of business and IT exists. This task looks at existing documented business principles and determines if there are additional business principles that need to be formulated to properly implement an SOA.

When identifying SOA business principles, follow these steps:

1. Interview key decision makers.
2. Document business and IT principles and policies.

The work products that will result from these steps include the following:

- Principles, policies, and guidelines (input)
- Principles, policies, and guidelines (output)

Task 1.2.3: Determine Existing Governance Structure

This task will document the organization's existing IT governance environment. It determines which individuals or groups are empowered with decision rights and the extent of those rights. A governance decision path workshop is conducted whose purpose is to engender discussion around the organization's current decision paths and discover other existing governance processes, mechanisms, and capabilities. The workshop is meant to highlight the as-is processes.

When determining the existing governance structure, use these inputs and create these outputs:

Input

- Current IT assessment
- Current organizational assessment
- Process identification
- Process definition

Output

- Architecture management framework
- IT architecture review and assessment
- Principles, policies, and guidelines
- Architecture metrics

Activity 1.3: Determine IT Governance Environment Readiness

Determining the readiness of the existing IT governance environment's ability to support the new SOA environment is a critical task that will have an impact throughout the implementation of the SOA Governance Model. During this activity, the engagement team will

- Measure governance capabilities using the SOA governance planning assessment
- Define and conduct the change readiness survey

Task 1.3.1: Tailor the SOA Governance Planning Assessment

Several international organizations have defined techniques to determine governance capability. This task uses the SOA governance planning assessment (see Chapter 2, "SOA Governance Assessment and Planning") to create a plan to improve upon some of the existing IT governance capabilities required for effective SOA governance.

When tailoring your SOA governance assessment, follow these steps:

1. Prepare the SOA governance planning assessment.
2. Select the appropriate participants for the assessment.

The work products that will result include the following:

- SOA governance planning assessment questionnaire (input)
- List of participants (output)

Task 1.3.2: Conduct the SOA Governance Planning Assessment

During this task, the SOA governance planning assessment that has been prepared in the previous task is distributed to the selected participants with instructions on its use. This can be done with a number of participants in a workshop or individually.

When conducting your SOA governance assessment, follow these steps:

1. Determine an assessment deployment method.
2. Conduct the assessment.

The work products that will result from these steps include the following:

- SOA governance planning assessment questionnaire (input)
- Completed SOA governance planning assessment questionnaire (output)

Task 1.3.3: Analyze Planning Assessment Results

After tailoring and administering the SOA governance planning assessment, the results are collected and analyzed. The analysis will help determine the additional SOA governance capabilities needed and their priorities.

When analyzing planning assessment results, follow these steps:

1. Collect the results from the assessment participants.
2. Review the results and score them.
3. Using the scores and results determine capability gaps.

Work products that will result from these steps include the following:

- SOA governance planning assessment questionnaire (input)
- A list of needed SOA governance capabilities (output)

Activity 1.4: Define Scope of SOA Governance and Management Model

The plan phase will update the activities and tasks that need to be completed in the define phase and will make recommendations concerning the set of governance processes that should be addressed in this governance iteration, processes to be governed, and SOA governance capabilities. In addition, SOA governance mechanisms that will be used in the SOA Governance Model will be selected. During this activity, the SOA governance team will

- Evaluate the current set of governance processes and recommend which processes should be defined or modified and implemented for this iteration
- Taking input from the SOA governance planning assessment, recommend which SOA governance capabilities should be defined or modified and for this iteration
- Evaluate the current set of governed processes and recommend which processes should be defined or modified and implemented for this iteration

■ Evaluate the usability of existing governance mechanisms and recommend changes or the establishment of a dedicated SOA CoE or similar organization

■ Update the define phase plan based on the recommendations and associated decisions

Task 1.4.1: Recommend Processes and Capabilities

This task is an essential element of the transition from the plan phase to the define phase and largely defines the scope of the define phase. After the analysis conducted in the previous tasks has been completed, the planning team will make recommendations to implement processes, capabilities, and mechanisms in the following areas.

To identify governance processes, processes to be governed, and SOA governance capabilities, follow these steps:

1. Conduct a workshop with the organization to discuss the recommended governance processes, processes to be governed and SOA governance capabilities for each iteration of the governance lifecycle and prioritize the order of development.
2. Define the level of effort (LoE) associated with the recommendations.

The work products that will develop from these steps include the following:

■ SOA processes to be governed (input)
■ Project plan (output)

Any governance process being defined must take into account four key process components, as described in Table 5.2:

Table 5.2 Governance Process Components and Description

Process Component	Governance Process Description
Compliance	Provides a mechanism for review and approval/rejects against the criteria established in the governance framework (that is, principles, standards, roles, responsibilities, and so on). This process can be performed at various points during the lifecycle.
Vitality	As documented in Chapter 1, "Introduction to Governance," and Chapter 7, "Governance Vitality," this maintains the applicability of the governance framework. It requires the governance framework to be current, reflecting the business and IT direction and strategy. It must also refine the governance processes and mechanisms composed of organizational entities and supporting roles to ensure ongoing usage and relevance to an implementation.
Exceptions and appeals	Allows a project to appeal noncompliance to established processes as defined within the governance framework, such as service funding, service ownership, service identification, and so on, and be granted an exception.
Communications	Aimed at educating and communicating the governance model across the organization. It includes ensuring that governance is acknowledged and understood and setting up environments and tools to allow easy access and use of the governance information.

The actual processes to be governed will need to be identified by the governance team. For example, for an end-to-end services development lifecycle (SDLC), the following processes should be considered by the governance team:

- SOA strategy
- Service funding and ownership
- Service architecture
- Service modeling
- Service design
- Service assembly
- Service testing
- Service deployment
- Service delivery

- Event management and service monitoring
- Security management
- Service support

For an enterprise service bus (ESB) lifecycle, the following processes should be considered by the governance team:

- Service opportunity identification
- Service discovery
- Service inception
- Service elaboration
- Service construction
- Service transition
- Manage services

Task 1.4.2: Make Governance Mechanism Recommendations

This task is designed to assist in the selection of the appropriate governance mechanism for the organization. If the client has a robust IT governance environment in place, usually accompanied by a fully formed enterprise architecture, the organization may choose to modify those existing mechanisms for an SOA. Many organizations, however, are inclined to launch and manage their SOA efforts around a CoE or equivalent type of organization. A CoE can provide a comprehensive approach to the establishment of the SOA and avoid the politics and complexities of existing mechanisms. Success rates are much higher with a CoE or similar organization mechanism.

When making governance mechanism recommendations, follow these steps:

1. Conduct a workshop with the organization to select the appropriate governance mechanisms for the organization.
2. Define the LoE associated with the chosen mechanisms.

Work products that will result from these steps include the following:
Input

- SOA Governance Model
- Project plan

Output

- SOA Governance Model—updated
- Project plan—updated

The Define Phase

"What is the quality of your intent?"

–Thurgood Marshall

In the define phase, as shown in Figure 5.3, the enablement team will execute a set of activities to build the new SOA Governance Model for the organization. This phase will take input from information discovered and understood about the organizations existing environment, principles, policies, procedures, goals, and vision in the plan phase. This phase will then start to build the processes, capabilities, and mechanisms recommended. Modifications are made to the identified reusable governance assets, and where necessary additions are put in place to support SOA. Plans for implementing and the ongoing operation of the governance model are defined, as is the mechanism to implement and support SOA.

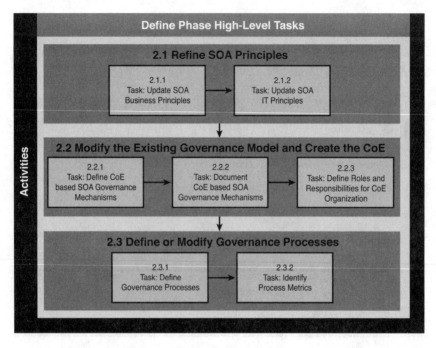

Figure 5.3   The Define Phase

Activity 2.1: Refine SOA Principles

Using the principles and standards reviewed and understood in the plan phase, make the necessary modifications that will enable alignment with the businesses SOA vision.

Task 2.1.1: Update SOA Business Principles

Business principles are the underlying construct that ensures IT aligns with business. This task looks at existing documented business principles and determines whether additional business principles need to be formulated to properly implement an SOA.

When updating SOA business principles, follow these steps:

1. Identify new business principles required for SOA.
2. Analyze, consolidate, and document the results.

Work products that will result from these steps include the following:

- Principles, policies, and guidelines (input)
- Principles, policies, and guidelines (output)

Task 2.1.2: Update SOA IT Principles

This activity enables the SOA enablement team to document the new or modified SOA IT principles. Updating and documenting new or modified SOA principles are essential steps in constructing SOA governance processes and mechanisms. The SOA principles are the basis for determining how well services are satisfying their objectives and whether the services are compliant with the SOA environment.

When updating SOA IT principles, follow these steps:

1. Create a starter set of IT principles for SOA.
2. Adapt the organization's IT principles to SOA.
3. Adapt an organization's system development lifecycle for SOA.
4. Adapt an organization's operational standards.

Work products that will result from these steps include the following:

- Principles, policies, and guidelines (input)
- Principles, policies, and guidelines (output)

Activity 2.2: Modify the Existing Governance Organizational Model and Create the SOA CoE

Our experience has been that establishing a dedicated SOA CoE is one of the most important organizational changes the governance planning team can make. It greatly increases the likelihood of a successful SOA governance and SOA implementation. It is an extremely valuable mechanism to ensure the ongoing success and continued maturity of SOA in any organization. In many of the organizations for which we have implemented SOA governance, the SOA enablement team was set up first and then drove all other SOA activities. As an organization continues to mature and improve their SOA, the SOA CoE will be at the center of the ongoing day-to-day operation and growth.

Task 2.2.1 Define CoE-based SOA Governance Mechanisms

SOA governance mechanisms are used to execute the governance of SOAs. This task identifies the mechanisms that need to be changed and updated for the SOA. SOA governance mechanisms are performed by members of both the IT and business communities. These mechanisms are the vehicles in which business and IT communicate and interact and in which decision rights are vested. It is not necessary to create an entirely new set of mechanisms for SOA governance. In many cases, existing mechanisms can easily be tailored to encompass the disciplines necessary for SOA.

The definition and implementation of these mechanisms may have significant political impact.

When modifying and defining the enablement team SOA governance mechanisms, follow these steps:

1. Define the SOA CoE mission and vision.
2. Review the SOA governance planning assessment to understand effectiveness of governance mechanisms.
3. Identify reusable mechanisms and required updates or build them.
4. Identify the scope of the chosen mechanisms.
5. Develop the CoE Organizational Model.

Work products that will result from these steps include the following:

Input
- Existing organizational structure
- SOA governance planning assessment

Output
- SOA governance plan (updated)
- Future organizational design

Task 2.2.2 Document SOA CoE Governance Mechanisms

This task documents changes made to the governance mechanisms and then elaborates upon them to complete the documentation required.

When documenting SOA CoE governance mechanisms, follow these steps:

1. Document governance mechanisms (SOA steering committee, SOA board, business/IT portfolio management board, IT councils, architecture working groups, architecture review board, and so on).
2. Update and complete documentation of the mechanisms, their descriptions and responsibilities.
3. Document CoE processes and metrics.

Work products that will result from these steps include the following:

Input
- Current organizational structure
- SOA governance planning assessment

Output
- Job roles: responsibilities and competencies
- Process definition, process metrics

Task 2.2.3 Define New Roles and Responsibilities for the CoE Organization

This step involves defining the basic roles and responsibilities and the associated organizational model to support SOA governance.

When defining new roles and responsibilities for the CoE organization, follow these steps:

1. Define roles and responsibilities to support updated mechanisms. Use a chart that documents the following for the mechanisms: responsible, accountable, consult, inform (RACI).
2. Identify new roles.
3. Define new responsibilities.
4. Define skills required for new roles.
5. Identify skill gaps.
6. Identify mentoring requirements.
7. Update the RACI matrix.

Work products that will result from these steps include the following:

Input

- Current organizational structure
- Current organizational description

Output

- Future organizational design
- Job roles: responsibilities and competencies RACI chart

Activity 2.3 Define or Modify Governance Processes

In these sets of tasks, we define the governance processes and the metrics that will measure their effectiveness.

Task 2.3.1 Define or Modify Governance Processes

This task is used to modify existing governance processes associated with the governance of an SOA. A major aspect of the project is the definition/modification of the governance processes that will be used to establish and maintain effective SOA governance. These governance processes need to be integrated into the existing software development lifecycle (SDLC) from a development perspective. Using the four governance processes that are listed and briefly described here as a guide, develop/update the process models to establish SOA governance. The governance processes were introduced in Chapter 1. They are inserted here in the task where they will be built.

When defining or modifying governance processes, follow these steps:

1. Conduct a workshop to define/modify governance processes.
2. Create and modify governance process diagrams: Level 0, 1, 2.
3. Update the organizational design with any new or changed mechanisms that are required for these processes.
4. Identify or modify the policy checkpoints within the process definition.
5. Develop the high-level RACI for each process and role description.

Work products that will result from these steps include the following:

Input
- Existing governance model
- SDLC

Output
- Updated governance processes model
- Updated SDLC
- RACI matrices
- Process metrics

Task 2.3.2 Identify Governance Process Metrics

Proper governance requires measurement, so that mechanisms can be assessed and improved. This task reviews the key performance indicators (KPIs) for SOA adoption and determines the measurements required. It also looks at the objectives for the processes adopted and determines the metrics required to facilitate process improvement.

This task is closely tied to what we want to measure as a result of the development or modification of the processes.

When identifying governance metrics, follow these steps:

1. Review the goals and objectives and SOA KPIs.
2. Define metrics for each business goal.

Work products that will result from these steps include the following:

Input
- Existing governance model
- SOA vision

Output
- Process metrics

The next set of activities and task completes the define phase, as shown in Figure 5.4.

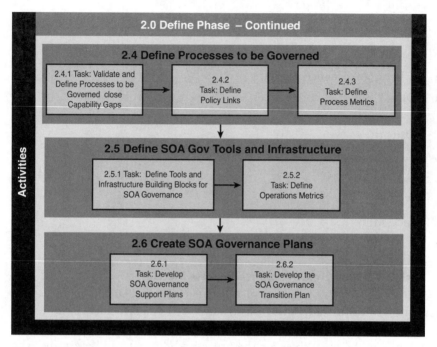

Figure 5.4   Define Phase 2

Activity 2.4: Define Processes to Be Governed and Close SOA Governance Capability Gaps

The definition of processes to be governed is key to defining and developing an SOA governance model. These processes form one of the most important elements of an SOA environment. The processes will define how the SOA environment will be governed and managed. As they are defined, metrics must be identified, and metric collections points must be inserted into each process. This is also true of policies. Policies, defined in another task, will be evaluated within each process. To that end, policy enforcement points need to be identified and inserted into each of the processes. Processes to be governed then need to be integrated with governance processes and the SDLC to achieve end-to-end control over the complete SOA lifecycle. The definition of the processes will determine which tools to use and how to use them. So, the importance of these processes cannot be underestimated.

Task 2.4.1: Validate and Define Processes to be Governed, Close Governance Capability Gaps

During this task's set of activities, the governance capabilities identified and prioritized in the plan phase will be developed and included in the SOA Governance Model.

Use and create these work products:

Input

- SOA governance planning assessment
- Prioritized governance capabilities list

Output

- Governance capabilities document

This task is used to modify existing business and IT processes and to identify the new processes associated with the governance of an SOA. A major aspect of the project is the definition/modification of the business and IT processes that will be used to establish and maintain effective SOA governance. The defined process models will be used to establish the SOA Governance Model, control gates, policy enforcement points, roles and responsibilities, standards, procedures and the metrics required to measure progress. See Chapter 1 for the list and descriptions of the processes to be governed.

The steps for validating and defining governed processes are as follows:

1. Select and prioritize the appropriate processes based on the project scope.
2. Conduct a workshop to define or modify governed processes.
3. Create and modify process diagrams (Level 0, 1, and 2).
4. Insert the appropriate steps for compliance, vitality, exceptions and appeals, and communications into each of the governed processes.
5. Identify or modify the policy check points within the process definition.
6. Develop the high-level RACI for each process and role description.

The work products that will result from these steps include the following:

- Business process model (input)
- Business process model (output)
- RACI matrices organizational design

Task 2.4.2: Define Policy Links

This task will define the policies that will be evaluated within each of the processes to be governed. It is key to define these policies so that we can determine whether the SOA governance model is adhering to its mission and goal.

The steps for defining policy links are as follows:

1. Conduct a workshop to insert policy links into governed processes.
2. Define the policy and evaluation steps for each policy in each governed process.
3. Update and verify the RACI for each policy.

The work products that will result from these steps include the following:

Input
- Process models
- RACI matrices

Output
- Process models
- RACI matrices

Task 2.4.3: Define Process Metrics

Proper governance requires measurement, so that mechanisms can be assessed and improved. This task reviews the KPIs for SOA adoption and determines the measurements required. It also looks at the objectives for the processes adopted and determines the metrics required to facilitate process improvement.

When defining process metrics, follow these steps:

1. Define metrics to assess the state of the KPIs.
2. Define metrics to assess the attainment of objectives for updated processes.
3. Define collection and analysis of measurements.

Work products that will result from this step include the following:

- Process models (input)
- Process metrics definition (output)

Activity 2.5: Define SOA Governance Infrastructure and Tools

In this activity, the SOA governance team working with information gathered during the plan phase will outline and suggest a set of tools that will be used to support the SOA Governance Model. These tools must fit with the existing architecture, and they must adhere to the standards and principles defined or modified earlier.

Task 2.5.1: Define Tools and Infrastructure Building Blocks for SOA Governance

The purpose of these steps is to determine which changes must be made in the organization's existing infrastructure to support the services lifecycle. The infrastructure provides full lifecycle support during service enablement, publishing, discovery, and management.

The steps to follow when defining the SOA governance infrastructure building blocks are as follows:

1. Determine what infrastructure components should be added to what exists in the environment today.
2. Plan implementation of the infrastructure to sustain the governance framework defined.
3. Document the process and findings in the key decision record.

The work products resulting from these steps include the following:

Input

■ Technology blueprint

■ Operational model

Output

■ Technology blueprint

■ Operational model

In addition, the governance practioner must determine what changes must be made in the client's organization's tool set to support SOA governance.

To define the tools for SOA governance, follow these steps:

1. Categorize the tools (such as registry, repository, portal, and so on).
2. Determine what standard products have already been shortlisted or are part of the enterprise architecture.
3. Refine the SOA governance tools shortlist.
4. Perform tool evaluation on the tools selected from the organization shortlist.
5. Determine which, if any, new tools should be added to what exists in the environment today.

The work products resulting from these steps include the following:

Input

■ Technology blueprint

■ Operational model

■ SOA development tools

Output

■ Operational model

■ SOA development tools

Task 2.5.2: Define Operations Metrics

Proper governance requires measurement, so that mechanisms, including tools and the associated infrastructure, can be assessed and improved. This task identifies the key metrics and measurements for infrastructure operations.

Follow these steps to define the tools for SOA governance:

1. Define metrics to support the SOA vision.
2. Define metrics to support service effectiveness.

The work products resulting from these steps include the following:

Input

- Operational goals
- Nonfunctional requirements

Output

- QoS monitoring plan
- SLA monitoring plan
- Service operational vitality report

Activity 2.6: Create SOA Governance Plans

During this activity, the governance plans will be created for implementation throughout each iteration of the SOA Governance Model.

Task 2.6.1: Develop SOA Governance Support Plans

In this step, the following plans are developed:

- **Communication plan.** This work product was defined in Chapter 3. This communication plan might include a self-service repository of information that can be accessed by consumers and developers of the services in the SOA. Usually, the communication plan's first iteration is created in the first few tasks of the plan phase as a means to communicate the ongoing development of the SOA governance effort, and it is updated here at the end of the define phase.

- **Mentoring plan.** This plan will outline how the CoE or boards with like responsibilities will assist consumers and developers of the services. It can be considered as part of the education and training plan.
- **Education and training plan.** This plan will describe the training and education that will be made available to help the consumers and developers of services successfully adopt SOA.

The steps to develop these plans are needed to implement the SOA Governance Model, but they will be continually modified and updated to reflect new initiatives and changes in the SOA. They are as follows:

1. Develop the SOA governance communications plan, which involves defining communication standards, identifying delivery channels, identifying an audience, and developing content.
2. Develop the SOA governance education plan, which involves defining education requirements, identifying delivery mechanisms, identifying an audience, and identifying content.
3. Develop the SOA governance mentoring plan, which involves defining mentoring requirements, identifying an audience, identifying mentors, and identifying a program structure.

The work products resulting from this task include the following:

Input
- SOA governance plan
- SOA development approach

Output
- Communications plan
- SOA education plan

Task 2.6.2: Develop the SOA Governance Transition Plan

The SOA transition plan provides a roadmap to implement SOA governance. It is the plan that will be used to create a WBS and a detailed project plan. This plan outlines and prioritizes the activities and tasks that will be executed. It is also a document that will be modified and updated during the life of the engagement and beyond depending on the scope of the organization's SOA vision.

Usually, the transition plan's first iteration is developed at the end of the plan phase and continually updated as the implementation continues. The steps for developing the SOA governance transition plan are as follows:

1. Define SOA governance transition steps.
2. Determine initiatives that further the business and corresponding IT goals.
3. Document each initiative required as part of the transition plan.

The work products resulting from this task include the following:

- Transition plan from plan phase, if available (input)
- Integrated transition plan (output)

Enable Phase

> *"At a time like this, scorching iron, not convincing argument, is needed."*
>
> —Frederick Douglas

During the enable phase, the defined solution is rolled out to the organization. Roles are assigned, staff are trained, the decision rights may be automated in workflow tools, and the metrics collection and reporting mechanisms are put in place. Figure 5.5 displays the activities and tasks of this phase of the enable phase.

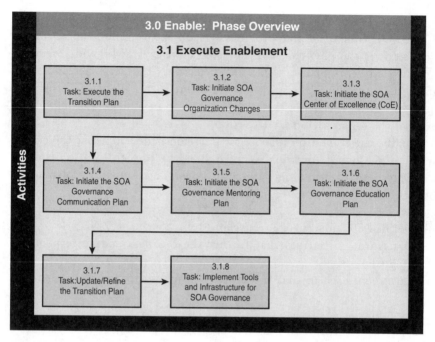

Figure 5.5   Enable Phase

Task 3.1: Execute Enable

Now that we have planned and defined the SOA Governance, it is time to implement. These tasks will walk us through the salient governance features and initiate the governance capabilities that have been approved.

Task 3.1.1: Execute the Transition Plan

In this task, we just execute the transition plan. The plan serves as the vehicle for the enablement team to marshal the resources and develop a WBS.

The steps for executing the transition plan are as follows:

1. Develop a resource plan which identifies the types of skills needed.
2. Develop a project plan that details the execution of the SOA governance project.
3. Identify resources to meet the skills needed and complete the team. This would include internal resources and resources from a service provider.

4. Develop kickoff meeting presentation material used to inform the initial SOA enablement team members and other stakeholders and initiate the enable phase. Also, review the material with key project members and stakeholders.

5. Schedule the kickoff meeting. Invite the enablement team and the stakeholders.

6. Conduct the transition kickoff meeting and deliver the presentation and other materials. Statements from key stakeholders about their objectives are desirable. Content from the following initiation tasks should also be included as part of the kickoff:

- Organizational change
- SOA enablement team
- Education and training
- Mentoring
- Communication

The work products resulting from this task include the following:

- Project plans (input)
- Project plans with resource plans (output)

Task 3.1.2: Initiate the SOA Center of Excellence (CoE)

This task will put the SOA Center of Excellence in place for the organization. The steps for incorporating governance mechanisms and the SOA CoE are as follows:

1. Create the CoE implementation plan and link to the overall project plan. This plan includes

- WBS detailing the steps needed to instantiate the CoE.
- Identification and assignment of resources with appropriate skills. These skills may be available through internal sources, or may have to be acquired from a service provider.
- Ensure that the requirements of the communication plan are represented in the WBS. This includes all project and stakeholder meetings.

2. Develop presentation material for the transition kickoff meeting. This material is intended to familiarize all team members and stakeholders on the key elements of the CoE and the tasks, schedule, and critical success factors to instantiate the CoE. Review this material with key SOA enablement team members and stakeholders.

3. Review the kickoff material with the SOA enablement team and essential stakeholders.

4. Deliver presentation material in a transition kickoff meeting.

5. Review and modify if needed the CoE mission statement developed in the define phase.

6. Review the organizational model developed in the define phase and modify if needed.

7. Assign the mechanisms to the resources.

8. Assign the processes and procedures to the mechanisms and resources.

9. Implement the mechanisms and processes.

10. Ensure the following plans, processes, and activities are assigned and initiated:
    - Education
    - Mentoring

11. Assign responsibility for and populate the documentation repository.

12. Initiate any mentoring roles that will be performed by outside organizations, by pairing the external resources with resources within the organization. (This is not necessarily a one-to one mapping.)

13. Update the following documents as necessary:
    - Mentoring plan
    - Procedures documentation
    - Architecture management or architecture management framework

Input

- Mission statement
- Future organizational design
- Process definition

Output

- Future organizational design
- Mentoring plan
- Architecture management framework
- Process definition
- Project plan

Task 3.1.4: Initiate the SOA Governance Education Plan

The initiation of the education plan will start the education of the organization involved with SOA. The steps for initiating the SOA governance education plan are as follows:

1. Review the education plan developed in the define phase. Modify the plan if needed.
2. Develop presentation material to include with the transition kickoff session that describes the education plan. The kickoff will be performed as part of the task to execute the transition plan.

The work products that result from these steps include the following:

- Education and training strategy (input)
- SOA education plan (output)

Task 3.1.5: Initiate the SOA Governance Mentoring Plan

This task will describe how the mentoring plan will be executed with the SOA initiative and start the process of mentoring the organization.

The steps for initiating the SOA governance mentoring plan are as follows:

1. Review the mentoring plan developed in the define phase. Modify the plan if needed.
2. Assign mentoring responsibilities to resources. Use the resources from the SOA CoE or from other SOA SMEs. These recourses can be assigned to individual projects or subject areas.
3. Develop presentation material to include with the transition kickoff session that describes the mentoring role and present it. The kickoff will be performed as part of the task to execute the transition plan.

The work products that result from these steps include the following:

- SOA education plan (input)
- SOA education plan, including mentoring plan (output)
- Presentation material

Task 3.1.6: Initiate the SOA Governance Communication Plan

This task initiates the communication plan that has been built for the project.

The steps for initiating the SOA governance communication plan are as follows:

1. Review the communication plan developed in the define phase. Modify the plan if needed. Ensure all required tasks are included in the overall project plans.
2. Present the communication plan during the transition kickoff meeting.

The work products that result from these steps include the following:

- Communication plan (input)
- Communication plan (output)

Task 3.1.7: Update/Refine the Transition Plan

The purpose of this task is to continually update the plan and keep it fresh. The plan should be updated to reflect new initiatives and approaches.

The steps for updating and refining the transition plan are as follows:

1. Monitor the transition processes that worked well and the ones that did not.
2. Document interim lessons learned. (Project lessons learned are traditionally harvested at project close.)
3. Review with the key team members and update the plan as necessary.

The work products that result from these steps include the following:

- Integrated transition plan (input)
- Integrated transition plan (output)

Task 3.1.8: Implement Tools and Infrastructure for SOA Governance

Steps for tools and infrastructure implementation needed to support SOA governance are as follows:

1. Review the key decision records for tools created in the define phase. Update the key decision records if required.
2. Prepare the environment.
3. Secure software and hardware.
4. Verify licensing for software tools.
5. Secure infrastructure components.
6. Configure hardware and infrastructure components.
7. Install selected tools.
8. Test installation.
9. Populate tools.
10. Develop an access control list and/or criteria.
11. Provide access.

12. Ensure that the communication plan is used to disseminate knowledge of the tools. Ensure that the education and training plan has provisions for the tools if training is required.

The work products that result from these steps include the following:

Input
- Key decision records
- Current IT environment
- Product selection alternatives and recommendations
- IT standards

Output
- Communications plan

Measure Phase

"However beautiful the strategy, you should occasionally look at the results."

—Winston Churchill

The measure phase is continually being performed. It is where the metrics defined in the define phase get captured and reported. This phase is where the SOA stakeholders will determine whether the services and the governance model are being effective. The measure phase monitors how well the processes, policies, and mechanisms put in place are meeting the SOA's need. It is the improvement opportunity, to add, modify, or remove processes based on their performance.

Figure 5.6 displays the activities and task used to measure the effectiveness of the SOA Governance Model.

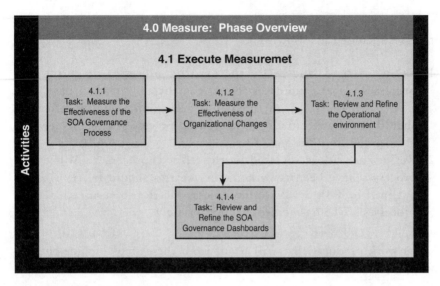

Figure 5.6   Measure Phase

Activity 4.1: Execute Measurement

In this activity, we execute measurement of the metrics developed in the define phase.

Task 4.1.1: Measure the Effectiveness of the SOA Governance Process

This task looks at the governance processes and may determine that

- Some processes are functioning:
    - Within bounds as currently defined and need no modifications.
    - Outside of the defined bounds and need to be refined.
- Some new processes have to be defined.
- Some processes are no longer required and can be retired.

The steps to measure the effectiveness of the SOA governance processes include the following:

1. Refine, extend, and retire the existing processes or define new processes. After candidates for refinement and creation have been identified, the steps outlined in process definition/modification should be followed to align the existing processes with the new target derived from the analysis.
2. Refine metrics associated with refined processes. When the processes have been reworked, the metrics should be revisited as outlined in Task 2.3.2 Define Process Metrics to ensure that these processes are being monitored appropriately.

The work products that will result from these steps include the following:

Input
- IT governance plan
- SOA governance plan (if any)

Output:
- SOA governance plan
- SOA governance vitality monitoring plan

Task 4.1.2: Measure the Effectiveness of Organizational Changes

Determine whether the defined roles and responsibilities are covering the necessary aspects of SOA governance and determine how well they are being performed. The steps to measure the effectiveness of organizational changes are as follows:

1. Assess effectiveness of SOA governance roles and responsibilities and make changes as needed.
2. Assess effectiveness of SOA governance mechanisms and make changes as needed.

The work products that will result from these steps include the following:

Input
- Process models
- Control point checklists

Output
- SOA governance plan (updated)
- SOA governance vitality monitoring plan
- Governance control point checklists

Task 4.1.3: Review and Refine the Operational Environment

To assess the effectiveness of the operational environment, gather metrics on the effectiveness of the SOA operational environment, and refine the environment as needed. The work products resulting from this task include the following:

Input
- Process definition
- Control gate checklist

Output
- Process definition
- Control gate checklist

Task 4.1.4: Review and Refine the SOA Governance Dashboards

Gather metrics on the effectiveness of the SOA governance dashboards and refine the environment as needed.

Case Study

> *"Organization can never be a substitute for initiative and for judgment."*
>
> —Louis Brandeis

After due consideration, Ideation leadership believes that it would have a better forum for initiative and judgment by implementing two new organizations. These include an SOA Center of Excellence (CoE) and an SOA executive review board (ERB). An architecture review board (ARB) already exists, but company leadership recognizes that the three groups will need to work with each other and that governance must define how.

Service Processes, Organizations, Roles, and Responsibilities

The first thing addressed is a mission statement for each of the two new organizations.

The CoE has the following mission statement:

The SOA Center of Excellence (CoE) is an IT cross-organizational team that has been established at Ideation to support and enable SOA governance and ensure the institutionalization of SOA. The CoE will specifically be responsible for the following:

- The CoE will be the implementation mechanism of SOA governance and is responsible for identifying and enabling the processes, standards, policies, mechanisms, and roles, and responsibilities for SOA governance.
- The CoE will work with the ARB to make sure that the necessary SOA patterns, policies, and standards are created, implemented, and maintained.
- The CoE will provide governance mechanisms and metrics for the quality review of SOA development, certification, and operations, and will validate that good governance is taking place with vitality.

- The CoE is the center of adoption, change, and vitality of the SOA architecture. The CoE will enable the communication and socialization of the CoE, SOA architecture, and architecture concepts as approved by the ARB.

- The CoE will identify the SOA skills gaps and training programs needed and will provide follow up to validate that training is successful and vital.

- The CoE will be a center of SOA skills and will consult on SOA projects and provide guidance on usage of SOA technologies.

- The CoE will provide an SOA registry/repository, and the CoE will manage the governance, control, and deployment of all operational services in the registry/repository.

- The CoE will ensure the project, architecture, and service assets are harvested and reused where appropriate.

The ERB has the following mission statement:

The SOA executive review board (ERB) is a linking mechanism that integrates business and IT with the appropriate stakeholders. Its purpose is to make key strategic and tactical decisions concerning the SOA journey and to investigate and resolve issues that require cross-organizational and business/IT decisions. It is a business and IT cross-organizational and cross line-of-business (LoB) team.

The ERB sets the direction and pace for services adoption and resolves or recommends solutions for exception requests, including business domain issues such as ownership, funding, and reuse policy. The board performs reviews of proposed investments to ensure commonality opportunities and reuse investments are considered.

- The ERB will resolve any issue needing resolution for an SOA project that involves a cross-organizational or cross-LoB issue. The ERB will do this in a timely fashion.

- The ERB will be the controlling organization for the strategic direction of creating business agility.

- The ERB will be the last review for any exception requests from an SOA program.

- The ERB will be the decision maker on all investments for the portion of the IT budget that is allocated for business agility.

- The ERB will be the primary communication mechanism for business agility and will work across both business and IT as necessary.

- The ERB will provide oversight and direction for the SOA Center of Excellence (CoE) and the architecture review board (ARB).

An organizational diagram was created that summarizes this arrangement in Figure 5.7.

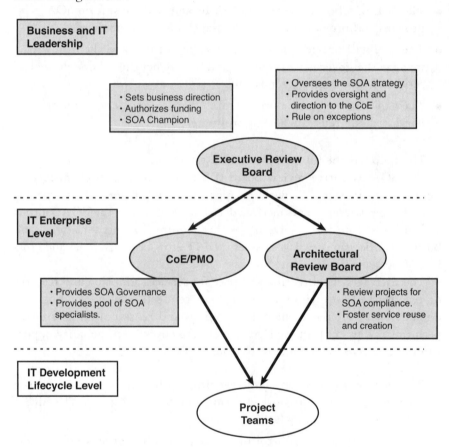

Figure 5.7   Ideation Organizational Chart for SOA Governance

Service Ownership and Funding

Almost immediately, an issue manifests itself that the ERB must resolve: SOA ownership and funding. All communication companies have a function called a rating, which provides for a specific price to be attached to a specific telecommunications transaction or set of transactions. As mentioned in the "Case Study" section of Chapter 3, ideation has a tactical business goal of creating a single rating function that spans all the LoBs. As Ideation has moved to offer more product bundling, the different pricing structures have led to a chaotic situation. In some cases, different pricing was available on the same service from a different sales group within the company. Consequently, one of the second-phase business agility projects is to create an SOA business service with the name Create Rating.

During the requirements phase, the service business analysts found that the different groups from the various LoBs would not cooperate. Information was withheld, meetings were missed, and it soon became clear that no amount of cajoling was going to get the team to a satisfactory solution.

The item was raised by the PMO via the CoE to the ERB. The business vice-president of operations, Gus Lee, is assigned to lead a group to address and resolve the requirements for this function. Gus has no direct involvement in rating, and was therefore considered a neutral business executive. In addition, Gus has an IT background from his time in the Army, and could work productively across business and IT. Gus selected one IT and one business colleague from the ERB, but also filled out his "tiger team" with an SME from an IT group that he believed would give him unbiased information.

Gus is busy running operations on a day-to-day basis, but he diligently holds meetings for one hour each day and made and followed up on assignments with his team. It soon became clear that this was not a technical or business issue, but a political one. The business director of each of the rating teams felt threatened by this business agility initiative, and based on past experience, thought that they could just wait out this passing storm and return to business as usual. Gus personally interviewed each of these leaders. His ERB colleagues on the tiger team were able to summarize statistics that showed that Ideation was losing about $50 million a year in revenue due to rating mistakes and another $100 million a year in opportunity cost due to an inability to respond to bundle-product pricing requests in a timely manner. The SME produced critical information about how each of the rating groups actually operated and how IT supported them with procedural code that was highly customized.

Gus assembled this information and then scheduled a meeting with the Ideation chief financial officer (CFO). The CFO pointed out that the $100 million "opportunity cost" was a soft number that he did not agree with, but the $50 million in lost revenue was well documented and could not be refuted. A week later, he called Gus into his office and told him that he was reorganizing all the rating groups into one organization immediately, and that David Croslin had been assigned to clean up the mess. Further, David had committed to providing timely requirements on the Create Rating service for the PMO and that he personally would review them and sign off.

The results were reported to the ERB at its next meeting, and the tiger team was duly terminated with a "job well done." The total time for the issue to be resolved was one month. The ERB had an SLA of three weeks for this type of issue, but it was agreed ahead of time that this was more complicated issue and the SLA would be relaxed by several weeks. Updates had been discussed at the weekly ERB meeting, and it was agreed that this pattern of issue resolution had worked well and should be repeated in the future.

Conclusion

In this chapter, we covered the activities and tasks needed to build an SOA Governance Model. Your implementation may vary depending on your scope and what's important for your organization at your level of maturity. Please see the documentation on this book's website (see Appendix B, "References") for a WBS that can be used to plan your implementation.

6

Managing the Service Lifecycle

"It's life, Captain, but not as we know it."

—Science Officer Spock

In Chapter 3, "Building the Service Factory," and Chapter 4, "Governing the Service Factory," we discussed the concept of setting up a production line for manufacturing and operating services. In Chapter 5, "Implementing the SOA Governance Model," we described the plan, define, enable, and measure flow to governance. This chapter adds additional detail on management of the services and automated processes as they progress along this production line. This will include giving insight into how the production line should work, so the governance specialist can then design their control points in an optimal manner. We also discuss service versioning and service granularity, because many organizations struggle with those topics.

Although we describe the stages of the service production line as a linear progression, the reality is that good service development practices use continuous feedback rather than a waterfall approach; each of the governance control points we discussed in Chapter 4 may send the service back for rework if errors, omissions, or additional requirements are found. In addition, the process of designing one service or modeling one process can uncover requirements for additional services or automated processes to be added to the service build plan.

It's a reasonable metaphor to treat software as if it were a kind of electronic life form, because software exhibits behavior remarkably similar to that of physical organisms. Some of the similarities include

- Life starts at conception.
- New individuals are hatched, budded, born, or delivered as infants.
- They grow, develop, and mature.
- They pass through adolescence into adulthood.
- They may have offspring of their own.
- They age, slow down, and gradually become less effective.
- Sometimes they get sick and need medical treatment.
- They retire or get replaced, and eventually die.

The *transitions* between states represent the key events in an organism's lifecycle—for example, *conception* is the transition from not living to living, *birth* is the transition from total dependence on a parent to the start of independence, and *death* is the final transition from living to not living. Among humans such lifecycle transitions often represent an occasion for a public ceremony or celebration to formally recognize the change in status.

The service factory consists essentially of a nursery of "production cells" in which specialists perform "'care and feeding" activities that develop services and transition them from one specific state to another specific state. The successful completion of each transition is monitored through a control point that validates that all the necessary conditions and approvals for that transition have been met. From a project management perspective, a best practice is to apply a principle from quantum mechanics, and assume that a task or work product can be in only one state at a given time; translation from any given state to a higher state requires the input of energy. It's a binary view—that is, a task is either *done* or *not done,* with no half measures allowed This approach may be mildly conservative but it's effective and avoids the problem of projects or tasks that remain at "90% complete" for years, long after their initial budgets have been exhausted.

There are seven distinct stages in the lifecycle of a service or automated process, each of which is governed by one of the control points described in Chapter 4. These stages are as follows:

- Requirements capture and service identification
- Solution architecture
- Service specification
- Service realization
- Service testing
- Service certification and deployment
- Service vitality

In Chapter 4, we described a set of control points to evaluate that services have successfully made the transition between each of these phases. Because this is a book about governance, not about service development, we describe the service lifecycle in terms of preparation for each of these control points.

Preparing for the Requirements Capture and Service Identification Control Point

> *"Can you build me a system that will tell me my requirements?"*
>
> —Scott Adams (Dilbert cartoon)

Although we propose a single control point to cover both the high-level requirements and the identification of candidate services that could implement them, we discuss requirements gathering and service identification separately.

Capturing Requirements "Top Down"

Obtaining good requirements is absolutely critical; without those, your SOA transformation is doomed to failure. *Top-down* analysis consists of capturing business requirements through the process of modeling the way the business works. The business heat map and services strategic blueprint work products described in Chapter 3 should help determine which business areas to focus on first. As we mentioned in Chapter 3, you will save yourself much work in the future if you maintain all your business requirements and rules in a searchable, enterprise-wide requirements and business rules catalog.

Remember that the end goal is to specify requirements in a sufficient level of detail that a developer can turn them into code. Ambiguity or a lack of precision is a recipe for disaster. The objective of this stage is to specify the business requirements in terms of well-defined processes and tasks:

Processes contain some elements of workflow and decision points. Executing a process typically takes minutes to days to complete. The structure of a typical process is:

1. Do the first step.
2. Then do the second step.
3. If the result is *x,* perform Step 3 and then go to Step 4; otherwise, go straight to Step 4.
4. Finish.

Tasks are fine-grained processes that can be performed in a single step by a single individual. A good means of distinguishing between tasks and processes is to ask the question, "I'm just about to pack up for the day, and I'm in the middle of something. If I can suspend it and complete it tomorrow, it's a process. If I have to complete it today or redo it from scratch tomorrow, it's a task."

Top-down business models should be expressed in terms of complete business processes, decomposed into subprocesses, sub-subprocesses and so on, until the leaf-level tasks have been defined. Generally, these leaf-level tasks are found around the third level of decomposition of a top-down business process model. Here's a simple example of process decomposition, describing making a purchase on the Internet:

First level (processes):

1. Buy something off the Internet.

Second level (subprocesses):

1. Search a product catalog.
2. Compare multiple items.
3. Add item to the shopping basket.
4. Check out.

Third level (tasks; in this case, tasks involved in the checkout subprocess):

1. Determine the total cost.
2. Establish a delivery address.
3. Select a payment method.
4. Authorize payment.
5. Confirm or reject purchase.
6. Notify the shipping department of the order.
7. Send an email to the customer to confirm payment.
8. Package the goods and ship them to the customer.

Tasks usually appear around the third level of decomposition, but occasionally a fourth or even a fifth level is necessary if the process is an especially complex one. Business rules that control this mechanism need to be clearly defined, and there are often subtleties that might not be immediately apparent. Even this simplest of business processes has more subtleties than may first be apparent. For example

- Many countries have rules that you must not take payment for any good unless you know that you will be able to deliver it within a certain time: hence the step Authorize Payment rather than Make Payment. The credit card company has guaranteed that it will reserve the required funds in the cardholder's account for a period to make that payment eventually (that is, when the goods leave the warehouse) but no actual funds have been transferred yet.

- In the United States, currently no state taxes are charged on purchases made from a state where the retailer does not have premises, and therefore if you purchase something from Amazon™, you only have to pay state taxes on that purchase if you live in the state of Washington.

Every industry has its own subtleties, and establishing good business models and rules takes time and requires much discussion and collaboration with business users.

The internal training department and QA may have interesting insight into how processes *should* be executed, and the individuals who perform those tasks can tell you how it is actually done in practice.

However, if you ask directly how they perform a specific task, they are likely to tell you how they think that task should be done, rather than what they actually do; few individuals will admit any shortcuts *they* regularly take or steps they ignore to do later, and it's important to understand the real picture. A technique used by the authors is to ask the professionals to describe a "day in the life" of a typical but imaginary colleague. It's often surprising how much truth those imaginary colleagues can reveal!

Requirements analysis should be commenced weeks to months before any IT solution is planned.

Capturing Business Requirements "Bottom Up"

Bottom-up requirements analysis is the derivation of business requirements from the analysis of how an existing IT system supports a business unit. If you plan to "wrap" any of your existing IT systems to expose them as services, this kind of analysis is essential. In the event that the source code of these systems cannot be changed (we see this a lot in practice), you are stuck with the function that's already there. Wrapping it as services can make it much granular; if you have additional requirements, however, you will have to develop those independently. Although it might seem inelegant to create a new IT solution from services that access a combination of old and new components parts, in practice it works well at much lower cost, and provides nearly as much flexibility as creating a totally new solution.

Even if you don't already have an existing IT asset that you want to expose as services, an examination of any commercial software packages that exist in that business area is always a good idea. You might learn some useful tricks and approaches, and who knows, you may be able to buy a package for less than it will cost you to build.

A disadvantage of the bottom up approach is that it can often entrench the existing approach to solving a business problem, reducing flexibility and impeding creativity. A good approach to counteract this is to use a "meet in the middle" technique, where you perform both top-down and bottom-up analysis and compare the results—a "sanity check" that ensures a good balance between theory and practice.

The last stage in requirements capture should be to prioritize requirements into

1. Absolutely essential
2. Nice to have
3. Ornamental

Generally, budget constraints will allow you to address all of the first category, maybe one or two of the second category, and none of the third.

Service Identification

In SOA, isn't everything a service? No, everything should *not* be a service. That's a costly mistake that we have seen many people and organizations make. One secret of success for SOA is choosing the right services to create, and avoiding creating the wrong ones. The other secret is about choosing business processes to automate. Don't forget that a large part of SOA is about the creation of executable business models, a powerful means of achieving business agility and flexibility.

Triage is essentially a classification process that involves assessing whether an IT asset should be created to support each business process or task, and if so, what type of IT asset it should be. This task includes determining the optimum scope of each candidate IT process or service operation, and then examining the organization's existing IT assets to determine whether there is a suitable existing IT asset that can be reused in whole or part

Figure 6.1 shows this triage process diagrammatically.

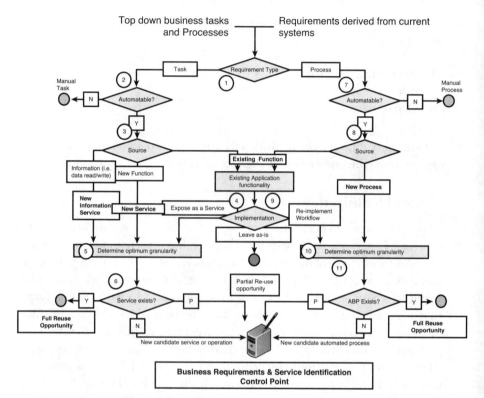

Figure 6.1 Triage Flowchart for Identifying Candidate Services and Automated Business Processes

The input to the triage process is a series of business processes, sub-processes, and tasks, defined using either top-down process decomposition or bottom-up analysis of an existing IT solution. The triage procedure is described here. The numbers equate to the numbers in the boxes on Figure 6.1.

1. The first step is to classify whether, from an IT perspective, we are dealing with candidate *processes* or candidate *tasks*. This needs to be a precise definition. Any of the Internet purchase components described earlier might be called business services, but if we are planning to construct an IT solution, we need to be more precise. Tasks represent discrete transactional units of work—that is, can be performed by one person in a single step, without outside intervention. Processes are more complex, and can take an extended time to perform.

2. The correct term for a specific invocation of a service is *operation.* Typically, each service will have multiple operations, each of which performs a specific task. Business tasks become candidate operations. At this stage, we need to determine whether the operation could be automated. This is a relatively simple test. Is the operation potentially able to be automated or performed by a program or application synchronously, and in a stateless fashion, without the need for session-specific context information? If the answer is yes, you have a potential candidate operation; otherwise, you have a manual operation. For the Internet purchase example, all tasks except "package the goods and ship them to the customer" could potentially be automated. If the candidate operation must be performed manually, exit the triage process at this stage.

3. The next step is to determine whether there is an obvious source for the functionality:

   - For straightforward data reads and for simple data writes (that is, that don't involve too complex data validation), you usually create an "information as a service" task. "Information as a service" tasks are almost always good candidates for becoming IT operations. Proceed to Step 4, where you determine optimum granularity.

   - For new business functionality for which you don't yet have an IT application that performs that task, you should also proceed to Step 4.

   - The case where there is an existing IT application that already performs that task is more complex. In this case, you need to decide whether to continue to use that application, to replace it because it doesn't perform the task the way you want it to, or to "wrap" it with code, exposing it as a service.

   In some cases, it should be possible to make some changes to the way the tasks, or modify the data inputs or outputs within the service itself, instead of changing the application. The service architect can make such decisions, based on the following criteria:

   - **Ease of use.** There are many potential consumers of that piece of functionality that do not need / do not want to learn to use the rest of the application. For example, you probably would not need (or want) to know how to use a complex supply chain package if you merely need to order some more stationery.

- **Flexibility of implementation.** If there is a plan to retire or replace a provider application, wrapping it as services allows it to be replaced at any time in the future without changing the service interfaces—that is, completely transparently to the service consumers. This can be an excellent migration strategy, or can help to reduce the number of competing IT solutions that you have to maintain.

- **Remote access.** There are third parties or remote users who need to given controlled and nonrepudiated (that is, auditable) access to certain functions. Services are an excellent way of providing this level of control.

Here are some reasons why you might choose *not* to wrap (or expose) an application as services:

- **"Chatty" interfaces.** Interfaces that require significant interaction between the user and the application are poor candidates for service because services are essentially transactional. For example, it would be unreasonable to attempt to wrap a product such as MS Word® or PowerPoint® as services.

- **Stable function provider.** If there is no plan to retire or replace an existing application, and there is no major expansion in the number of users that need to be supported, wrapping it as services may be overkill.

- **Frequency of use.** If the application can support most or all of the user's role (for example, end users would spend hours each using that application), it is worth investing their time to become experts in that application, rather than wrapping it as services.

- **Technical complexity.** Sometimes it can be too difficult to break down a complex application into services; we are used to dealing with a lack of documentation, but a lack of the original source code is generally a show stopper. In this case, you must either put up with the status quo or look to sourcing a suitable replacement.

4. This is the vital stage of determining the correct granularity or the scope of the operation. This is a complex task that we have seen many people struggle with, so we've included a detailed example of determining service granularity later in this chapter.

5. The final stage is to determine whether you already have an existing service that implements all or part of the functionality that you need. If that is the case, you can achieve at least some level of reuse, and you should record that as an SOA success. You might find that that will involve creating a new version of an existing service. Managing multiple service versions is a complex activity, and so we have also included a section on service versioning later in this chapter.

6. Next, look at the branch of the flowchart that covers candidate automated business processes: Again, the first procedure is to determine whether the process or subprocess being examined is potentially capable of being automated. Most business processes can be automated to a considerable degree. Automated processes can invoke manual tasks or subprocesses, and it's generally a good practice to automatically monitor manual processes. It's generally a good idea to start with triaging the leaf-level subprocesses first, because completely automating a complex business process is resource intensive, and you may well be able to achieve your business flexibility and agility key performance indicator targets by simply focusing on a subset of the business subprocesses.

7. Just as for services, the next stage is to determine whether there is any existing process automation or workflow embedded in existing IT solutions that currently support the business area being analyzed. If the current systems do not provide any workflow to support, proceed directly to Step 8.

   Many traditional applications "hard code" the sequence of tasks that need to be performed, and in such cases, it can be difficult to modify that workflow, or to allow an external workload management or process control engine to replace it. In such cases, unless you have explicit plans to replace such applications, the lead service architect should make any decisions to reengineer a hard-coded workflow, because it's a technical minefield.

8. As for services, the next step in the triage process is to determine the scope of any process you choose to automate, and you should try to determine the maximum benefit you can achieve with the minimum of effort. Pick the low-hanging fruit first!

9. Just as for services, the final step in triage of automated processes is to look for existing executable models that either already perform the business process, or that perform something similar. For executable Business Process Execution Language (BPEL) models, the question of whether there is an existing implementation is not nearly as binary as for service operations. Extending an existing BPEL model (for example, to add additional branches or rules) is relatively straightforward and, unlike modifying services, creates no version management issues.

After a candidate set of services, operations, and processes to be automated has been created, they should be disseminated to all business analysts. The program or project management office, and of course the business service champion, determines which other lines of business (LOB) might be able to reuse them.

Determining who the potential future consumers are of each service or automated process has two important benefits: It establishes the reuse potential, and it gives an opportunity to capture their requirements before the service is designed.

There will inevitably be more candidate services proposed than resources available to design, develop, and deploy them, so some means of assigning development priority is essential. This is where effective service portfolio management should be used to determine that the services and automated processes that get developed are the ones that are most strategic.

The Service Prioritization Checklist Work Product, described in Chapter 3, describes our recommended means of assigning priorities; ideally, candidate service priorities should be established in group sessions.

Naturally, when any candidate is a prerequisite of another candidate, it should save the same or higher development priority. There may be some special cases that mandate the development of a specific service (for example, when an operation or automated process is essential for ensuring regulatory compliance, or to meet the needs of a specific customer or supplier). Remember that not all operations of a given service need to have the same development priority.

While this assessment will necessarily be subjective, and the difference in priority between two candidates thathave similar overall scores is insignificant, this process should make a clear distinction between high-impact / low-cost services and high-cost / low-impact services. It works especially well in group sessions, with the whole of the SOA enablement team voting on the relative priorities.

Once the candidate services have been prioritized, you should now be ready to conduct the business requirements and service identification control point; in practice, these group sessions can generally be combined to reduce the number of meetings involved. The service identification control point should establish ownership of each candidate asset and confirm that there is outline funding available to begin the design stage.

Assets that successfully pass the business requirements and service identification control point should be added to the services build plan work product. This is intended to act as a mechanism to disseminate the current build priorities and inform every potential service consumer what services and automated processes are planned and when they will be created, ensuring that all potential stakeholders are informed in time for their individual requirements to be considered.

Preparing for the Solution Architecture Control Point

"Good judgment comes from experience. Experience comes from bad judgment"

—Barry LePatner

In the solution architecture phase, service architects and service designers confirm the scope of each service or automated process, make technical decisions about how any IT solutions will be constructed (for example, what design patterns should be used), and determine what nonfunctional requirements should be applicable. Nonfunctional requirements should include outline systems monitoring and management needs, and what key performance indicators and business metrics should be captured.

The team creating these solution architecture decisions and nonfunctional requirements should include a business service analyst or business process analyst (depending on whether the planed asset is a service or automated process), a service architect, and a service designer. The outputs from this team should be formally reviewed in the solution architecture control point by a meeting of all business service, process analysts, service architects and designers, the business service champion, and the SOA governance lead.

Preparing for the Service Specification Control Point

"A verbal contract isn't worth the paper it's written on"

—Samuel Goldwyn

Creating the *service externals* part of the service specification is a collaborative, incremental exercise. Although the business services analyst will take the lead in the production of each service specification, he or she may not have the necessary skills to develop the models and some of the data elements. A data architect might be asked to assist in defining the service signature (that is, the details of the inputs and outputs to each operation) in accordance with the enterprise's Messaging Model (MM).

One reason for delivering both the service externals and service internals in a single service specification work product is that there are strung dependencies between them. For example, when attempting to expose part of an existing IT solution as a service operation, the service designer first has to determine whether it is physically possible to transform the data derived from that system to "to-be" MM schema. In the event that it is impossible to mediate between the desired and existing data format or content, the service designer and service architect determine a satisfactory outcome, and then record it in an architectural decision. Potential outcomes include the following:

- Changing the MM to match existing data, or deciding not to comply with an industry reference model.
- The creation of a new database or table in the desired format and migration of existing data into it. This may require creating a mechanism to synchronize the new and old tables going forward.

- As a last resort, create modified versions of the existing application to return the appropriate data, or consider replacing it with a new more pliable system.

The service specification contains content intended for both technical and nontechnical audiences. The authors of service externals should write them as public documents, and not include any information that is proprietary to the enterprise. They should also avoid using terminology that might be unfamiliar to any business partners. The service registrar should approve any descriptive text.

The *service internals* part of the service specification should be initiated at the same time as the service externals, since the service level agreements (SLAs), which should also be defined at this stage, will depend to some extent on the internals of the service design.

The service specification control point is essentially a QA review of the service externals and SLAs. The service registrar is responsible for the quality of the service description that goes into the service registry.

Preparing for the Service Design Control Point

> *"Design is not just what it looks like and feels like. Design is how it works"*
>
> —Steve Jobs

Good design should be an iterative approach with much consultation. Design walkthroughs are an excellent mechanism for helping ensure quality and consistency, and help to spot any cases where standards or best practices are not followed. Minutes of design walkthroughs also help determine any systemic issues that can be corrected by more education or better working practices.

The service internals should consist of a set of models and notes that are considered to be private to those individuals who are developing and testing the service code or process BPEL. Such information should not be shared with potential service consumers, who have no need to know it.

In the case where a service is used to wrap an existing application (termed a service provider), it is essential that the interfaces to that application are well defined. It is important to record any dependencies between calls to the existing systems, such as state dependencies, or that there is a required sequence of execution of calls. An excellent way to do this is to use an interaction diagram that shows the detail and sequence of messages and responses.

Creating content to the appropriate quality and ensuring that there is complete continuity between the service specification, interface specifications, and service design documentation will require an incremental approach to each of these tasks, with frequent reviews between the team members associated with each task and with the SOA enablement team as a whole.

In practice, creating a hard-copy service specification will be a process of collating a series of report outputs from various tools. For example

- The service overview and operation descriptions will probably be maintained in a service registry tool rather than in simple text documents, but should be able to be output by the registry tool in an appropriate format.
- Process models, interface class models, Web Service Definition Language (WSDL), and BPEL will be generated directly from the tools used by the service designers; and where necessary, these tools will generate models in printable format.

In the case of automated processes, the design process consists of progressive refining of the executable model. The distinction between design and realization of such models is a fine one.

The test plan should also be created at this stage, because it is an essential tool for the service developers to use to determine whether their code actually works as intended.

The acid test of the level of completeness and accuracy of a service specification package is that it contains no ambiguity and that it provides a reasonably skilled developer with all the information necessary to develop a high-quality code deliverable without the need for asking any questions to clarify any item it contains.

The service design control point review is a QA audit of the service internals and test plan, to ensure that they meet the necessary quality and that they comply with the appropriate architectural decisions and standards—or that compliance exemptions have been explicitly granted in the case where compliance is not possible.

Preparing for the Service Realization Control Point

> *"Continuous effort—not strength or intelligence—is the key to unlocking our potential."*
>
> —Winston Churchill

The actual code development occurs in this task, a large part of which consists in generating code artifacts via tooling. The most efficient development style is model driven (that is, most of the developer's efforts go into the creation and progressive refinement of models), and the physical code is generated by a software tool, rather than hand-coded. Development of the executable models that automate business processes is an extreme form of model-driven development; in this case, the model *is* the final deliverable.

In creating service operations, much of the development task is the assembly of existing simple services or service fragments into more complex and functionally rich operations. An operation that combines several existing operations together with some logical flow is called a *compound* operation. Simple operations without logical flow are termed *atomic* operations. Compound operations typically take much longer to execute than atomic operations, so their nonfunctional requirements have to be managed carefully.

From a technical perspective, there is much similarity between operations where the service provider application uses a common technology. For example, all operations that access a relational database will have a similar structure, as will all operations that access a mainframe transaction-processing system, such as IBM's Customer Information Control System® (CICS®).

The enterprise's SOA infrastructure should be able to handle most of the housekeeping and routine activities for each service invocation, such as the following:

- Establishing the identity of the requestor
- Establishing that the requestor is authorized to make the request
- Recording details of the request (who made it, when it occurred, what the result was, and how long it took) and raising alerts in the case of SLA violations

- Reporting any faults or problems that occurred during service execution, and taking appropriate actions to handle these exceptions

The service build control point is essentially a code walkthrough review to determine that the service was coded as designed, meets the required standards, and conforms to the relevant architectural decisions. It also verifies that the build management processes are being followed correctly.

Preparing for the Service Testing Control Point

"I didn't fail the test, I just found 100 ways to do it wrong."

—Benjamin Franklin

Testing should be a way of life, not just an afterthought. Incremental testing is vital to ensure that the final code deliverables fully meet their functional and nonfunctional requirements without the need for extensive rework.

While formal testing of both functional and nonfunctional requirements is essential, it should be rare for significant errors to be found at this stage if the service developers are doing their job well. Services and automated processes should be stress tested, and testing should ensure that they behave as predicted even in error conditions. For example, all service operations should issue and log an error in the event of malformed input data. New versions of every operation need extensive regression testing. They should go through the identical testing disciplines as new operations. Any maintenance work on a service component should be considered to invalidate all operations and services that use it, and require them all to be regression-tested.

Exhaustive testing takes time and should wherever possible be automated, but many useful service testing tools are beginning to appear in the marketplace.

The test plan should include operating all services and automated processes in an environment that is as close to production as possible. Component failures should be simulated to determine that the correct systems management events and alerts are generated. It is also good practice to try some system crash testing, where, literally, you pull the plug on one component in the SOA infrastructure to see what happens.

Naturally, in-flight service executions may not complete, but there must never be any loss of data integrity, and long-running automated processes should resume normally when the component is restored.

Automated processes are especially hard to test because of the complex logic required to back out of a running process in the event of a component failure, or to handle unusual combinations of branches in the decision logic. However, testing must assume that all possible logic branches will occur in practice some day, and should test to see that there is no combination that causes unexpected behavior.

Preparing for the Service Certification and Deployment Control Point

"Trust, but verify."

—Ronald Regan

The most important transition in the life of each service is its migration to production, when it ceases to be a burden on its developer "parents" and sets off to earn its own living. Adding a new service or automated process to the set of enterprise assets requires a way to announce its status and display details to its potential consumers, so that the service can start earning its keep. Service certification and publishing is a vital process for SOA adoption.

Although this is not an entirely new step within IT operations procedures today, there are aspects such as the loosely coupled nature and new interoperability challenges that are new to services and that must also be addressed. This is an area where technology standards and tools (registry, repository, and so on) are rapidly evolving.

Service certification is a critical part of SOA governance. The main objective of certifying services is to actively encourage their reuse by warranting quality and ensuring potential new users of the service that it will be fully supported. Success in SOA is all about establishing a relationship of trust with the consumers.

Such assurance may be achieved by requiring additional accountability requirements and by publishing the details of such additional certification for the benefit of potential consumers of the service. Service certification should be carried out under the control of the quality assurance (QA) department.

The certification step builds on the effort already undertaken during the service identification around reuse and due diligence in identification of potential service consumers.

Various details that were developed and documented during the service design and development phase such as the SLAs and the nonfunctional requirements will contribute to the certification process. This final certification review step formalizes the QA process prior to physically publishing the service as being "enterprise ready," with an assured quality of service and a full and complete set of support materials.

For example, certification ensures that information such as a version number, ownership, who is accountable for the service, and that classification and availability of the service are published as mandatory service metadata.

Certification and publishing services also serve the following purposes:

- It helps the IT operations staff capture and document service related metadata. This benefits visibility and system analysis for later projects that may require such information of existing systems and services.

- During early stages of SOA adoption, it provides feedback channel from IT operations to design and development teams. This may result in additional design time discipline toward services by prompting reuse questions and considerations from operational aspects of services.

- The process of certification ensures the correctness of service contracts created as part of service specification.

- It establishes the source for communication related to service lifecycle, usage, and subscription information.

- It demonstrates that the service has adhered to the required sequence of steps for the service lifecycle status, including intermediate peer reviews.

- It ensures that all the necessary monitoring and systems management is in place before the service is used in production.

The service certification and deployment control point review results in a pass or fail status for the service in consideration. Pass status indicates that the service is ready to be published. Fail status indicates that further work needs to be done before this can be certified as a service.

Preparing for the Service Vitality Control Point

> *"It is not the strongest of the species that survives, nor the most intelligent, but the one most responsive to change"*
>
> —Charles Darwin

Service vitality covers many aspects and deserves a chapter of its own. Chapter 7, "Governance Vitality," covers this topic in depth.

Many of the reports described in Chapters 3 and 4, such as the SOA reuse and ROI report, the business flexibility and business agility reports, SLA monitoring reports, and service construction metrics are designed to help monitor vitality. The SOA governance vitality report monitors the vitality of SOA governance. Less-formal lessons learned work products contain a finer level of detail. Every three to six months, the SOA enablement team should meet to analyze all these reports, and determine any improvements that can be made, in a service vitality control point review.

The overall popularity of individual services, and the relative utilization of each of their current versions should be reviewed every six months or so, using the service usage data work product described in Chapter 4.

Service and Process Lifecycles: Overview

> *"Good management is the art of making problems so interesting and their solutions so constructive that everyone wants to get to work and deal with them"*
>
> —Paul Hawken

Implementing SOA is a complex task, but the activities within the service factory needed to analyze, design, develop, and deploy services and to automate business processes are predictable and repeatable. That said, they are not simple tasks, even when the best possible set of tools is used to automate them. As for most other human activities, the quality of the end result depends on the abilities of the individuals involved in their creation. Good governance can help avoid problems and identify issues early, but having real experts in the SOA enablement team is still essential.

Because there are some subtle differences in the lifecycles of services and of automated processes, we have created two different figures, one for service and one for process automation. The governance mechanisms are essentially the same for both services and automated processes, but the timings differ.

Figure 6.2 shows diagrammatically the service lifecycle.

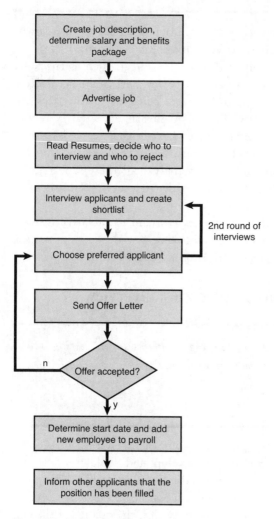

Figure 6.2   The Services Lifecycle

Figure 6.3 shows the lifecycle of automated processes, ones that have passed the business requirements and service identification control point.

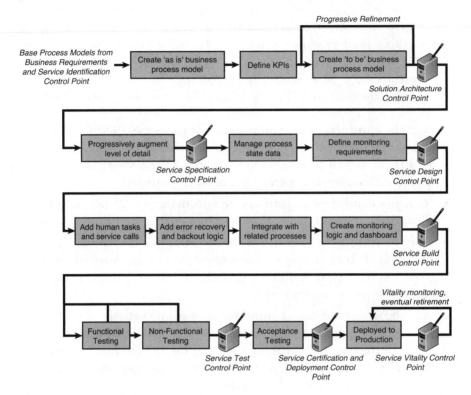

Figure 6.3   The Automated Process Lifecycle

Regulating Service Granularity

"Size does matter"

—USA Today (in reference to new research that shows that class size does affect student academic performance)

This section contains a set of notes to assist business services analysts in the task of identifying candidate services of the correct granularity. The process begins with the identification of a conceptual need for an IT solution to support a business task or activity.

This checklist should be completed by the business analyst responsible for service identification, after a through peer review of the list of candidate operations by other business analysts and service designers.

To give context for making correct decisions on service granularity, we use a worked example, Employee Hire, because most people are familiar with this process and it has few industry dependencies. We demonstrate a top-down modeling approach.

Here are the questions that the business service analyst should ask:

- **Are the candidate operations tasks or processes?** Does each candidate service operation represent a discrete synchronous task (that is, a task that can be performed as a single stateless logical unit of work, without interruption or human intervention)?

- **Can the candidate operations be automated?** Can they be performed or supported by an IT system rather than by a human being?

- **Are the candidate operations really reusable?** Is each candidate operation defined at a level of granularity that maximizes its reuse potential (that is, it performs a specific, unique task that has value to multiple service consumers)?

- **Are the scopes of each candidate operation realistic?** Are the conceptual inputs and outputs of the operation defined (that is, in terms of the business entities passed to/from the service). Is the candidate operation stateless, and is the volume of input and output data both predictable and reasonable?

- **Does each candidate operations have visible business value?** Are the candidate operations discrete logical tasks with obvious business value that a nontechnical business user would understand and want to use?

Step 1. Are the Candidate Operations Tasks or Services?

To distinguish between candidate services and candidate automated services, you need to perform or validate existing business process decomposition until there is a clear distinction between business processes and potential candidate services. You must ask the following question: Is it a task or process?

Employee Hire is clearly not a task but an extended business process that takes days or weeks to complete. Employee Hire may be a good candidate for an automated business process, but it is too complex and too asynchronous to be a candidate for a service.

Because Employee Hire is too complex to be a candidate service, let's decompose it further to identify candidate business services within the hiring process. The first-level decomposition shown in Figure 6.4 shows that the hiring process consists of the following set of subprocesses or tasks.

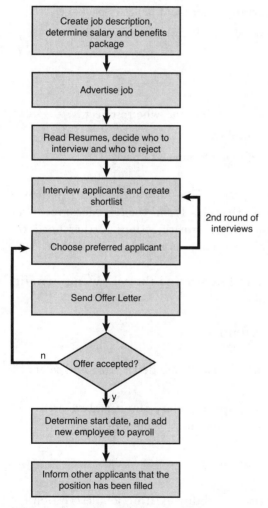

Figure 6.4 Employee Contractor Hire Process: Employee Hire at First Level of Decomposition

If we reapply the "is this a task or a process" test, we get the following results:

Tasks:

- Send offer letter
- Inform other candidates that the position is filled

Processes:
- Create job description, determine salary and benefits package
- Interview candidates and create shortlist of suitable candidates

Undetermined:
- Advertise job
- Read resumés, decide who to interview and who to reject
- Choose preferred candidate employee
- Determine start date and add new employee to payroll

Such ambiguity is not acceptable. The solution to this problem is the same as for the activities that clearly fail the test: decompose the business processes and the indeterminate actions further until the distinctions become clear. More analysis reveals the following sub-processes.

Create a job description and determine the salary and benefits package:

- Option 1. Use an existing definition:

  - Search HR database for an existing job description and salary range
  - Validate existing job description, salary range, and advertisement copy (that is, text and graphics to be published)

- Option 2. Create a new definition:

  - Create new job description / modify existing job description, salary range, and advertisement copy
  - Obtain HR approval for new/modified job description and salary range

Interview candidates and create a shortlist of suitable candidates:

- Determine whether applicant has been previously employed by the organization
- Determine whether applicant has been previously interviewed and rejected by the organization
- Schedule interview
- Perform interview
- Assess suitability of each applicant
- Rank applicants in terms of suitability for the job and track record
- Write to references for leading applicants (optional)
- Interpret reference replies
- Adjust applicant's relative rank

Advertise jobs:

- Establish the correct channel for advertising the position
- Establish agreements with channel owners (for example, newspapers, magazines, online job agencies)
- Send advert copy for publication
- Pay advertiser

Read resumés and decide who to interview and who to reject:

- Assess resumé to qualify the suitability of an applicant. For each resumé, determine whether the candidate has the skills and experience to perform the job. Assign a provisional rating—excellent fit, good fit, possible fit, overqualified, not qualified.
- Record applicant details.
- Add applicants that are an excellent fit, good fit, and possible fit to the potential interviewees.
- Trim the set of potential interviewees to an acceptable size, rejecting the possible fit and good fit applicants if the number of potential interviewees is too large.

Determine start date and add employee to payroll:

- Assign an unique employee number for the new employee
- Create or update a personnel record for the new employee
- Add new employee to the payroll system when he or she starts work

Experience suggests that by the third or fourth level of decomposition you should have identified most candidate operations.

The set of candidate operations for the Employee Hire process has now grown to 26, as shown in the following list:

Employee Hire—First List of Candidate Services

1. Send offer letter
2. Send rejection letter
3. Search HR database for an existing job description and salary range
4. Validate existing job description, salary range, and advertisement copy
5. Create new job description/modify existing job description, salary range, and advertisement copy
6. Obtain HR approval to new/modified job description and salary range
7. Determine whether applicant has been previously employed by the organization
8. Determine whether applicant has been previously interviewed and rejected by the organization
9. Schedule interview
10. Perform interview
11. Assess applicant suitability
12. Record applicant details
13. Rank applicants in terms of suitability for the job and track record
14. Add/remove applicant to/from the shortlist
15. Write to referee for leading applicants (optional)
16. Interpret referee reply
17. Adjust applicant's relative rank
18. Establish the correct channels for advertising the position
19. Establish agreements with advertising channel owners
20. Send advert copy for publication

21. Pay advertiser
22. Assess resumé to qualify the suitability of an applicant
23. Add/remove applicant to/from potential interviewee list
24. Assign employee ID number
25. Create/update employee personnel record
26. Add employee to payroll system

For further analysis, it is convenient to group these operations into categories (that is, services) in terms of the business entities that are involved. This will produce the result shown in Table 6.1.

Table 6.1 Employee Hire: First List of Candidate Services Organized by Business Entity

Service or Business Entity	Operation
Communication	Send offer letter Send rejection letter Send advert copy for publication Write to referee Interpret referee reply
Job description	Look up job descriptions Validate job description Create/update job description Approve job description
Calendar	Schedule interview Perform interview
Job applicant	Assess applicant resumé Assess applicant suitability post interview Rank a set of applicants Record applicant details Adjust applicant rank Add to/remove from interview list Add to/remove from shortlist Search for historical applicant record
B2B	Establish the correct channels for advertising the position Establish agreements with advertising channel owners Pay advertiser
Employee	Record/update employee profile Assign new ID number Add to payroll system Look up historic employee records

Step 2. Can the Candidate Operations Be Automated?

Now it's time to decide whether each of these tasks could potentially be automated. This is a relatively simple question to answer. The following activities need to be performed by humans rather than machines:

- Interpret referee reply
- Validate job description
- Approve job description
- Perform interview
- Assess applicant resumé
- Assess applicant post interview
- Rank a set of applicants
- Establish the correct channels for advertising the position

Some of the other tasks that remain would need to be performed by humans, but services that record the results of a human activity could provide useful support. These include the following:

- Create/update job description
- Record applicant details
- Adjust applicant rank
- Add to/remove from interview list
- Add to/remove from shortlist

After applying the manual or automated test to the list of candidate operations, the size of candidate IT operations is narrowed to 17, as shown in Table 6.2.

Table 6.2   Employee Hire: Tasks That Could Potentially Be Automated

Service or Business Entity	Operation
Communication	Send offer letter
	Send rejection letter
	Send advert copy for publication
	Write to referee
Job description	Look up job descriptions
	Create/update job description

Service or Business Entity	Operation
Calendar	Schedule interview
Job applicant	Record applicant details
	Adjust applicant rank
	Add to/remove from interview list
	Add to/remove from shortlist
	Search for historical applicant record
B2B	Pay advertiser
Employee	Maintain employee profile
	Assign new employee ID number
	Add to payroll system
	Look up historic employee records

Step 3. Are the Candidate Operations Really Reusable?

The next step is to consider how reusable these candidate operations would be. Considerations for this include the following:

- Does each operation implement a business task that is of business value to multiple potential users?
- Does each operation represent a distinct, unique task, rather than a minor variation on an existing task?
- Could each operation be made more reusable by making it more generic?

These questions can be answered by first grouping related or similar operations, and then assessing whether they can be combined into a single, more generically applicable operation. After this task has been completed for groups of operations, it can be repeated for single operations. Following is how communication and job applicant might be grouped.

Communication

For example, the following operations seem to be minor variants on each other:

- Send offer letter
- Send rejection letter
- Send advert copy for publication
- Write to referee

Each of these operations applies to hiring employees and to no other process. While there are multiple operating groups that need to hire employees, if every individual form letter needs to be created by an individual service, a much better option would be to create an operation that

- Takes as input a form letter template or template number and a set of recipient profiles
- Creates and customizes individual text by merging name and address information with the form letter
- Chooses the optimum delivery channel using the recipient's contact preferences (for example, email, fax, printed letter)
- Records the fact that the communication has been sent

Job Applicant

Similarly, most of the operations of the job applicant service can be better combined into a single operation. The original set of operations included

- Record applicant details
- Adjust applicant rank
- Add to/remove from interview list
- Add to/remove from shortlist

If we added information to the applicant profile that defined his or her rank, and whether the candidate was on the interview list or the shortlist, all these operations could be merged into a single *maintain applicant profile* operation.

By a similar set of reasoning, a generic *process invoice* operation of the B2B service would be much more reusable than an operation that is restricted to B2B partners that are advertisers.

The reuse potential of the adding new employee ID number operation is low, and it's a granular operation, but it's certainly a necessary piece of functionality, and we cannot eliminate it yet.

Our candidate operations list has now shrunk to 11 candidate operations, as shown in Table 6.3.

Table 6.3 Employee Hire: Reusable Candidate Operations

Service or Business Entity	Operation
Communication	Send form letter
Job Description	Look up job description
	Create/update job description
Calendar	Schedule interview
Job Applicant	Maintain applicant profile
	Look up applicant profile
B2B	Process invoice
Employee	Maintain employee profile
	Assign new employee ID number
	Add to payroll system
	Look up historic employee records

Step 4. Are the Scopes of Each Candidate Operation Realistic?

The next step is to determine that the technical scope of each candidate operation is reasonable. We want to ensure that each candidate service represents a stateless transaction whose inputs and outputs are of a reasonable and predictable size.

The term *stateless* implies that the operations inputs and outputs consist of data representing business entities only and do not contain context or session-related information. The service messages contain information that defines who is invoking the service, enabling service security mechanisms to be enforced. Business entities passed to or from a service will include data that represents the state of that business entity. To be reusable, the execution of services should be independent of

- The specific application that the service consumer is using to invoke the service
- What GUI screen or page the user is at

It is extremely poor design to pass such context or session-related information into service operations.

At this stage, the inputs and outputs of each operation need be defined at a conceptual level only, in terms of business entities defined in the MM.

Services of reasonable granularity should involve relatively few instances of business entities. A rule of thumb is that input and output data lengths should be less than around 250K, although this recommended limit is increasing as SOA technology matures. This number should be reviewed and updated at least annually. The input and output sizes determined here are estimates only. The actual service data input/output sizes will be determined during nonfunctional testing.

In most cases, this is relatively simple to achieve. Lookups or searches present potential problems because of potential for an unpredictable number of hits. A search for employee records for "Ichiro Suzuki" in Japan or "John Smith" in Australia, the United States, or the United Kingdom would probably return so many results that the service execution time would be unacceptable if the full profiles of every matching employee were returned.

A pattern that has proven effective at solving this mega-data problem is for the operation to return the full profile only when there is a single hit, and return summary profiles (e.g., name, address, job, work location, date of birth only) if there are multiple hits. Consider an example, for Employee Hire, in Table 6.4.

Table 6.4 Employee Hire: Logical Inputs and Outputs

Service or Business Entity	Operation	Logical Inputs	Logical Outputs
Communication	Send form letter	Form letter number, set of recipient profiles	Confirmation
Job Description	Look up job descriptions	Partially complete job profile	Set of matching job profiles
	Create/update job description	Job profile (new or updated)	Confirmation
Calendar	Schedule interview	Job profile	Interview slot
Job Applicant	Maintain applicant profile	Applicant profile (new or updated)	Confirmation
	Look up applicant profile	Applicant profile fragment	Set of matching applicant profiles (current and historic)

Service or Business Entity	Operation	Logical Inputs	Logical Outputs
B2B	Process invoice	Invoice details	Confirmation of payment
Employee	Maintain employee profile	Applicant profile or updated employee profile	Confirmation
	Assign new employee ID number	Applicant profile	Updated applicant profile
	Add to payroll system	Employee profile	Confirmation
	Look up historic employee records	Employee profile fragment	Set of matching employee profiles

Step 5. Does Each Candidate Operation Have Visible Business Value?

The final test is that each operation should be discrete, usable as a standalone task, and have meaning to a business user. The operative words here are *discrete* and *standalone.* Good operations should be valuable individually, not as part of an extended sequence.

All of the operations pass this test except for *assign new employee ID number.* When would this ever be used other than as part of creating a new employee personnel record? There are two alternative solutions:

- Keep an assign new employee ID number operation, but do not make it visible in the catalog (that is, it is available to applications that need it but not made visible in the service registry to potential consumers).
- Perform that action in a larger, composite operation, such as *maintain employee profile,* that could assign employee ID numbers for new profiles.

The latter option is probably the best as it reduces the number of code assets that have to be separately maintained.

Notes on Granularity of Data-Related Services

Many services involve reading or writing of data, with little or no application logic. Some additional considerations apply in such cases.

Services That Read Data

Many services consist of simple data lookups (for example, look up job description, look up applicant profile, and look up historic employee records). Special considerations apply to such read-only services:

- Security considerations, such as controlling and recording access to sensitive data may take priority over service execution efficiency, and it is reasonable that such services may have smaller-than-usual granularity

- There may be many alternative ways to search for or look up records. For example, you might want to search for employees by name, serial number, Social Security number, department, and so on. This can lead to a proliferation of related services, such as look up by name, look up by serial number. An accepted leading practice is to avoid such proliferation by creating a single *Lookup* service invocation. The input to this invocation is a partially completed employee profile containing some mix of parameters such as name, serial number, and so on. Logic in the service determines the optimum search algorithm, hiding such complexity from the service consumers. Similarly, if there are multiple records that fit the search criteria, logic within the service can filter the results to reduce the overall volume of data returned, by returning only summary data if there are too many "hits." This style of using a partially complete input XML document, and returning zero to many more complete documents is called "Wrapped Document Literal." (See, for example, www-128.ibm.com/developerworks/webservices/library/ws-whichwsdl/.)

Services That Update Data

As for read-only services, granularity assessments may be relaxed where security is a major factor. However, exposing the ability to write to an organization's operational database introduces some additional security considerations. Services provide a means of insulating service consumers from the underlying implementation, but they also insulate the service provider from the technology of the service consumer:

- Because the internal workings of the service consumer cannot be inspected, the service designer should assume that all such services treat all clients as "untrusted" clients, and implement a vigorous and complete check for data integrity before any physical data writes occur.

- Similarly, each data writing service should insulate its consumers from its implementation technology. The need for separate *Create* (Insert), *Update*, and *Delete* operations for each data row is a characteristic of relational technology, not a physical law, and exposing these operations as separate service invocations would make it difficult to change the technical implementation of services in the future. A much better solution is to create a single *Maintain* service invocation that, if necessary, determines internally whether it needs to insert, create, or delete individual records in relational databases.

Managing Service Versioning

"All human situations have their inconveniences. We feel those of the present but neither see nor feel those of the future; and hence we often make troublesome changes without amendment, and frequently for the worse."

—Benjamin Franklin

Let's be clear about service versioning. It's a pain. Like changing the mirror on the Hubble telescope once it was in orbit, it's an impressive feat, but it would have been much better for all concerned if NASA had got it right in the first place.

Replacing an existing service with a new version of a service may cause every consumer of that service to change the IT systems that use it and require a significant effort in regression testing, potentially expending significant IT resources for additional functionality the consumers might not need. Alternatively, IT operations would have to manage and maintain multiple versions of every deployed service forever.

Unfortunately, change is inevitable. There will be new requirements, new regulations, new business initiatives, and the goal of SOA is to increase the enterprise's agility, not to ossify it. So, what can be done to enable changes to be made to working services with minimum inconvenience to existing consumers? There are two main ways to do this: using good design practices to make most services future-proof, and good communications and consultation with service consumers.

Designing Future-Proof Services

The first prerequisite for creating future-proof services is to ensure that the MM is mature for the business entity or entities involved. Changing the name of an entity or an attribute (data item) for an entity forces all service consumers to have to change their code.

Ideally, operations should be designed to be forward compatible; that is, adding additional business rules, new attributes, or relationships to the MM entities should be transparent to existing users unless they specifically want to take advantage of them.

The second prerequisite is to allow a reasonable degree of flexibility in the data sent to and from service operation invocations. Applications or processes that invoke services operations are generally able to ignore any additional unfamiliar items without complaint. You should use the Wrapped Document Literal style of invocation described earlier in this chapter, because it helps establish forward compatibility.

WSDL is XML-based and it includes the ability to use style sheets to enforce validation of input and output data. There is an important trade-off between using this feature and forward compatibility. Simply put, if you rigidly enforce data validation using this mechanism, you will never be able to change the structure of that data. That is, the operations cannot be forward compatible.

We recommend that data validation be carried out inside the service code, rather than as the service request is transmitted. The service WSDL should describe all service attributes and relationships as optional.

Using a consistent set of naming standards also helps to promote reuse. We suggest that service names should be based on the corresponding component or domain (for example, *Customer*, *Agreement*, *Product*) and that operation names take the following form:

    <Business Entity> <action> <version><release>

Following is what each part represents:

- **<Business Entity>.** This is the service name based on the principal business entity involved, such as Customer, Agreement, Product, and so on. This does not imply that the operation can only receive and send instances of that entity; receiving and sending multiple instances of multiple entities as operation arguments is perfectly valid.

- **<action>.** A mandatory element, this defines the type of operation being performed, such as *search, update.* These names need to be consistent and captured in the business requirements and rules catalog. The Open Applications Group provides a set of standardized terms that may be used to provide precise and unambiguous operation names. See www.openapplications.org/ for more information.

- **<version>< release>.** We believe that version control should be exercised at the operations level rather than the service level. Why should a consumer be forced to upgrade to a new service version if the few operations they need are unchanged? Releases should represent upward-compatible additions to the operation, while new versions represent changes for which consumers need to perform maintenance. Hence, moving from operation 1.2 to 1.3 should require no action by consumers, but moving from 1.3 to 2.0 will require maintenance activity. Examples of changes that can be release changes only include the following:

  - Adding new data attributes to one or more entities in the operation arguments or return data (assuming that all attributes have been defined as optional)
  - Changing the business logic within the operation

  Examples of changes that would be version changes include the following:
  - Changing the name or data type of any attribute passed into or from the operations execution call
  - Forcing any data attribute to be required

Communicating with Service Consumers

SLAs define the contractual terms agreed to by service consumers, and these should include commitments on how many versions of an individual operation should be maintained at any given time and for how long. When any new version or release of a service is planned, the existing consumers should be kept informed early and questioned to determine whether they have any specific individual requirements that need to be addressed in the new version.

Anyone who has used the Internet is aware of the frustration caused by products that seem to require a new version to be downloaded and installed every few weeks or less. Because new versions are disruptive, service consumers need to be treated with consideration, and kept well informed when new versions are planned.

Case Study

"A pessimist sees the difficulty in every opportunity; an optimist sees the opportunity in every difficulty."

—Winston Churchill

Although the SOA pilot had been judged a success, one area of difficulty is the service certification. Truth be told, from an IT governance point of view, Ideation has never had a smooth handoff procedure from development and test to operations. The operations group complains continuously that programs are dumped on their department without the necessary documentation and without their approval.

Service Certification

Gus Lee, vice-president of operations, gained significant credibility based on his success in solving the rating problem. In conjunction with the CoE leader, Ike Elliott, they decided to bring before the ERB the problem of service certification. Both had reviewed the process used during the SOA pilot and pronounced it "severely inadequate." IT had been able to ignore operations in the past, but because of the governance that was being put in place and the increasing power of the ERB, they were no longer able to do so. Tom Baker, an ace service architect on the CoE, was asked by Gus and Ike to lead a tiger team to solve the service certification problem. His instructions were to find a methodology for adding a new "service" entity to the set of enterprise assets that operations would support and which would be readily available and documented to potential service consumers.

Based on his experience, Tom recognized that although this was not an entirely new step within IT operations procedures, there were interoperability challenges new to services that had to be addressed. He believed that technology standards and tools (registry, repository, and so on) were quickly evolving and might be useful here. Tom drafted two SMEs in the area of requirements and operations to assist him. To understand the additional accountability requirements that were needed, the SMEs interviewed stakeholders in operations, business analysis, and potential service consumers for the rating service that is being built. They reported the results to Tom and further recommended that service certification should be carried out under the control of the Ideation Quality Assurance department. This process needed to include various details that are developed and documented during the service design and development phase, such as SLA and QoS. It is believed by Tom and his team that this final certification review step would formalize the QA process before physically publishing the service as being "enterprise ready," with an assured QoS and a full and complete set of support materials. This would also provide approval for deployment to production and update of the service registry and repository.

Their published requirements identified that certification should ensure that information such as a version number, ownership, who is accountable for the service, and classification and availability of the service be published as mandatory service metadata. They also required that documentation be provided that helps the IT operations staff understand the service and be able to support it for all levels of operation (first through fourth). Requirements for certification need to ensure the correctness of service contracts created as part of service specification and that it could be demonstrated that the service has adhered to the required sequence of steps for the service lifecycle status, including intermediate peer reviews. The purpose of defining formal service statuses and allowed status transitions is to clearly provide information related to the stage in which the service is at a given point in time. The certification review results in a pass or fail status for the service in consideration. Pass status indicates that the service is ready to be published. Fail status indicates that further work needs to be done before this can be certified as a service.

It is recommended that the SOA CoE assist IT operations with the service certification during the adoption phase of SOA.

As a result of these requirements, Tom and his team create the service certification checklist shown in the following tables. The final report is reviewed and accepted by the ERB and then implemented via the PMO and the CoE.

The Ideation Service Certification Header is shown in Table 6.5.

Table 6.5 Ideation Service Certification Header

Certification Item	Certification Explanation
Description	Ensure that each service passes all necessary certification criteria before it is deployed to production.
Governance goal	Reduce risk.
Governed entities	Type: Deployed services.
Inputs	Deployed services, test results.
When to apply	This checklist should be completed before any service is deployed to production.

The Ideation Service Certification Detail is as follows:

Ideation Service Certification Detail

☐ Functional test plan is at a level of rigor and detail appropriate for a core software asset?

☐ Functional test plan has been completed satisfactorily?

☐ Nonfunctional testing, including performance testing, is complete?

☐ Service meets security architecture requirements?

☐ Risk assessment conducted according to existing risk management framework. Where the risk assessment shows a residual risk greater than LOW, approval for deployment of the service must be sought from the security architect. Residual risk of EXTREME must be referred to CIO for approval.

☐ Performance engineering—design of the service has involved those parties with responsibility for production support of all platforms that the service touches and all agree that the service can be deployed without adversely affecting performance.

☐ Performance engineering team has been engaged and agree the service levels for availability can be met.

☐ Response times adequate and fit within a broader end-to-end performance budget.

☐ Deployment plan is complete (need to review the existing template and augment where necessary)?

☐ Does the operational area know how to deploy the service?

☐ Are all the dependencies identified in the plan?

☐ Organizational issues related to maintenance of the service have been resolved?

☐ Does the operational area know where errors (fatal, warning, informational) will be reported at runtime?

☐ Does the operational area know how to react to runtime errors?

☐ Is the service (or supporting runtime environment) able to report that it's under stress?

☐ Does the operational support area have processes for escalating production issues?

Conclusion

"There's nothing wrong with staying small. You can do big things with a small team"

—Jason Fried

This chapter discussed the lifecycles of services and automated processes, and described how relatively lightweight governance control points can be used to verify that they are ready to progress from one intermediate state to the next one during the whole of their lifecycle—from "inspiration to expiration."

The SOA enablement team does not need to be large, and the governance of it need not be onerous if it relies on collaboration and cooperation. Implementing governance should be about reducing cost, by reducing unnecessary work and improving value and quality, rather than about adding unnecessary overhead.

Unless existing IT governance processes, governing bodies and roles are missing or are completely dysfunctional, you should extend and enhance them to include SOA-specific aspects, rather than duplicate or replace them.

7

Governance Vitality

"If you don't know where you are going, any road will get you there."

–Lewis Carroll

The vitality of SOA governance is defined by the ability to keep the various dimensions of the governance framework relevant, current, and at the right level as required by the business. Vitality maintains the applicability of the governance framework. It requires the governance framework to be current, reflecting the business and IT strategy and their direction. To maintain the vitality, the governance processes and mechanisms, comprising organizational entities and supporting roles, need to be refined and enhanced to ensure ongoing usage and relevance to an implementation.

We have referred to governance vitality in many areas of the book. This chapter addresses the aspects of SOA governance vitality: the goals and measurements, effective reporting on the sustenance of the vitality, and using the feedback from the current and previous iterations of SOA implementations to develop a continuous cycle of improvement.

Goals and Measurements

> *"Always bear in mind that your own resolution to succeed is more important than any one thing."*
>
> —Abraham Lincoln

The IT adage "you cannot manage what you cannot measure" applies to SOA governance as much as, if not more than, it applies to any other discipline within IT. The promise of SOA is to align IT initiatives directly to the business goals, vision, and drivers; to foster reusability; and to drive down total cost of ownership (TCO). The measurements of the results of the attainment of such alignment, therefore, assume a lot of importance. SOA governance is the framework that incorporates such measurement as one of its key responsibilities.

Goals remain merely of a theoretical significance unless a mechanism exists to measure the ability of the execution team to meet the goals. Measurements of goals along with a supporting management structure help an enterprise to judge the effectiveness of the institutionalization of a given discipline. SOA governance, like any other discipline, needs to first define a set of goals that it strives to achieve. A base set of metrics should also be defined to measure the goals that the governance framework sets forth to achieve.

Michael Treacy and Fred Wiersema, in their book *The Discipline of Market Leaders,* postulate that a fundamental tenet of success for any company is to identify its strength and then define a value proposition around that strength. They recommend that each enterprise should have a business operating model that matches its strength to deliver value. Keeping a strong business focus rather than broadening it is the secret to sustained success. At the heart of the operating model is a set of core business processes that defines the business structure, management systems, and organizational culture. Different operating models demand a different set of business processes. The industry landscape can be broadly classified into three distinct operating models: operational excellence, product leadership, and customer intimacy. The business goals for each of the operating models differ, and their metrics and measurements are potentially unique.

It is the responsibility of the SOA governance executive review board (ERB) to define a set of its goals that are traceable to the business goals for the enterprise. The SOA governance goals hinge around the processes and techniques used to define an optimal set of monitorable metrics that maximizes the use of SOA to assist the business to meet or realize its business goals. Each metric is made actionable by defining a set of measurements that needs to be documented by the SOA governance stakeholders.

There are many different ways of arriving at the set of goals and metrics. The first way is to start top down, wherein the enterprise operating model is used as the starting point to identify the goals and metrics that can be derived from the operating model. The second approach is a bottom-up approach, in which a set of goals and metrics are defined based on the various dimensions of SOA governance (for example, design time, runtime, planning time). These goals and metrics are then mapped back to the business goals of the operating model that is chosen for the enterprise. Both approaches are applicable, and the one chosen is based on the skill set, culture, and organization of the members in the governance review board.

In the top-down approach, we start with the business/enterprise operating model, and then identify, derive, and develop the SOA governance goals from them. Taking a cue from Treacy and Wiersema's work, they define the following set business focus areas for each of the operating models:

- **Operational excellence.** Product supply, expedient customer service, demand management, always low price, and so on
- **Product leadership.** Invention, product development, market exploitation, and so on
- **Customer intimacy.** Advisory services, relationship management, and so on

Without going into the details of any specific operating model, let's look at how we can derive some SOA governance goals, metrics, and measurements from each of the operating models.

For operational excellence, to ensure the lowest price, here is an example of a decomposition and a metric derivation technique:

Business goal—Minimize cost of basic services

SOA governance goal—Minimize the cost of developing, building, and orchestration of business processes

SOA governance metric—Cost of the business process orchestration to support new business processes

Measurement—Number of services that are reused from the service portfolio

One can derive multiple IT goals and their metrics for a given business goal. For example, for the same operating model and the business goal, we can derive the following:

SOA governance goal—Implement SOA governance planning around identifying low-cost service providers that can participate in business process orchestrations and thereby reduce the TCO

SOA governance metric—1. Ease of swapping existing services in a business process and replacing it with other services; and 2. Adherence to service interoperability standards

Measurement—1. Number of occurrences of swapping services in an existing business process; and 2. Number of exceptions around standards noncompliance in service implementation

For the operating model product leadership, one of the value propositions is to be able to come up with and sustain the best product in the market. The following can be derived:

Business goal—Develop the capability to react to market conditions and changes before the competitors can

SOA governance goal—Create the ability to change business processes based on business imperatives

SOA governance metric—Service development techniques used to develop reconfigurable services

Measurement—Number of times the same service is reconfigured to meet the changing business process requirements

For the operating model around customer intimacy, one of the value propositions is to sell products and services that cater to specific customer needs. The following can be derived:

Business goal—Maximize customer retention

SOA governance goal—Increase the maturity of the service portfolio by adding more information services

SOA governance metric—Methodology used to identify, design, and implement information services; reusable value of the information services in the context of customer related business processes

Measurement—Number of SOA implementation initiatives in which the methodology is used to identify, design, and implement information services that are used in implementing the customer service-related business processes

In the bottom-up approach, the members of the SOA governance ERB define a set of goals to effectively measure the relevance and significance of the governance framework in the broader corporate context. The goals are identified through business value alignment, prior experiences in the art, and through formal definitions of each of the various facets of the framework. The framework provides this base set of goals and metrics, which are then customized in the context of an enterprise's implementation of SOA governance. The customization may require the alignment or association of the goals to the business operating model or the modification of the base set of goals to align with the business goals that already exist in the enterprise. The rest of this section provides a set of governance goals and metrics that we recommend as a good starting point on which to build upon.

1. **Service reuse**
   a. Goal
      i. Maximize the reuse of services across multiple business processes, IT projects, and so on.
   b. Metrics & Measurements
      i. Number of new services developed versus existing services reused. A larger percentage value is a cause for concern.
      ii. Number of SOA assets (enterprise services) reused.
      iii. Number of requests for reuse that are rejected by the service owner.
2. **Service total cost of ownership (TCO)**
   a. Goal
      i. Reduce the TCO for a service or a set of services.

   b. Metrics & Measurements
      i. Total cost for service design, development, deployment, and operational and maintenance costs
     ii. Number of times an existing service is reused versus new services that had to be designed and implemented.

3. **Return on investment (ROI) on the service portfolio**
   a. Goal
      i. Increase the ROI from SOA investment.
   b. Metrics & Measurements
      i. Revenue generated from each SOA asset, such as reused services, departmental earnings from cross-departmental usage, and corporate earnings from service consumer usage.
     ii. Service TCO metrics around cost of design, development, deployment, and maintenance.

4. **Business to IT alignment through SOA**
   a. Goals
      i. Increase the traceability of IT assets to business goals and drivers.
     ii. Ensure services commissioned for development have direct traceability to business goals.
   b. Metrics & Measurements
      i. Number of services in the portfolio that have direct traceability to a business goal.
     ii. Number of services that pass the business alignment service litmus test. The service litmus test is a part of the RUP-SOMA method, which, in essence, provides a filtering mechanism to assess and evaluate which services should be exposed and hence implemented as a service.

5. **SOA reference architecture**
   a. Goals
      i. Compliance to SOA reference architecture.
     ii. Minimize number of exceptions to architecture compliance.
   b. Metrics & Measurements
      i. Number of exceptions for all assets (that is, services' compliance to the reference architecture and justifications for the exception condition)
     ii. Number of architecture decisions documented for compliance and for noncompliance

       iii. Number of architecture board reviews conducted; the review reports; ensuring that the recommendations are understood and incorporated

6. **Service vitality and maturity index**
   a. Goal
      i. Increase the service maturity index with each new development opportunity
   b. Metrics & Measurements
      i. Revenue generated from a service or a set of services as a percentage of the total IT revenue. Average revenue generated per service
      ii. Percentage of services that were upgraded from simple invocations to policy driven invocations
      iii. Number of versions that exist for a given service or SOA asset

7. **Governance process compliance**
   a. Goal
      i. Reduce the number of exceptions to the process
   b. Metrics & Measurements
      i. Number of exceptions to the implementation or execution of the governance process
      ii. Number of services that did not meet the compliance criteria
      iii. Number of projects that attempted to be deployed to production, but could not meet the compliance requirements (that is, the percentage of compliant projects)

8. **Service identification technique**
   a. Goal
      i. Follow a well-established and proven service modeling design and architecture methodology for SOA implementations
   b. Metrics & Measurements
      i. Number and percentage of services identified from goal service modeling. Goal service modeling that assists in the identification of business services by analyzing and decomposing the business goals into actionable items and associating services to the actionable items

  ii. Number and percentage of services identified through a top-down approach using domain decomposition and business process modeling

  iii. Number and percentage of services identified through a bottom-up approach by extracting high-value business functions from existing legacy and packaged systems

9. **Application portfolio rationalization**
   a. Goals
      i. Reuse existing applications
      ii. Develop a strategy for aging and closing down of legacy applications that have a high cost of maintenance and dated technology
   b. Metrics & Measurements
      i. Number of existing applications that have been identified as candidates for service enablement
      ii. Number of applications that are closed down by leveraging SOA as the major contributor

10. **Governance process maturity**
    a. Goal
       i. Increase the robustness and maturity of the SOA governance process and framework so that it justifies the corporate investment on SOA governance
    b. Metrics & Measurements
       i. Number of exceptions encountered while implementing the process and framework artifacts
       ii. Number of feedback items from the *continuous feedback loop* that has been incorporated into the framework and process
       iii. Increase or decrease in the time spent, such as the effort and commitment demonstrated by stakeholders to the ERB (also known as the governance council)
       iv. Increase or decrease in the incorporation of SOA governance activities and tasks in the project plan of a typical SOA implementation project

11. **Service response time**
    a. Goal
       i.   Meet service runtime service level agreements (SLAs)
    b. Metrics & Measurements
       i.   Elapsed time for request fulfillment by service provider
       ii. Elapsed time at the consumer layer of the service invocation
       iii. CPU cycles and time used for each service invocation
       iv. Number of times redundant (failover) services are invoked.
            Note: This is contingent upon the fact that a service redun-
            dant strategy is in place
12. **Service broker usage**
    a. Goal
       i.   Ensure a well-architected and efficient use of the SOA infra-
            structure
    b. Metrics & Measurements
       i.   Number of times the enterprise service bus (ESB) / broker is
            leveraged for message transformation or translation, for
            mediation, and for routing
       ii. Number of times the ESB/broker is used for security
            functions
       iii. CPU time spent during the execution of the broker/ESB
            functions
       iv. Number of services provisioned in the service repository and
            the number of times the repository search capabilities are
            used to find the correct service provider

Although this outline of goals and metrics is a good starting point, it
is by no means an exhaustive list of SOA governance goals and metrics
that the framework can use as the basis for further elaboration and customization. You should create goals and metrics for your SOA governance planning and implementation that align with your organization's
business and IT needs and drivers.

Governance Reporting

"Nothing is as approved as mediocrity, the majority has established it and it fixes its fangs on whatever gets beyond it either way."

—Blaise Pascal

The SOA governance council (or ERB) has representatives from both the business and IT groups in the organization. The governance framework leverages the council members by assigning and empowering the right individuals with decision rights and management activities that ensure the meeting of a predefined set of desirable behaviors that are expected from the execution of the governance framework and its associated processes. SOA governance forms the liaison between the business and IT; and although it is expected to have adequate representation from these two corporate wings, it is imperative that an effective communication mechanism be enforced to keep the business stakeholders apprised of the SOA adoption progress. The most typical form of communication is through well-structured reporting targeted at different roles and individuals in an organization. Reporting can be categorized broadly into planning and organization reporting, service development reporting, service runtime reporting, and operational reporting.

In the planning and organization governance report, metrics are used to assess whether the services align with business initiatives—services must be funded through their lifecycles with an identified business stakeholder as the service owner. Metrics for the revenue generated from the service consumption should be presented in the report. The service development cost for each service, consolidated up to each SOA project initiative, is used as the basis to report on how the service development cost is amortized across multiple projects. The report also calls out how many services are implemented and provisioned in a given time period and also how many services found an owner to sponsor the entire lifecycle funding. Based on the maturity index defined by the governance council, the report documents the success or failure of attainment of the predefined maturity index. The strategy and planning phase of SOA governance assists the governance council to justify the enterprises' decision to invest in SOA governance as a part of its corporate IT strategy. The outcome of the activities executed in this phase is documented and communicated to the business stakeholders of the organization through a well articulated report.

In the service development SOA governance report, the main artifacts documented are the number of projects that follow and comply with the chosen enterprise service analysis and design method, real metrics and data points for the achievement of service reusability that is fostered by the adherence to method guidance, and the number of wrongly engineered or designed services that resulted in method noncompliance. Compliance to the usage of the registry and repository, which enables service provisioning, usage, and search, is also documented and reported for each SOA initiative that is undertaken. Such a report from the SOA governance ERB assists in instilling the confidence in the business and IT stakeholders that the enterprise service portfolio is being developed in adherence with the design and implementation best practices and guidelines of SOA.

Reports on the testing of services and the associated infrastructure components are highly recommended documentation artifacts. Many governance activities are carried on after the services are implemented. A formal process around testing of each service for compliance to the SLAs is a key governance step, the output of which is consolidated and documented as a report. Such documentation assists in exercising a continuous feedback loop that helps to fine-tune the process in subsequent iterations—reports generated for both compliance and noncompliance to SLA metrics. The report is usually generated for two different audiences. A report containing a high-level synopsis of the outcome from the execution of the activities from the SOA governance process steps that are exercised on the service testing is generated for the business stakeholders. A more detailed technical version of the exact steps in the testing instrumentation that shows failures and exceptions to each of the SLAs that occurred is also developed. The detailed report is addressed to the IT design and implementation team.

Such reports not only assist in analyzing the design and implementation flaws that attributed to the exceptions and failures, but also foster a learning process through which better, more compliant services can be developed in subsequent projects and initiatives. The technology architecture components provide a set of products that make up the SOA infrastructure landscape. Documentation of whether the right set of infrastructure components (that comply with corporate standards) are used in a specific SOA implementation is also recommended. Reports addressing the usage of ESBs, registries, repositories, mediations, technology adapters, and so on are strongly recommended. Such reports help ensure whether the right artifacts from the SOA reference architecture are adhered to and used.

SOA governance reports that address the service runtime components of SOA implementations are critical to ensure the vitality of the governance framework. Service monitoring and management is as imperative as the planning, design, and implementation of services: Reporting on the key metrics of the SOA runtime is important. The service usage information is a key metric that needs to be documented. The following data points are worth documenting and reporting on:

- The service consumers who invoked the service.
- Any time-based invocation statistics that may help in selective tuning of the service availability. An example is a larger number of a *placeOrder* service during the holiday season.
- Time taken to fulfill the service request on the service provider side.
- SLA metrics that were met and the ones that were not met, along with the type of faults, if any.
- Service availability during service invocation.
- Operational support for service consumers on issues such as service outage, SLA noncompliance reports, and so on.

Reporting on the service runtime aspects of an SOA enables the governance council to identify the most frequently used (i.e., potentially the highest value) business services, the real-time compliance conformance data, possible issues that consumers face from service usage, and so on. Such reports help maintain the vitality of the service portfolio and provide key metrics to help prioritize service enhancements in the subsequent iterations.

In addition to the various aspects of the SOA governance that we recommend be documented, reporting the total cost of each SOA project or initiative must be meticulously documented in an itemized manner. A cost analysis helps the SOA governance ERB keep a close watch over the IT budget, thereby influencing the business to foster a controlled and prioritized release of the IT investment. Business dashboards are increasingly used as the standard for reporting business metrics. IT metrics from the various layers of the SOA solution stack are collected, analyzed, and consolidated into various business metrics that are predefined during the Plan & Organization phase of the SOA governance framework and model. Role-based business metrics are developed, and the business dashboard is leveraged to provide a personalized view of metrics to the various business and IT stakeholders.

Reporting also helps the SOA governance framework document the results of the execution of each of its phases (in the context of each of the individual SOA initiatives) and develop a continuous feedback mechanism. Such a feedback enables the refinement of the framework, keeping the framework current and taking it to the next higher level of maturity.

Feedback for Continuous Improvement

"Opportunity is missed by most people because it is dressed in overalls and looks like work."

—Thomas Edison

It is imperative for any discipline that wants to reach the next higher level of maturity to not only encourage a formal feedback process that ideally comes from the direct users of the discipline, but also to institutionalize feedback as a mandatory part of the formal process. Feedback fosters a cycle of continuous improvement based on its real-world usage scenarios. SOA governance is an emerging discipline in the broader spectrum of SOA, but nonetheless, it is one of the most important success factors for organizations that are serious about harnessing its true and potential benefits. A formal feedback process is highly recommended as an integral part of the SOA governance framework. Feedback fosters improvement through evaluation, and it vitalizes the governance model through an assessment and appraisal of the compliance-related results. In SOA governance, and specifically from the execution of the enablement phase activities, the feedback from a given project execution is collected. The feedback is based on the service lifecycle execution, the organizational execution capabilities, and the process execution results. The results and findings are summarized for communication with the stakeholders.

We recommend that the feedback process be broken down into three main phases:

- Evaluate management performance
- Assess governance capability
- Develop governance enhancements

The rest of this section discusses these three activities in further detail.

During the *evaluate management performance* phase, the efficiency (doing the things right) of the management participants, along with their involvement in the governance lifecycle of a project execution, is evaluated. The service lifecycle execution results are also assessed against the performance and evaluation criteria. This phase might consist of three main activities:

- **Analyze management execution.** During this activity, the performance of the ERB (a.k.a. management in the context of SOA governance) is evaluated in the context of a given project's execution. Information that pertains to the ability of review board members to participate in project reviews, to address raised issues and concerns in a timely fashion, and to be accountable for the governance process-related activities is gathered. Information about the efficiency of the project manager to execute project-specific governance activities in the correct sequence and at the correct time in the project is also gathered. Essentially, the ERB members are evaluated based on a performance metric.
- **Analyze service lifecycle execution.** During this activity, the existing service lifecycle phases are analyzed against the actual lifecycle phases that were implemented in a given project. The existing lifecycle may need to change (for example, adding new activities or deleting existing activities). The implemented services are also evaluated against the performance criteria (for example, key performance indicator [KPI], SLA) to identify the gaps in the achievements of the service goals.
- **Confirm performance metrics.** During this activity, the performance evaluation criteria is revisited based on the experience gathered from actual executed projects. The performance criteria may have

been too strict or too loosely defined. Based on this analysis of project outcomes, the metrics may require revision and modification before the next iteration of governance process is executed.

During the *assess governance capability* phase, the governance process that was executed in a given project is analyzed, and possible improvement activities are suggested. The organizational capability and behavior that are demonstrated to execute the change in processes and principles are also evaluated; and possible refinements and improvements are suggested. This phase also has three main activities:

- **Analyze governance processes.** During this activity, the governance process is analyzed for effectiveness (doing the right things). The checkpoints and the decision rights are analyzed after being executed in a given project. The checkpoints might need further refinement or augmentation based on the knowledge gained from the project execution. The decision rights matrix (that is, which individual is empowered to take which decisions) is also carefully analyzed for opportunities for improvement or tuning based on project execution feedback.

- **Analyze organization.** During this activity, the organization capabilities are assessed. When a given project is executed, the organizational impact of the execution is analyzed and the issue of resource-based bottlenecks (based on time constraints, lack of decision rights, lack of required expertise and domain knowledge, ineffective escalation procedure, and so on) is assessed. The defined roles are assessed for granularity and organizational applicability. Based on the results of the execution of a project lifecycle, the skills required to support the governance council may need to be acquired and augmented. The method adoption workshops might also need to be restructured. The support structure needs to be analyzed based on the following:

  - Whether white papers or other formalized analysis are created, reviewed, and enhanced as a result of project findings
  - Whether resources need to be allocated for knowledge harvesting and feedback mechanism; whether the correct level of knowledge is disseminated to the correct audience and whether the feedback loop is implemented with the correct stakeholder involvement

- **Confirm value creation.** During this activity, the value of governance is revisited and illustrated with tangible benefits and outcomes from the execution of a project under the governance umbrella. Every aspect of the value proposition for governance might not be realized through a given project lifecycle, but this activity strives to confirm and assure the value of governance in the form of time and cost factors and also showcase, the positive cultural and organizational changes and their acceptance across the enterprise.

During the *develop governance enhancements* phase, potential changes are suggested, and a consensus among the council members and stakeholders is obtained on the suggested changes and improvements (in process, technology, and organizational change) before they are finally incorporated into the SOA governance framework. This phase also has three main activities:

- **Refine service lifecycle.** During this activity, the service lifecycle definition, and its various phases or stages, is refined or enhanced based on the findings from a project that has completed its execution. During a project execution, new lifecycle steps may be identified (for example, service versioning/decommissioning). These findings are used as inputs for the subsequent refinement activities.

- **Address feasibility and adaptability.** During this activity, feasibility and adaptability factors in SOA adoption are assessed, and the outcomes of the analysis are subsequently used as inputs into maturing the governance process in the subsequent iterations. The feedback is obtained based on the gradual and continual work efforts of implementing additional governance processes that are deemed as pertinent to the client environment and organizational culture. Stakeholder feedback also ensures their commitment to and acceptance of the gradual implementation of governance.

- **Recommend potential changes.** During this activity, recommendations are aggregated, consolidated, documented, and presented to management for consideration. Whereas some recommendations are for management to accept, fund, and implement, others are to improve the technical vitality of the governance process. These recommendations, typically, are outcomes from the culmination of an execution cycle and are expected to be incorporated or implemented before the start of a new one.

Case Study

> *"Nature knows no pause in progress and development, and attached her curse on all inaction."*
>
> —Johann Wolfgang von Goethe

Ike Elliott, the Ideation CoE Lead, is charged with creating metrics that will assist in measuring the progress of creating business agility and providing vitality measurements that can enable the CoE to change the governance processes when needed.

Service Governance Vitality

First, Ike reviews the business goals from the original study chartered by the Ideation board of directors, restated here:

- Be able to create new product bundles in 6 months' time measured from product marketing ideation to product offering in the marketplace.
- Decrease the operating run rate by 10%.
- Create upsell opportunities with our current customers that result in an increased average revenue per user (ARPU) by 5 percent.
- Create a common services organization and merge duplicative corporate capabilities into this single organization. This will include finance, HR, and data center support.
- Create and implement a business agility capability that includes a governance organization and appropriate business-IT linking groups to work with enterprise architecture, the business, and IT and bring quality to Ideation's business and IT.

The last item is satisfied by the implementation of the CoE and the ERB, and it is agreed that these were performing well. In particular, the metric of measuring how long it took to resolve issues brought before the ERB had been an excellent way to keep the focus on resolving issues expeditiously (with an average of three weeks). The planning for the common services organization has been ongoing for several months, and an announcement from the CEO was scheduled to be made next week.

The first three items from the board are quite strategic and need some tactical planning around them to be meaningful. To this end, Ike assembled a team that included Lance Miller, chief architect and head of the architecture review board (ARB), two key subject matter experts from the ARB, and Katherine Bull, vice-president of finance and a standing member of the ERB.

For example, the requirement for the run-rate cost reduction required Katherine to work with Lance to identify the tactical means of such a reduction. As a result of this analysis, the following metrics are created by Katherine to measure the plan for decreasing the operating run rate by 10%:

- **METRIC**: Percentage of automated flow through for provisioned orders
  - **DEFINITION**: Percentage of provisioning orders provisioned by fulfillment function without human intervention ("no-touch orders")
  - **GOAL**: 75% automated flow through for provisioning by end of year (estimated $111M savings)
    - **SUBGOAL**: 90% of disconnect orders automated
    - **SUBGOAL**: 80% of supplement orders automated
    - **SUBGOAL**: 95% of orders with all correct information at initial order release
- **METRIC**: Percentage of no-touch orders for operations
  - **DEFINITION**: Percentage of network operations requests from trouble tickets that can be responded to without human intervention
  - **GOAL**: 50% no-touch orders for operations by end of year (estimated $17M savings)
- **METRIC**: Percentage of repairs that can be performed remotely
  - **DEFINITION**: Percentage of repair requests that can be performed without a truck roll by using remote and automated capabilities to resolve network operations requests from trouble tickets that can be responded to without human intervention
  - **GOAL**: 30% remote repair for operations by end of year (estimated $39M savings)

While Katherine and Lance continue this pattern to create metrics for the other two Ideation strategic goals mentioned previously, Ike is working with some of his CoE governance specialists to analyze the areas within the implemented governance processes where vitality is a concern. In particular, Ike wants to make sure that the right metrics are in place for the service development lifecycle so that the CoE can adjust the tightness of governance for the various control points.

Ike creates multiple metrics for each of the control points, with two of those noted here:

- METRIC: Percentage of development trouble tickets caused by inadequate requirements
    - DEFINITION: Development trouble tickets are assigned a root cause with "inadequate requirements" being one of the root causes. To test the efficacy of the business requirements control point, measure the percentage of all tickets caused by bad requirements.
    - GOAL: After establishment of a six-month baseline, expect this percentage to continually decrease.
    - VITALITY: Further analyze the causes of inadequate requirements and make and implement changes to the business requirements control point as needed.
- METRIC: Number of violations of architecture standards, policies, and reference architectures in solution architecture
    - DEFINITION: The solution architecture control point checks compliance with the architecture standards, policies, and reference architectures as created and approved by the ARB. In the review, the number of violations will be tracked.
    - GOAL: After establishment of a six-month baseline, expect this percentage to continually decrease.
    - VITALITY: Further analyze the causes of violation and decide whether the policies, standards, and reference architectures are inadequate, or whether further training needs to take place to make the solution architects more conversant with them.

Case Study Conclusion

It's been six months now since you took over as head of the SOA governance function. During that time, you've initiated an SOA governance planning assessment and addressed the governance of the areas of service transaction planning, the service development lifecycle controls, service processes, organization, roles and responsibilities, service ownership and funding, service certification, and service governance vitality.

Six months ago, you never would have believed that you could have accomplished so much. Good thing you bought that great book on SOA governance and applied everything you learned!

Conclusion

Maintaining the vitality of the SOA governance framework is the key to sustaining a robust and efficient SOA governance council in the corporate enterprise. The vitality (the process behind the framework) of the SOA governance framework is defined by the service identification, specification, realization, testing, deployment, management, and monitoring techniques; the relationship between the IT architecture and the business architecture as it pertains to their convergence and linkage based on SOA principles, best practices, and guidelines; the continuous feedback mechanism to keep enhancing and modifying the governance framework to tie the loose ends and process artifacts that do not seem to work in the real-world implementations; and so on. Each of these dimensions requires a keen focus commensurate with its maturity level in the organization—the dimensions that are less mature need more elaboration and refinement, whereas the more mature dimensions require sustenance.

It is the vitality of the SOA governance framework that enables the corporate funding around it to be justified in the eyes and minds of the business stakeholders!

8

SOA Governance Case Study

"Far better is it to dare mighty things, to win glorious triumphs, even though checkered by failure... than to rank with those poor spirits who neither enjoy nor suffer much, because they live in a gray twilight that knows not victory nor defeat."

—Theodore Roosevelt

We are taking the point of view for this book on SOA governance that a case study approach will help to drive home the points and help you understand and apply the practical aspects of planning and building a governance capability.

The case study uses some of the salient aspects of SOA governance from the book to provide an example of the application of the governance needs of a fictional company. This company, Ideation Communications, does not exist, and any resemblance to an existing company is purely coincidental.

Introduction: Case Study Background

> *"Walking is a man's best medicine."*
>
> –Hippocrates

Ideation Communications started as local, independent communications service provider in the rural areas of the Midwestern portion of the United States, offering Plain Old Telephone Service (POTS) to satisfy the communication needs of a largely agrarian customer base separated by long distances.

Despite its business being initially rural, Ideation has always placed an emphasis on implementing technological innovation as quickly as it makes sense, for the benefit of its customers and workers. Ideation was one of the first communications providers to offer 100% dial service with no manual operators needed. Ideation employed microwave towers in the 1970s in its territory and leased the bandwidth to truckers and local companies. This soon grew into a national footprint that provided a long-distance telephony service that grew profits explosively. Data capabilities with ATM (Asynchronous Transfer Mode) and Frame Relay were added due to corporate demand. Ideation was one of the first companies to see the value of the Internet and chose to purchase a company (Inet) that had created an Internet network capability that both commercial and residential customers use.

Cell (mobile) phone was seen as a strategic differentiator, and Ideation built a strong presence of cell towers and service in its territory and has been trying to expand into a more national presence. There is a repeated emphasis on "the customer comes first," and the company strives to give customers the services that they want at a fair price, while at the same time providing a quality customer service experience at all of their stakeholder touch points.

On the employee side, Ideation has had another point of emphasis on "safety first." For example, in the 1950s, all field personnel involved in truck rolls were equipped with nylon body belts and climber straps when those were first available. Workers have been treated with respect, and their ideas are continuously solicited by management for getting the job done better, faster, and cheaper. As a result of the new markets that

Ideation has entered over time, there have continuously been new opportunities for personnel, and this, combined with the progressive treatment by management, has led to a high degree of worker loyalty and commitment.

Ideation is currently experiencing tough times, though. Long distance, a cash cow for several decades, has now been commoditized as a result of deregulation and usage of Voice over IP (VoIP) by many of its former and even current subscribers. Revenue has continued to decrease in this area by 10% a year, and shows no signs of stopping despite repeated marketing campaigns by Ideation's customer service centers. Its ATM and Frame Relay revenue and customers have also atrophied in favor of Internet services such as virtual private network (VPN). Cell phone service has grown about 15% per year, but is now coming under attack from bigger and better capitalized national providers.

Increasingly, management attention has been drawn to the many different systems and operations groups and the various networks that Ideation maintains, as something that is impacting their margins (see Figure 8.1).

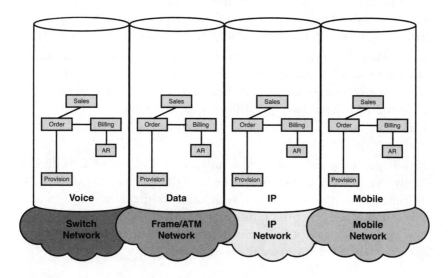

Figure 8.1 Ideation Systems and Networks

There are many different ordering systems, provisioning systems, billing systems, and network management systems. Each of these systems has its own support structure, subject matter experts, business analysts, management structure, and development cycles. Because the business has required products that involve bundles of existing network capabilities, the amount of time to get a new release out has continually increased with missed schedules, project de-scope, budget over runs, or all three.

A year ago, at the direction of the board of directors, Ideation assembled its best and brightest and some industry consultants to analyze the corporate and industry trends and the current situation for Ideation and to come up with the business goals and objectives that would enable it to reverse the negative trends. Some of their conclusions on the current state of Ideation included the following:

- We built up rapidly because of market opportunities and never took the time to integrate our business well. As a result, we are characterized by many separate lines of business (LoB).

- Our cost structure is too high. We have much duplication of services across our various LoB, and this is hampering our ability to significantly reduce costs and increase margins.

- Our ability to offer bundles is constrained by the silos that have been built up in our IT infrastructure. Integrating any of our products requires a huge IT effort with a minimum time frame of two years. This is constraining Ideation's ability to react to market opportunities.

- Our ability to gather information about our customers and to exploit our strategic relationship with them to sell new products and services is severely constrained. Customer data is distributed in various LoB databases, each having a different customer ID and name. Ideation is losing out on market opportunities against our current customer base as a result.

- Ideation is too small to survive as an independent entity. It is highly likely that we will be bought in the next three years. Our value will be enhanced to the degree that we are able to integrate our LOB and operations, decrease costs, improve margins, and improve our business agility. We have 12 months to get this going before we will be constrained by the investment environment.

In consultation with the board, Ideation Communications created the following business goals for the next year:

- Be able to create new product bundles in six month's time measured from product marketing ideation to product offering in the marketplace.
- Decrease the operating run rate by 10%.
- Create upsell opportunities with our current customers that result in an increased average revenue per user (ARPU) by 5%.
- Create a common services organization and merge duplicative corporate capabilities into this single organization. This will include finance, HR, and data center support.
- Create and implement a business agility capability that includes a governance organization and linkage to the business so that they can work together. For example, groups such as enterprise architecture, the business, and IT must work together to bring quality to Ideation's business and to achieve the goals Ideation has outlined.

The path ahead is a difficult one for Ideation. Although they still have a positive corporate culture, Ideation experienced its first layoff this year, and the staff is wary of any changes. Rumors about a merger with an acquiring company have been floating around for some time, further inflaming the angst of the staff.

You have been selected by the CIO to lead the governance organization and are working with a highly intelligent and motivated team that has been charged with the task of creating business agility. The first order of business is to do a governance planning assessment.

SOA Governance Assessment and Planning

"Let the young know they will never find a more interesting, more instructive book than the patient himself."

—Giorgio Baglivi

Now that the CIO has assigned you the task of implementing the SOA governance function at Ideation, your first step is to understand all the governance items that you must address. Although you know that you won't be able to attack all of them at once, nevertheless you want to get the big picture first.

SOA Planning Assessment

The first order of business is to use the SOA governance planning assessment that was discussed in Chapter 2, "SOA Goverance Assessment and Planning," to understand Ideation's current state from an SOA governance and SOA program point of view.

You need to assess not only where the organization is today, but also the areas of greatest program and governance need. This enables you to establish priorities for the governance transition plan to be created. This not only gives you a structured planning tool, but it also gives you metrics to measure the success of the transition plan at periodic milestones. It also helps you by giving some standard metrics for the necessary discussions that you need to periodically have with the SOA program and governance executive leadership to communicate progress and accept feedback on areas to be focused on.

Using the SOA governance planning assessment, you will interview various stakeholders from both business and IT. This will consist of some 1:1 sessions so that you can get frank and open comments and in some team sessions where you will get information from the right people in a particular area. Topics will include the SOA governance assessment areas domains of Plan & Organize, Program Management Controls, Service Development Lifecycle, and Service Operations.

At Ideation, the assessment information you are getting is eye opening even though you thought you knew the organization quite well. The development process in the various organizations is haphazard and not well structured. One highly respected subject matter expert (SME) says to you, "The inmates are running the asylum here. I'm really not sure how we get anything done. It's only because we have heroes who step in at the last second and save the day that we get any releases out. Even then, we've cut so much of the scope that I wonder why we bother at all." Another manager says, "Of course we do everything right, but all of the other groups are idiots. How they keep their jobs, I'll never know." A project manager says to you, "There is no consequence management. The same people screw up, and everyone just shrugs. I'm sick of spending so many hours here to make things work when management doesn't seem to know or care."

Whew! You have to take a step back and think after the interview sessions. The reactions were passionate, and the people involved kept looking at you with a mixture of hope and cynicism. "Nothing around here ever really changes, will it?" one tester questions you. "When the going gets tough, the execs around here will always compromise doing something meaningful and with quality for the sake of looking good to their bosses and meeting their dates." You patiently explain that that's why governance is being assessed and that their leadership, ideas, and passion are needed now more than ever.

Although there are many issues that governance should eventually address at Ideation, a few key ones stand out:

- The lack of a consistent process, repeatability, best practices, and quality controls are obvious. When some of those things have been tried in the past, they usually end up sacrificed upon the altar of project dates. Problems that should have been caught and resolved during business requirement, solution architecture, and design find their way to testing, where it is expensive and time-consuming to fix. Something that must be redesigned, recoded, or reassembled and retested is a long process.

- The company has been thinking about ideas around creating business agility, particularly across LoB. There's a strategy group somewhere in corporate that is alleged to have done some thinking about this, but some quick checking determines that the strategy group is an "ivory tower" organization that is not steeped in the realities of the business. Apparently, no group is really charged with the responsibility of figuring out what business services make sense, and consequently, each project team must figure it out on their own or just write something that works for their LoB. Chances of cross-organizational cooperation and success are low without planning and real thinking in this area. Also, there are some common IT services, but it is unclear what they are and who owns or maintains them. You know that there need to be some ground rules around service ownership and funding, especially when they affect cross-organizational projects that must come together as a program.

- It is not clear how the cross-department organizations should interact with each other. Who makes decisions when the various LoB disagree with each other and the goal is to create a capability that is cross organization? How does the work get managed across groups? How are common standards and principles set and promulgated across the organizational? How are reference architectures created and accepted and architectural decisions made? How does IT interact with the business? All of these must be addressed by governance, and the rules of engagement must be specified.

- Service certification has been a disaster. The rules of engagement are unknown, and operations continually complain that they are not consulted until it is too late and they have to fix things in production. Most of second- and third- level support are burned out after being called in continually on nights and weekends and several have quit.

- There is no vitality in any of the processes that do exist. *"Process"* is probably too strong a term for what actually happens; organized chaos is probably closer to reality. "If you don't measure it, you can't improve it," one program manager says to you, and you wholeheartedly agree.

You present the results of the survey to the Ideation leadership team from the SOA planning assessment, as noted in Table 8.1 with the values corresponding to the maturity levels noted in Chapter 2. It is agreed to go forward with the steps necessary to define the first phase of an SOA governance transition plan.

Table 8.1   SOA Governance Planning Assessment Results for Ideation

SOA Governance Planning Assessment	Ideation Rating	Desired Ideation Rating
Plan and Organize		
Services Transformation Planning	1.67	4.00
Information Transformation Planning	1.00	3.83
Technology Transformation Planning	2.12	4.17
Service Processes, Organizations, Roles & Responsibilities	1.00	4.00
Manage the Service Investment	0.50	4.50
Business Vision & IT Alignment	1.75	3.50
Service Portfolio Management	1.83	4.33
Service Ownership & Funding	2.00	4.00
Service Governance Vitality	0.00	3.00
Service Communication Planning	2.00	4.00
Service Education & Training	1.17	4.00
Plan and Organize Average	1.37	3.94
Program Management Controls		
Enterprise Program Management	1.50	3.50
Change Management	1.00	3.00
Procurement of Resources	1.00	3.00

SOA Governance Planning Assessment	Ideation Rating	Desired Ideation Rating
Vendor Management	1.50	3.00
Identify and Allocate Costs	0.50	2.50
Monitor Business Benefits of SOA	0.50	3.00
Program Management Controls Average	1.00	3.00
Service Development		
Service Development Lifecycle Controls	1.00	4.00
Manage Business Requirements	1.00	4.00
Service Identification	0.50	3.00
Service Specification	1.00	3.00
Service Realization	1.50	3.50
Service Certification	0.33	3.50
Service Development Average	0.89	3.50
Service Operations		
Service Execution Monitoring	2.00	3.00
Service Operational Vitality	1.67	3.00
Service Support	1.33	3.00
Service Operations Average	1.67	3.00
SOA Governance Planning Average	1.21	3.51

Building the Service Factory

"In all planning you make a list and you set priorities"

—Alan Lakein

Now that you have successfully completed the SOA governance planning assessment, you are keen to consider the various SOA governance capabilities and figure out where you should be focusing your limited resources.

Service Transformation Planning

You have agreed with the stakeholders about the immediate areas that need to be addressed in phase one of the SOA governance definition and enablement. A heat map has been created to show the results (see Figure 8.2).

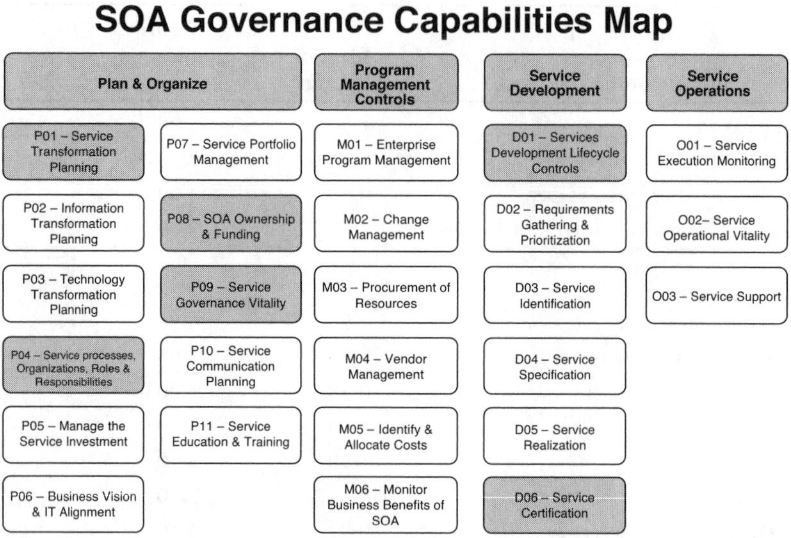

SOA Governance Capabilities Map

Plan & Organize		Program Management Controls	Service Development	Service Operations
P01 – Service Transformation Planning	P07 – Service Portfolio Management	M01 – Enterprise Program Management	D01 – Services Development Lifecycle Controls	O01 – Service Execution Monitoring
P02 – Information Transformation Planning	P08 – SOA Ownership & Funding	M02 – Change Management	D02 – Requirements Gathering & Prioritization	O02– Service Operational Vitality
P03 – Technology Transformation Planning	P09 – Service Governance Vitality	M03 – Procurement of Resources	D03 – Service Identification	O03 – Service Support
P04 – Service processes, Organizations, Roles & Responsibilities	P10 – Service Communication Planning	M04 – Vendor Management	D04 – Service Specification	
P05 – Manage the Service Investment	P11 – Service Education & Training	M05 – Identify & Allocate Costs	D05 – Service Realization	
P06 – Business Vision & IT Alignment		M06 – Monitor Business Benefits of SOA	D06 – Service Certification	

Figure 8.2   SOA Governance Capabilities Heat Map for Ideation

Service transformation planning is an area that many of the most important stakeholders are concerned about. Business agility is one of the main drivers for SOA adoption, and creation of a service transformation plan is important in leading the organization to that goal. SOA governance must ensure that the right resources are engaged in this task.

The Enterprise Architecture (EA) group at Ideation has been studying this and has decided to use a standard industry business function map that can be used to map the enterprise's current business processes. They want to use this map to identify the current business groups and map their business responsibilities to standard business functions to understand how business opportunities can be grouped together. The EA group will use a gap and overlap analysis to identify areas of strength and areas of opportunity for business agility.

Ideation chose to use the TeleManagement Forum (TMF) Next Generation Operating System Support and its standard business process framework called enhanced Telecommunications Operations Map (eTOM; www. tmforum.org/browse.aspx? catID=1648). Figure 8.3 shows some of the standard Level 2 business functions that a typical telecommunications firm would be using, as per the industry TeleManagement Forum.

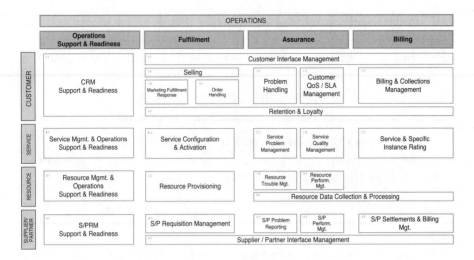

Figure 8.3   Use an Industry Functional Component Model to Guide the Business Agility Discussion

For Ideation, the enterprise architecture group uses their industry function map in interviews with the business units and identifies that four separate business groups perform the business function of "2.5 Instance & Service-Specific Rating." In some cases, different pricing is available on the same service from a different sales group within the company. Consequently, it is a business goal to create a single rating function for all Ideation Communication products, and an SOA business service has been created with the name Create Rating. This service then consists of a set of subservices—Mediate Usage Records, Rate Usage Records, and Analyze Usage Records—as per the eTOM Level 3 business functional map.

In this manner, an industry business process map drives both a business discussion that results in measurable benefit to the business and the planning of the SOA business services creation strategy. In addition, the business agility discussion is a good time to establish key performance indicators (KPIs). In the example on rating, an obvious KPI created might be "single source of pricing for all products by the end of the year." A more business-focused KPI in this case might be "DSL product margin increase 2% due to elimination of pricing mistakes."

As a result of this analysis, the EA group creates a business architecture that identifies service domains, business processes, and an optimal set of business services that are prioritized as to usefulness to Ideation.

The SOA governance function ensures that this standard is used in areas such as investment decision making and opportunities for service creation, to inform and expedite the creation of these business services.

Governing the Service Factory

"To regret one's own experiences is to arrest one's own development. To deny one's own experiences is to put a lie into the lips of one's life. It is no less than a denial of the soul."

—Oscar Wilde

Service transformation planning was one of the capability priorities that SOA governance needed so that it could work with the EA group and help govern the resultant business service priorities. Service development lifecycle controls (SDLCs) represent another area of great concern. After all, the adherence to best practices and a consistency of approach across the development organizations are needed, especially to help enforce the results of the service transformation planning.

Service Development Lifecycle Controls

Ideation has known for some time that it needs a common and structured development process. Some groups perform peer reviews from time to time on their code, but the reviews tend to be haphazardly completed.

Another group at Ideation is considering a standardized development approach. Your SOA governance team has been asked to propose governance control gates for the service development lifecycle of

- Business requirements
- Solution architecture
- Service identification and specification
- Service build
- Service test
- Service certification

Control Gates for Ideation

In consultation with the development stakeholders, you decide to create the following control gates for the Ideation SDLC:

- Business Requirements control gate
- Solution Architecture control gate
- Service Design control gate
- Service Build control gate
- Service Test control gate
- Service Certification and Deployment control gate

As a first step, you create the template for the Business Requirements control gate and elicit feedback, as shown in Table 8.2.

Table 8.2 Ideation Business Requirements Control Gate

Section	Contains	Definition
Name	Control gate name	Business Requirements.
Motivation	The justification for this control gate.	We must have a consistent and well-formed set of business requirements to create services that give us the greatest amount of agility and reuse. This requires that we have a consistent and repeatable approach to the specification of requirements and that this specification gives the required information for the rest of the development lifecycle.
Objective	The output objective	Ensure that the business requirements have a sufficient level of content regardless of form so that development can deliver on the requirement; IT will have a true specification of the business need and objective. This better enables IT to size and estimate this project. Enables the alignment of cross-functional teams on the delivery of the business requirement.
Trigger	Triggering event	Complete business requirements are delivered by the business to the project manager.

Table 8.2 Ideation Business Requirements Control Gate (continued)

Section	Contains	Definition
Scale / Applicability Guidance	Indication of what scale/ style of review is appropriate for the circumstance	Perform if project is > $100K in size.
Review type	General classification of review types: ■ Peer review ■ Submission to approver ■ Workshop ■ Formal meeting	A workshop to review the requirements artifact and identify that the correct level of detail per the executive design authority standard for business requirements specification has been followed. The following roles are represented at the workshop: Application architect Process analyst Business architecture Business analyst Requirements analyst Solution designer Project manager
Concept/approach	Description of how the review is conducted and how it supports the objective	The project manager schedules and leads the workshop. The application architect, business analyst, requirements analyst, and solution designer must validate the requirements while meeting the needs of the next steps of the development lifecycle. That is, they have the information they need to do a good job and the requirements are understood.
		The business architecture must validate the requirements by following the architecture review board (ARB) requirements standard.
		Needed updates to requirements are noted and assigned for follow up, or requirements are approved or disapproved (with updates required).
	Governing authority	Business architecture is the governing authority responsible for validating form and that all standards for business requirements are followed.
	Responsible/manages	The project manager schedules and leads the workshop.

Section	Contains	Definition
	Accountable - approves/ conditional approval/rejects	The head of line of business (LoB) must be accountable and approve the business requirements with a final signoff.
	Consults/supports/performs	The application architect understands the requirements and ensures all the requirements information needed for the high-level solution architecture (the architecture solution document) is there.
		The process analyst answers queries about the business process and ensures that the rest of the requirements conform to the applicable processes.
		The business analyst is responsible for delivering the requirements and is available to answer questions about the requirements or to follow up with any updates needed.
		The requirements analyst understands the requirements, creates the specification, and identifies the specifications applicable to each development group (to understand which areas are impacted).
		The solution designer understands the requirements and will take the architecture solution document from the application architect and create the solution design (end-to-end solution). The solution designer also oversees the components of the solution design. Test/QA—Is this requirement sufficiently articulated to be validated?
	Informed	All participants, governance specialist.
Artifacts to be made available	The input that is required	Business requirements should be circulated before the workshop to all participants. (A customer service level agreement [SLA] needs to be considered and agreed to.)
		Opinions must be sought from the application architect, business analyst, requirements analyst, and solution designer to validate the requirements.

Table 8.2 Ideation Business Requirements Control Gate (continued)

Section	Contains	Definition
	What opinions to be sought	The application architect, business analyst, requirements analyst, and solution designer must validate that the requirements meet the needs of the next steps of the development lifecycle. That is, they have the information they need to do a good job, and the requirements are understood.
Key review criteria	Highlights the key criteria	The business requirements standard must be adhered to, including the following: ■ Consistency of requirements within the business requirements package
		■ Adherence of business requirements to business processes
		■ Adherence of business requirements to regulatory and organization compliances and standards
Key work product acceptance criteria	Key acceptance criteria to be met for successful review of work product	Consistency and completeness of the business requirements must be followed. Any inconsistencies or gaps or opportunities for improvement or rework of the business requirements must be specified. Record next steps, work assigned, and schedule agreed. Any follow up agreed.
Checklist	Sets a suggested process for the review. Provides objective support for recommendations, rework requests, and signoffs.	Business requirements checklist will be used.
Escalation process	Name of escalation process to be used to request an exception to the control gate result	Escalates a decision to the program management office (PMO) to drive the business requirements process to conclusion.
Measurements	Metrics to be captured during or at the end of this control gate	Governance metrics on this gate, including incrementing the number of times this gate has been implemented, incrementing the number of times this business unit has been through this gate, and the results (pass, fail, pass with conditions), and the checklist score.

Section	Contains	Definition
Outcomes	Who is responsible for final signoff, who gets notified, and who are the results delivered to?	Final signoff—Head of the LoB. Notification—All on the informed list and service registrar. Delivery—The PMO will be the official owner of the results.

As a next step, you need to create and get feedback on the control gate for the Solution Architecture control gate, as shown in Table 8.3.

Table 8.3 Ideation Solution Architecture Control Gate

Section	Contains	Definition
Name	Control gate name	Solution Architecture
Motivation	The justification for this control gate	Approval to proceed with proposed solutions presented in conformance to technology standards and principles: ■ To confirm deliverables are encompassing and "fit for purpose" ■ To promote deliverable integration and support ■ To proactively understand impacts before further investment
Objective	The output objective	To assess deliverable's impact on member domains and resulting consideration: ■ To agree on integration, interfaces, and support of deliverables ■ To ensure alternative approaches and solutions ■ To approve new IT solutions presented
Trigger	Triggering event	Project manager receives completed solution architecture document.
Scale / applicability guidance	Indication of what scale/ style of review is appropriate for the circumstance	Perform if project size > $100K.

Table 8.3   Ideation Solution Architecture Control Gate (continued)

Section	Contains	Definition
Review type	General classification of review types: ■ Peer review ■ Submission to approver ■ Workshop ■ Formal meeting	A workshop to review the requirements artifact and identify that the correct level of detail per the guidelines has been specified. The following roles are needed: Application architect Process analyst Business architecture Business analyst Requirements analyst Solution designer Head of line of business
Concept/approach	Description of how the review is conducted and how it supports the objective	The business analyst must validate the requirements as meeting the standards for requirements, and must then trigger the business requirement review workshop to be scheduled and completed.
Participants, roles, and interests	Governing authority	ARB.
	Responsible/manages	Project manager—Trigger the meeting and provide follow up and results.
	Accountable - approves/ conditional approval/rejects	Lead architect—Responsible for presenting and answering questions on the architecture solution document.
	Consults/supports/performs	Solution designer—Responsible for representing the technical expertise of standards and policies and evaluating the architecture solution document end-to-end solution as being feasible. Business analyst—Responsible for representing the business client and validates that the solution meets needs of the business and accepts or declines proposed trade-offs. Architecture executives—Provide guidance, review output, and ensure governance. Infrastructure architect (if heavy infrastructure in solution)—Have provided infrastructure architecture in the architecture solution document and answer questions as needed.

Section	Contains	Definition
		Infrastructure designer—Validate the solution architecture for structural feasibility.
		Requirements analyst—Review and understand the high-level solution architecture and context of downstream requirements and analyst comments.
		Data architect—Provided data architecture in the architecture solution document and answers questions as needed.
	Informed	All participants, Center of Excellence (CoE).
Artifacts to be made available	The input that is required	Architecture solution document
	What opinions to be sought	The solution designer, solution architect, infrastructure designer, and the requirements analyst must validate the architecture solution document as meeting the needs of the next steps of the development lifecycle. That is, they have the information they need to do a good job, and the high-level design is understood.
Key review	Highlights the key criteria	The architecture solution document criteria must comply with architectural standards, policies, and patterns.
		The architecture solution document conforms to existing application future views where those views exist.
		The architecture solution document highlights key infrastructure impacts and requirements.
		Have services been identified and classified, and are they at the correct level of granularity (services litmus tests)?
Key work product acceptance criteria	Key acceptance criteria to be met for successful review of work product	Consistency and completeness of the high-level design must be followed. Any inconsistencies or gaps or opportunities for improvement or rework of the high-level design must be specified. Record next steps, work assigned, and schedule agreed. Any follow up agreed.

Table 8.3   Ideation Solution Architecture Control Gate (continued)

Section	Contains	Definition
Checklist	Sets a suggested process for the review. Provides objective support for recommendations, rework requests, and signoffs.	Follow the architecture solution document checklist.
Escalation process	Name of escalation process to be used to request an exception to the control gate result	Exceptions to demands for rework can be approved by the ARB. Where the issue is a dispute on service identification, the ARB shall send that issue to the CoE for resolution.
Measurements	Metrics to be captured during or at the end of this control gate	Governance metrics on this gate, including incrementing the number of times this gate has been implemented, incrementing the number of times this lead architect has been through this gate, the results (pass, fail, pass with conditions), and the checklist score
Outcomes	Who is responsible for final signoff, who gets notified, and who are the results delivered to?	Final signoff—ARB lead. Notification—All participants are notified, service registrar. Handoff—The PMO will be the official owner of the results.

Implementing the SOA Governance Model

> *"Organization can never be a substitute for initiative and for judgment."*
>
> —Louis Brandeis

After due consideration, Ideation leadership believes that it would have a better forum for initiative and judgment by implementing two new organizations. These include an SOA Center of Excellence (CoE) and an SOA executive review board (ERB). An architecture review board (ARB) already exists, but company leadership recognizes that the three groups will need to work with each other and that governance must define how.

Service Processes, Organizations, Roles, and Responsibilities

The first thing addressed is a mission statement for each of the two new organizations.

The CoE has the following mission statement:

The SOA Center of Excellence (CoE) is an IT cross-organizational team that has been established at Ideation to support and enable SOA governance and ensure the institutionalization of SOA. The CoE will specifically be responsible for the following:

- The CoE will be the implementation mechanism of SOA governance and is responsible for identifying and enabling the processes, standards, policies, mechanisms, roles, and responsibilities for SOA governance.
- The CoE will work with the ARB to make sure that the necessary SOA patterns, policies, and standards are created, implemented, and maintained.
- The CoE will provide governance mechanisms and metrics for the quality review of SOA development, certification, and operations, and will validate that good governance is taking place with vitality.
- The CoE is the center of adoption, change, and vitality of the SOA architecture. The CoE will enable the communication and socialization of the CoE, SOA architecture, and architecture concepts as approved by the ARB.
- The CoE will identify the SOA skills gaps and training programs needed and will provide follow up to validate that training is successful and vital.
- The CoE will be a center of SOA skills and will consult on SOA projects and provide guidance on usage of SOA technologies.
- The CoE will provide an SOA registry/repository, and the CoE will manage the governance, control, and deployment of all operational services in the registry/repository.
- The CoE will ensure the project, architecture, and service assets are harvested and reused where appropriate.

The ERB has the following mission statement:

The SOA executive review board (ERB) is a linking mechanism that integrates business and IT with the appropriate stakeholders. Its purpose is to make key strategic and tactical decisions concerning the SOA journey and to investigate and resolve issues that require cross-organizational and business/IT decisions. It is a business and IT cross-organizational and cross line-of-business (LoB) team.

The ERB sets the direction and pace for services adoption and resolves or recommends solutions for exception requests, including business domain issues such as ownership, funding, and reuse policy. The board performs reviews of proposed investments to ensure commonality opportunities and reuse investments are considered.

- The ERB will resolve any issue needing resolution for an SOA project that involves a cross-organizational or cross-LoB issue. The ERB will do this in a timely fashion.
- The ERB will be the controlling organization for the strategic direction of creating business agility.
- The ERB will be the last review for any exception requests from an SOA program.
- The ERB will be the decision maker on all investments for the portion of the IT budget that is allocated for business agility.
- The ERB will be the primary communication mechanism for business agility and will work across both business and IT as necessary.
- The ERB will provide oversight and direction for the SOA Center of Excellence (CoE) and the architecture review board (ARB).

An organizational diagram was created that summarizes this arrangement (see Figure 8.4).

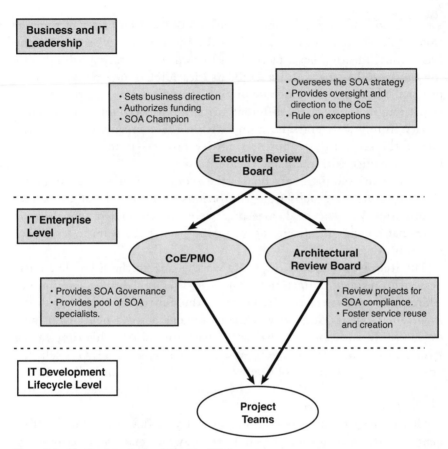

Figure 8.4 Ideation Organizational Chart for SOA Governance

The first SOA project for Ideation is a pilot, and things go well. On the other hand, there is no need for governance for the pilot project itself, because all the work is performed within a single organization. Several programs, which are enterprisewide and cross LOB and IT department fiefdoms, are up next.

Service Ownership and Funding

Almost immediately, an issue manifests itself that the ERB must resolve: SOA ownership and funding. All communication companies have a function called a rating, which provides for a specific price to be attached to a specific telecommunications transaction or set of transactions. As mentioned in the "Building the Service Factory" section of the Case Study, Ideation has a tactical business goal of creating a single rating function that spans all the LOB. As Ideation has moved to offer more product bundling, the different pricing structures have led to a chaotic situation. In some cases, different pricing was available on the same service from a different sales group within the company. Consequently, one of the second-phase business agility projects is to create an SOA business service with the name Create Rating.

During the requirements phase, the service business analysts found that the different groups from the various LOB would not cooperate. Information was withheld, meetings were missed, and it soon became clear that no amount of cajoling was going to get the team to a satisfactory solution.

The item was raised by the PMO via the CoE to the ERB. The business vice-president of operations, Gus Lee, is assigned to lead a group to address and resolve the requirements for this function. Gus has no direct involvement in rating, and was therefore considered a neutral business executive. In addition, Gus has an IT background from his time in the Army, and could work productively across business and IT. Gus selected one IT and one business colleague from the ERB, but also filled out his "tiger team" with an SME from an IT group that he believed would give him unbiased information.

Gus is busy running operations on a day-to-day basis, but he diligently holds meetings for one hour each day and made and followed up on assignments with his team. It soon became clear that this was not a technical or business issue, but a political one. The business director of each of the rating teams felt threatened by this business agility initiative, and based on past experience, thought that they could just wait out this passing storm and return to business as usual. Gus personally interviewed each of these leaders. His ERB colleagues on the tiger team were able to summarize statistics that showed that Ideation was losing about $50 million a year in revenue due to rating mistakes and another $100 million a year in opportunity cost due to an inability to respond to bundle-product pricing requests in a timely manner. The SME produced critical information about how each of the rating groups actually operated and how IT supported them with procedural code that was highly customized.

Gus assembled this information and then scheduled a meeting with the Ideation chief financial officer (CFO). The CFO pointed out that the $100 million "opportunity cost" was a soft number that he did not agree with, but the $50 million in lost revenue was well documented and could not be refuted. A week later, he called Gus into his office and told him that he was reorganizing all the rating groups into one organization immediately, and that David Croslin had been assigned to clean up the mess. Further, David had committed to providing timely requirements on the Create Rating service for the PMO and that he personally would review them and sign off.

The results were reported to the ERB at its next meeting, and the tiger team was duly terminated with a "job well done." The total time for the issue to be resolved was one month. The ERB had an SLA of three weeks for this type of issue, but it was agreed ahead of time that this was a more complicated issue and the SLA would be relaxed by several weeks. Updates had been discussed at the weekly ERB meeting, and it was agreed that this pattern of issue resolution had worked well and should be repeated in the future.

Managing the Service Lifecycle

"A pessimist sees the difficulty in every opportunity; an optimist sees the opportunity in every difficulty."

—Winston Churchill

Although the SOA pilot had been judged a success, one area of difficulty is the service certification. Truth be told, from an IT governance point of view, Ideation has never had a smooth handoff procedure from development and test to operations. The operations group complains continuously that programs are dumped on their department without the necessary documentation and without their approval.

Service Certification

Gus Lee, vice-president of operations, gained significant credibility based on his success in solving the rating problem. In conjunction with the CoE leader, Ike Elliott, they decided to bring before the ERB the problem of service certification. Both had reviewed the process used during the SOA pilot and pronounced it "severely inadequate." IT had been able to ignore operations in the past, but because of the governance that was being put in place and the increasing power of the ERB, they were no longer able to do so. Tom Baker, an ace service architect on the CoE, was asked by Gus and Ike to lead a tiger team to solve the service certification problem. His instructions were to find a methodology for adding a new "service" entity to the set of enterprise assets that operations would support and which would be readily available and documented to potential service consumers.

Based on his experience, Tom recognized that although this was not an entirely new step within IT operations procedures, there were interoperability challenges new to services that had to be addressed. He believed that technology standards and tools (registry, repository, and so on) were quickly evolving and might be useful here. Tom drafted two SMEs in the area of requirements and operations to assist him. To understand the additional accountability requirements that were needed, the SMEs interviewed stakeholders in operations, business analysis, and potential service consumers for the rating service that is being built. They reported the results to Tom and further recommended that service certification should be carried out under the control of the Ideation Quality Assurance department. This process needed to include various details that are developed and documented during the service design and development phase, such as SLA and QoS. It is believed by Tom and his team that this final certification review step would formalize the QA process before physically publishing the service as being "enterprise ready," with an assured QoS and a full and complete set of support materials. This would also provide approval for deployment to production and update of the service registry and repository.

Their published requirements identified that certification ensured information such as a version number, ownership, who is accountable for the service, and classification and availability of the service be published as mandatory service metadata. They also required that documentation be provided that helps the IT operations staff understand the service and be able to support it for all levels of operation (first through fourth). Requirements for certification need to ensure the correctness of service contracts created as part of service specification and that it could be demonstrated that the service has adhered to the required sequence of steps for the service lifecycle status, including intermediate peer reviews.

The purpose of defining formal service statuses and allowed status transitions is to clearly provide information related to the stage in which the service is at a given point in time. The certification review results in a pass or fail status for the service in consideration. Pass status indicates that the service is ready to be published. Fail status indicates that further work needs to be done before this can be certified as a service.

It is recommended that the SOA CoE assist IT operations with the service certification during the adoption phase of SOA.

As a result of these requirements, Tom and his team create the service certification checklist shown in the following tables. The final report is reviewed and accepted by the ERB and then implemented via the PMO and the CoE.

The Ideation Service Certification Header is shown in Table 8.4.

Table 8.4 Ideation Service Certification Header

Certification Item	Certification Explanation
Description	Ensure that each service passes all necessary certification criteria before it is deployed to production.
Governance goal	Reduce risk.
Governed entities	Type: Deployed services.
Inputs	Deployed services, test results.
When to apply	This checklist should be completed before any service is deployed to production.

The Ideation service certification detail is listed here.

Ideation Service Certification Detail

☐ Functional test plan is at a level of rigor and detail appropriate for a core software asset?

☐ Functional test plan has been completed satisfactorily?

☐ Nonfunctional testing, including performance testing, iscomplete?

☐ Service meets security architecture requirements?

☐ Risk assessment conducted according to existing risk management framework. Where the risk assessment shows a residual risk greater than LOW, approval for deployment of the service must be sought from security architect. Residual risk of EXTREME must be referred to CIO for approval.

☐ Performance engineering—design of the service has involved those parties with responsibility for production support of all platforms that the service touches and all agree that the service can be deployed without adversely affecting performance.

☐ Performance engineering team has been engaged and agree the service levels for availability can be met.

☐ Response times adequate and fit within a broader end-to-end performance budget.

☐ Deployment plan is complete (need to review the existing template and augment where necessary)?

☐ Does the operational area know how to deploy the service?

☐ Are all the dependencies identified in the plan?

☐ Organizational issues related to maintenance of the service have been resolved?

☐ Does the operational area know where errors (fatal, warning, informational) will be reported at runtime?

☐ Does the operational area know how to react to runtime errors?

☐ Is the service (or supporting runtime environment) able to report that it's under stress?

Governance Vitality

> *"Nature knows no pause in progress and development, and attached her curse on all inaction."*
>
> –Johann Wolfgang von Goethe

Ike Elliott, the Ideation CoE Lead, is charged with creating metrics that will assist in measuring the progress of creating business agility and providing vitality measurements that can enable the CoE to change the governance processes when needed.

Service Governance Vitality

First, Ike reviews the business goals from the original study chartered by the Ideation board of directors, restated here:

- Be able to create new product bundles in 6 months' time measured from product marketing ideation to product offering in the marketplace.
- Decrease the operating run rate by 10%.
- Create upsell opportunities with our current customers that result in an increased average revenue per user (ARPU) by 5%.
- Create a common services organization and merge duplicative corporate capabilities into this single organization. This will include finance, HR, and data center support.
- Create and implement a business agility capability that includes a governance organization and appropriate business-IT linking groups to work with enterprise architecture, the business, and IT and bring quality to Ideation's business and IT.

The last item is satisfied by the implementation of the CoE and the ERB, and it is agreed that these were performing well. In particular, the metric of measuring how long it took to resolve issues brought before the ERB had been an excellent way to keep the focus on resolving issues expeditiously (with an average of three weeks). The planning for the common services organization has been ongoing for several months, and an announcement from the CEO was scheduled to be made next week.

The first three items from the board are quite strategic and need some tactical planning around them to be meaningful. To this end, Ike assembled a team that included Lance Miller, chief architect and head of the architecture review board (ARB), two key subject matter experts from the ARB, and Katherine Bull, vice-president of finance and a standing member of the ERB.

For example, the requirement for the run-rate cost reduction required Katherine to work with Lance to identify the tactical means of such a reduction. As a result of this analysis, the following metrics are created by Katherine to measure the plan for decreasing the operating run rate by 10%:

- METRIC: Percentage of automated flow through for provisioned orders
  - DEFINITION: Percentage of provisioning orders provisioned by fulfillment function without human intervention ("no-touch orders")
  - GOAL: 75% automated flow through for provisioning by end of year (estimated $111M savings)
    - SUBGOAL: 90% of disconnect orders automated
    - SUBGOAL: 80% of supplement orders automated
    - SUBGOAL: 95% of orders with all correct information at initial order release

- METRIC: Percentage of no-touch orders for operations
  - DEFINITION: Percentage of network operations requests from trouble tickets that can be responded to without human intervention
  - GOAL: 50% no-touch orders for operations by end of year (estimated $17M savings)

- METRIC: Percentage of repairs that can be performed remotely

  - DEFINITION: Percentage of repair requests that can be performed without a truck roll by using remote and automated capabilities to resolve network operations requests from trouble tickets that can be responded to without human intervention
  - GOAL: 30% remote repair for operations by end of year (estimated $39M savings)

While Katherine and Lance continue this pattern to create metrics for the other two Ideation strategic goals mentioned previously, Ike is working with some of his CoE governance specialists to analyze the areas within the implemented governance processes where vitality is a concern. In particular, Ike wants to make sure that the right metrics are in place for the service development lifecycle so that the CoE can adjust the tightness of governance for the various control points.

Ike creates multiple metrics for each of the control points, with two of those noted here:

- METRIC: Percentage of development trouble tickets caused by inadequate requirements

    - DEFINITION: Development trouble tickets are assigned a root cause with "inadequate requirements" being one of the root causes. To test the efficacy of the business requirements control point, measure the percentage of all tickets caused by bad requirements.
    - GOAL: After establishment of a six-month baseline, expect this percentage to continually decrease.
    - VITALITY: Further analyze the causes of inadequate requirements and make and implement changes to the business requirements control point as needed.

- METRIC: Number of violations of architecture standards, policies, and reference architectures in solution architecture

    - DEFINITION: The solution architecture control point checks compliance with the architecture standards, policies, and reference architectures as created and approved by the ARB. In the review, the number of violations will be tracked.
    - GOAL: After establishment of a six-month baseline, expect this percentage to continually decrease.
    - VITALITY: Further analyze the causes of violation and decide whether the policies, standards, and reference architectures are inadequate, or whether further training needs to take place to make the solution architects more conversant with them.

Conclusion

It's been six months now since you took over as head of the SOA governance function. During that time, you've initiated an SOA governance planning assessment and addressed the governance of the areas of service transaction planning, the service development lifecycle controls, service processes, organization, roles and responsibilities, service ownership and funding, service certification, and service governance vitality.

Six months ago, you never would have believed that you could have accomplished so much. Good thing you bought that great book on SOA governance and applied everything you learned!

A

Glossary

ACORD—Association for Cooperative Operations Research and Development (ACORD) is the insurance industry's nonprofit standards developer, a resource for information about object technology, EDI, XML, and electronic commerce in the United States and abroad.

Architectural Decision—Documented decisions about any aspect of the architecture, including the structure of the system, the provision and allocation of function, the contextual fitness of the system, and adherence to standards.

Architecture Principle—Underlying guidelines that hold true across the architecture of multiple systems. These guidelines define the essence of the architecture by capturing the thinking behind it, and they provide a decision framework that enables the process of making decisions on the architecture.

Best Practice—A process or method that is generally recognized to produce superior results. The application of these should result in a positive, measurable change.

Business Process Management (BPM)—The general term for the services and tools that support explicit process management (such as process analysis, definition, execution, monitoring, and administration), including support for human and application-level interaction.

Business Process Modeling Notation (BPMN)—Standardized graphical notation for drawing business processes in a workflow.

Business Service—A service that performs a repeatable business task or a key step of a business process.

CBM for the Business of IT (CBM-BOIT)—A representative model of the nonoverlapping components of an IT organization. It is modeled as a stand-alone entity that is developed with an enterprise to identify opportunities for innovation/improvement in the IT organization.

Communications Process—A specific governance process aimed at educating and communicating the governance model across the organization. It includes ensuring that governance is acknowledged and understood and setting up environments and tools to enable easy access and use of the governance information.

Compliance Process—A process that provides a mechanism to review approvals or rejects against the criteria established in the governance framework (i.e., principles, standards, roles, responsibilities, policies and so on). This process can be performed at various points during the SOA governance lifecycle.

Component Business Modeling (CBM)—A technique for modeling an enterprise as nonoverlapping components to identify opportunities for innovation/improvement.

Component Infrastructure Roadmap (CIR)—A plan created via a current state / desired state gap analysis to optimize the strategic IT components or building blocks for the organization.

Control Objectives for Information and Related Technology (COBIT)—An IT governance framework and supporting toolset that allows managers to bridge the gap between control requirements, technical issues, and business risks. COBIT enables clear policy development and good practice for IT control throughout organizations. COBIT is managed by the IT Governance Institute and the Information Systems Audit and Control Foundation® (ISACF).

Corporate Governance—The system by which business corporations are directed and controlled. The corporate governance structure specifies the distribution of rights and responsibilities among different participants in the corporation, such as the board of directors, managers, employees, shareholders, and other stakeholders, and spells out the rules and procedures for making decisions about corporate affairs.

Corporate ICT Governance (AS8015)—The Australian standard for corporate governance of information and communication technology (ICT). This standard provides guiding principles for directors of organizations (including owners, board members, directors, partners, senior executives, or someone in a similar position) with regard to the effective, efficient, and acceptable use of ICT in their organizations. The standard applies to the governance of resources, computer-based or otherwise, used to provide information and communication services to an organization.

Critical Success Factor—Those things which must go right for the organization to achieve its mission.

Domain—A large business area or a logical grouping of business capabilities that provide related business functions and require similar skills and expertise (for example, financial services management, product development, business administration). SOMA domains correspond to CBM competencies.

Domain Decomposition—The activity of identification and analysis of business architecture elements such as business functions, processes, and business rules into specific areas of interest.

Enterprise Architecture—Defines the business, application, technical, and information architectural models, governance, and transition initiatives needed to effectively coordinate stakeholders of the enterprise toward a common goal. Aligns IT with business goals and includes both the architecture models and the management processes to support these models.

Enterprise Governance—Focuses on the "management of the management process" and on such strategic aspects of governance as operational controls, communications, and strategic planning and alignment with the goals of the enterprise.

eTOM—enhanced Telecom Operations Map. The most widely used and accepted standard for business processes in the telecommunications industry. The eTOM model describes the full scope of business processes required by a service provider and defines key elements and how they interact.

Event Management and Service Monitoring—This governed process monitors workload and system events that could cause service outages/problems.

Exceptions and Appeals Process—A governance process that allows a project to appeal a noncompliance decision to an established process as defined within the governance framework, such as service funding, service ownership, service modeling, and so on and be granted an exception.

Functional Area—A grouping of business functionalities that are easily identified by business analysts in their business domain.

Functional Component—Provides business functionality and collaborates with other functional and technical components as part of a service component to realize business-aligned services. See also: Technical Component, Service Component.

Governance—Addresses the need for a mechanism to ensure compliance with the laws, policies, standards, and procedures under which an organization operates.

Governance Capabilities—A specific area of the end-to-end business and IT lifecycle that must be managed competently to have an optimally governed organization.

Governance Mechanisms—Provide the structure required to implement and operate governance. They specify and describe organizational structures, roles and responsibilities, functions, purpose, and lifecycles.

Governance Process—The steps that must be followed and that describe who, what, where, when, and why for the management of a specific IT or business task that must be governed.

Governed Process—The specific IT or business task that a governance process is addressing.

Guideline—An indication or outline of policy or conduct. Adherence to guidelines is recommended but is not mandatory.

IBM Tivoli® Unified Process (ITUP)—Provides detailed documentation of IT service management processes based on industry best practices, enabling users to significantly improve their organization's efficiency and effectiveness. ITUP is designed to enable users to easily understand processes, the relationships between processes, and the roles and tools involved in an efficient process implementation.

Information Framework (IFW)—A framework of related business models that describes different aspects of the analysis and design required to support a financial institution. The IFW process models are detailed business process models capturing the end-to-end processes of the financial institution.

Information Technology Information Library (ITIL)—A series of documents used to aid the implementation of a framework for IT service management (ITSM). This framework defines how service management is applied in specific organizations. Being a framework, it is completely customizable for an application within any type of business or organization that has a reliance on IT infrastructure. Although the U.K. government created the ITIL, it has rapidly been adopted across the world as a standard for best practice in the provision of IT service.

IT Governance—Addresses the application of governance to an IT organization and its people, processes, and information to guide the way those assets support the needs of the business. It may be characterized by assigning decision rights and measures to processes.

J2EE— Java 2 Platform, Enterprise Edition. A platform from Sun Microsystems® for building distributed enterprise applications. Its core component is Enterprise JavaBeans (EJBs), followed by JavaServer Pages (JSPs) and Java servlets and a variety of interfaces for linking to the information resources in the enterprise.

Java Server Pages (JSP)—A collection of application programming interfaces (API) that allows a software developer to add dynamic content to web pages using the J2EE platform and the Java language.

Java Servlet—Java technology that allows software developers to dynamically generate HTML, XML, or other types of documents in response to a web client request. The technology allows Java code and certain predefined actions to be embedded into static content.

Key Performance Indicator—Quantifiable, measurable objectives agreed to beforehand and that reflect the critical success factors of an organization.

Monitors and Metrics—Measure and report on the performance of an item of interest. This could be a governance process, a key performance indicator, a particular aspect of the SOA lifecycle, or equivalent.

.NET—Software technology that is available with several Microsoft Windows® operating systems. It includes a large library of pre-coded solutions to common programming problems and a virtual machine that manages the execution of programs written specifically for the framework.

Nonfunctional Requirements (NFR)—Technical requirements for an IT system, including performance, reliability, security, monitoring, and operational environments.

Organization for the Advancement of Structured Information Standards (OASIS)—A global consortium that drives the development, convergence, and adoption of e-business and web service standards.

Organizational Change Management—Governance planning, talent management, service ownership, business responsiveness, and the organization redesign that must occur to get the agility that stems from any paradigm shift such as SOA.

OSGi—An open standards organization developing specifications. The core part of the specifications is a framework that defines an application lifecycle management model, a service registry, an execution environment, and modules. Based on this framework, a large number of OSGi layers, APIs, and services have been defined.

Policies—A deliberate plan of action to guide decisions and achieve rationale outcomes.

Principles—Defines the underlying general rules that an organization uses to utilize and deploy all business and IT resources and assets across the enterprise.

Procedure—A method, process, or particular way that is established by an organization as the correct way of accomplishing a desired result. Adherence may be mandatory or optional, depending on the degree of impact or risk.

Process Reference Model for IT (PRM-IT)—An ITIL-aligned comprehensive model that covers all the activities under the purview of the office of the CIO. PRM-IT was jointly developed by IBM Global Services and IBM Tivoli.

Responsible/Accountable/Consulted/Informed (RACI)—A manner of documenting roles and responsibilities. Generally represented by a matrix, roles are graphed on one axis, and decisions are graphed on the other.

REST—Representational State Transfer. A style of software architecture for distributed hypermedia systems such as the World Wide Web. REST strictly refers to a collection of network architecture principles that outline how resources are defined and addressed.

Security Management—This governed process covers the lifecycle of security concerns, including planning, operational measures, evaluation, and audit.

Service—An abstraction that encapsulates a software function. The value of any abstraction is in reducing conceptual burden. A service-oriented abstraction models only the details necessary and relevant to use the service, while hiding the technical details of the implementation.

Service Architecture—Defines the SOA reference architecture, including architectural models, standards and design, development, and infrastructure design techniques.

Service Assembly—A governed process that ensures that developers create new services that follow predefined rules and use processes based on defined architectural standards.

Service Component—A logical grouping of functionally cohesive business-aligned services that is managed and governed as an enterprise asset. Services may be exposed at the edge of the enterprise or business unit. Service components are a programming model concept subject to service level agreements, and provide a base abstraction to express the important properties of existing programming model work products.

Service Delivery—A governed process that manages the realization of service levels, customer satisfaction, and service availability, along with addressing capacity requirements.

Service Deployment—A governed process that manages the registration and configuration of services and release into production. Service changes and versioning are also managed by this process.

Service Design—A governed process that addresses the detailed design and specification of services based on design techniques, patterns, and standards.

Service Design Category—A collection of SOA processes used to develop the SOA architecture and model and design services.

Service Funding—A governed process that establishes the rules for service funding for new and enhanced services and for the mechanisms used to provide incentives for service reuse.

Service Integration Maturity Model (SIMM)—A process for measuring and achieving desirable stages of SOA maturity. The level of decoupling and amount of flexibility achievable at each stage of maturity are what make up the seven levels of maturity.

Service Level Agreement (SLA)—A formal negotiated agreement between two parties. It is a contract that exists between customers and their service provider, or between service providers. It records the common understanding about services, priorities, responsibilities, guarantees, and so on, with the main purpose to agree on the level of service.

Service Model—Information including details of service portfolio, service hierarchy, service exposure, service dependencies, service composition, quality of service, service messages, realization decisions, and state management decisions.

Service Modeling—A governed process that defines the key activities required for the analysis to build services and the techniques required for the identification, specification, and realization of services.

Service Operations—A collection of SOA processes used to manage service performance, security, and problems.

Service Orientation—A way of integrating a business process as linked business services and the outcomes they achieve.

Service-Oriented Architecture (SOA)—An architectural style for creating an enterprise architecture that exploits the principles of service orientation to achieve a tighter relationship between the business and the information systems that support the business.

Service-Oriented IT Governance—Disciplines that transcend architecture and a proper governance model in a service-oriented context that must address IT issues that fall outside the realm of architecture.

Service-Oriented Modeling and Architecture (SOMA)— A method for modeling and supporting a structured approach for creating a Service Oriented Architecture (SOA).

Service Ownership—A governed process that identifies and manages service domains and service ownership.

Service Support—A governed process that manages problems, incidents, and the interaction with service users.

Service Testing—A governed process that ensures that services are tested at multiple levels so that the service meets the stated functional and nonfunctional objectives according to the service contract criteria.

Six Sigma – Lean Sigma—A set of practices originally developed by Motorola to systematically improve process quality by producing output within specification. Lean Sigma combines Lean Manufacturing (focusing on speed) with Six Sigma (focusing on quality).

SOA Governance—An extension of IT governance focused on the business and IT lifecycle of services to ensure business value.

SOA Governance and Management Method (SGMM)—An end-to-end methodology for constructing and implementing SOA governance and maintaining the model over the SOA governance lifecycle.

SOA Solution Stack—Provides a way to understand all the necessary "moving parts" of an SOA and its role in supporting service orientation.

SOA Strategy—A process that defines the desired degree of service orientation and service maturity. This process provides a mechanism to evaluate initiatives/projects with regard to the corporation's desired degree of service focus.

SOA Vision—The plan for transformation of an enterprise to one characterized by reusable business services that allows for rapid changes to the business process and therefore a business that is agile.

Standard—A rule, policy, principle, or measure either established by an organization or established by a recognized standards body and adopted by that organization. Adherence is expected and mandatory until revoked or revised. Exceptions are allowed provided appropriate process is followed.

Technical Component—Provides technical/infrastructure services that are reusable components that address all operational aspects. They are reusable and can be implemented as libraries or shared services. See also: Functional Component, Service Component.

The Open Group Architecture Forum (TOGAF)—An industry consortium to set vendor- and technology-neutral open standards for enterprise architecture.

Vitality Process—The process by which an existing procedure is assessed and changing needs are identified and accommodated by changes in the procedure.

Web 2.0—A trend in the use of World Wide Web technology and web design that aims to facilitate creativity, information sharing, and, most notably, collaboration among users.

Web Services Description Language (WSDL)—An XML-based language that provides a model for describing Web services.

B

References

Ang, J.; L. Cherbakov; M. Ibrahim. *SOA Antipatterns,* IBM developerWorks, November 2005.
http://www.ibm.com/developerworks/webservices/library/ws-antipatterns/

Arsanjani, A. and K. Holley. *Increase Flexibility with Service Integration Maturity Model (SIMM),* IBM developerWorks, September 2005.
http://www.ibm.com/developerworks/webservices/library/ws-soa-simm/

Bieberstein, N.; R. Laird; K. Jones; T. Mitra. *Executing SOA—A Practical Guide for the Service-Oriented Architect.* Indianapolis: IBM Press, 2008.

Cantor, M. and J. Sanders. "Operational IT Governance," IBM developerWorks, 17 May 2007
http://www.ibm.com/developerworks/rational/library/may07/cantor_sanders/

Mitra, Tilak. *Avoiding Common Pitfalls in SOA Adoption,* IBM developerWorks, June 2006.
http://www.ibm.com/developerworks/library/ar-soapit/

A Case for SOA Governance, IBM developerWorks, August 2005. http://www.ibm.com/developerworks/webservices/library/ws-soa-govern/

Michael, P. *Competitive Strategy: Techniques for Analyzing Industries and Competitors*. New York: Free Press, 1998.

Slack, S. E. "Five ways to identify whether your organization is truly agile," IBM developerWorks, 16 October 2007, http://www.ibm.com/developerworks/library/ar-agileorg/

Treacy, Michael and Fred Wiersema. *The Discipline of Market Leaders: Choose Your Customers, Narrow Your Focus, Dominate Your Market*. New York: Basic Books, 1997.

Weill, P., and J. Ross. *IT Governance*. Harvard Business School Press, 2004.

Website for book—www.ibmpressbooks.com/soagovernance

Index

J-K

L

N-O

P

Q-R

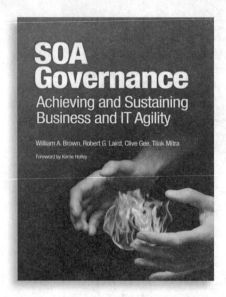

FREE Online Edition

Your purchase of **SOA Governance: Achieving and Sustaining Business and IT Agility** includes access to a free online edition for 45 days through the Safari Books Online subscription service. Nearly every IBM Press book is available online through Safari Books Online, along with more than 5,000 other technical books and videos from publishers such as Addison-Wesley Professional, Cisco Press, Exam Cram, O'Reilly, Prentice Hall, Que, and Sams.

SAFARI BOOKS ONLINE allows you to search for a specific answer, cut and paste code, download chapters, and stay current with emerging technologies.

Activate your FREE Online Edition at www.informit.com/safarifree

> **STEP 1:** Enter the coupon code: QXEGJGA.

> **STEP 2:** New Safari users, complete the brief registration form. Safari subscribers, just log in.

If you have difficulty registering on Safari or accessing the online edition, please e-mail customer-service@safaribooksonline.com